SADHGURU

Sadhguru

More Than a Life

ARUNDHATHI SUBRAMANIAM

PENGUIN
ANANDA

PENGUIN ANANDA
Published by the Penguin Group
Penguin Books India Pvt. Ltd, 11 Community Centre, Panchsheel Park, New Delhi 110 017, India
Penguin Group (USA) Inc., 375 Hudson Street, New York, New York 10014, USA
Penguin Group (Canada), 90 Eglinton Avenue East, Suite 700, Toronto, Ontario, M4P 2Y3, Canada (a division of Pearson Penguin Canada Inc.)
Penguin Books Ltd, 80 Strand, London WC2R 0RL, England
Penguin Ireland, 25 St Stephen's Green, Dublin 2, Ireland (a division of Penguin Books Ltd)
Penguin Group (Australia), 707 Collins Street, Melbourne, Victoria 3008, Australia (a division of Pearson Australia Group Pty Ltd)
Penguin Group (NZ), 67 Apollo Drive, Rosedale, Auckland 0632, New Zealand (a division of Pearson New Zealand Ltd)
Penguin Group (South Africa) (Pty) Ltd, Block D, Rosebank Office Park, 181 Jan Smuts Avenue, Parktown North, Johannesburg 2193, South Africa

Penguin Books Ltd, Registered Offices: 80 Strand, London WC2R 0RL, England

First published in Penguin Ananda by Penguin Books India 2010

12 11 10 9 8 7 6 5

ISBN 9780670085125

Typeset in Adobe Garamond by InoSoft Systems, Noida
Printed at Chaman Offset Printers, Delhi

Contents

Preface

This book is a subjective account of one man's life journey—or more accurately, life journeys. It is emphatically not a biography, if the word evokes expectations of an authenticated catalogue of dates, times and events. It is based on my conversations with the subject, with those acquainted with him, as well as on archival material from the Isha Yoga Centre in Coimbatore.

When the subject happens to be a mystic, one inevitably enters the realm of the hyper-subjective. I have relied largely on Sadhguru's version of events—inner and outer—in the early part of his life. Subsequently, I have relied on the views and impressions of those who happened to be around him as his mission as a guru unfolded.

I decided to implicate my own journey as a seeker in the story primarily as a contextual device. It also seemed only fair to give the reader an idea of my own position (with its implicit biases and limitations) rather than assume a bogus omniscience as storyteller. It became increasingly apparent to me as the narrative progressed that it would be impossible to play the consistent role of an impersonal third-person narrator. As a result, I have consciously inserted myself into the tale at certain points, to ask my share of questions and counter-questions that I assume several readers will share.

I am grateful to all those at the Isha Yoga Centre who delved into personal memory and shared some of their deepest life experiences with me. This book would not have been possible without their generosity, their honesty, their insight. There are as many versions of Sadhguru as there are people who know him, and I encountered many simmering potential biographers on the way. This book claims to be no more than one non-definitive version of Sadhguru's life and the birth of Isha. Hopefully, there will be others.

My special thanks to Maa Gnana at the Isha Archives who attended to my many diverse requests with unflappable calm and an unwaveringly radiant smile; to Swami Chitranga and Swami Devasatwa who helped design the cover; and to Ravi Singh and Kamini Mahadevan of Penguin for the sensitivity and attention that they brought to the birthing of this book.

I am grateful, above all, to Sadhguru for the freedom he allowed me over this manuscript, for his ability to home in on detail without turning micro-managerial—and for the almost terrifying élan with which he leaves his life 'open', allowing readers of all persuasions to draw their own conclusions.

Introduction

I thought gurus happened to other people. Let me confess to my snobbery right away. I thought they happened to a certain kind of safari-suited Indian man and his docile status quoist wife. I thought they happened to those who knew the finer points of ritual red-tapism and pundit protocol, those who knew how to dive at holy feet and look ecstatic at *satsanghs*.

That's true on one level, but a somewhat facetious level, I admit. Let me also say that as a seeker (with my own share of torment and yearning), I had read enough to know all that stuff about masters appearing when students are ready. But what are the chances anyway of a master appearing on a peak-hour Mumbai local? Or at a poetry reading? Or a city bookshop or theatre or café? And what are the chances of a master speaking my particular language, figuring out my convoluted inner geography—my simultaneous need for guidance and dislike of guides, my need for a vocabulary that is sacred and yet secular? And what about my ability to turn mentors into tormentors?

No, gurus didn't happen to contemporary urban women. Psychotherapists happened to us. Books and conversations happened to us. Wittgenstein-and-Kierkegaard-and-Krishnamurti spouting friends happened to us. Gurus belonged to another era, another world—a simpler world where there were simpler divides between the leader and the led. The only guru I could envisage was the sage in a B-grade Indian mythological movie with a candyfloss beard and an air of constipated benignity.

Dead gurus were fine. They left behind words that provoked, challenged. That was a manageable bequest. But live gurus were unthinkable. Or to put it another way, I knew I didn't have the qualifications—social, cultural or historical—to deserve them.

Existential qualifications? I thought I had some. That is, if qualifications meant an absence. The unease, the out-of-kilter feelings, the 'what-does-it-all-add-up-to' questions, the sudden fear of death 'on dawn visits to the bathroom'—I'd been there, done that. And while some of those clammy moments could be addressed by a poem, or love, or sex, or travel, or a book, or even chocolate, I knew there were others that couldn't.

And yogis? I thought they were a bit like unicorns. Near mythic. I thought they were to be found in remote Himalayan caves or in exotic spiritual literature (like Paramahansa Yogananda's *Autobiography of a Yogi*). The only yogis I knew of were the kind who held classes two days a week to 'beat stress' and 'combat diabetes'.

Then I met Sadhguru.

Many things changed in my life after that encounter six years ago. I learnt, for one, that yogis exist. I mean, real yogis. I learnt that they aren't mere contortionists or New Age faddists; that they have at their disposal a time-tested and sophisticated technology of transformation capable of radically empowering the seeker on the path to self-understanding.

I learnt that enlightenment isn't the sole prerogative of the Buddha or Christ or Akka Mahadevi or Ramakrishna—or any of those conveniently dead and buried. That it is possible to meet a man who can address the questions of life and death with the crisp authority of an adept, but also talk with childlike enthusiasm about a motorcycle, a Salman Rushdie novel or a game of golf. A man who can read minds, heal, talk about past and future lives, yet remain rational, scientific, down-to-earth, devastatingly logical. A man who can discuss karma, nirvana and ancient spiritual traditions, yet remain liberal, provocative, contemporary.

A website describes him as 'a self-realized yogi and profound mystic of our times, a visionary humanitarian and prominent spiritual leader'. He is all that and more. Sadhguru is the founder of the Isha Foundation in Coimbatore, an organization with well over a hundred centres in India and other parts of the world. Today the centres boast of millions of practitioners of Isha yoga in various parts of the country, the US, UK and Europe. With his razor-sharp intelligence, astringent wit, modern-day vocabulary and commitment to varied social causes, he is in growing demand as an international speaker. He is equally at home in a satsangh for thousands of meditators in India as he is at the World Economic Forum in Davos; equally at ease with a group of Tamil peasants or prisoners as he is at the United Nations Millennium Peace Summit.

But that's just bio-note stuff. It conveys nothing of the man himself. A man who is a mystic, not a metaphysician. A sage, not a scholar. A guru, not a godman. An exuberantly vibrant human being, not a beaming plaster saint.

This is a book about the kind of person I never expected to meet. A person whom I consider to be a guru simply because he doesn't fit into any of the other categories I know. I've tried to give the relationship a name. Friendship comes closest. But it's not just that either.

I'm not given to easy adoration. I have long suffered from an affliction that I term 'insubordination'—a primal discomfort with authority figures and gatekeepers of all kinds. And with it goes a dislike of the mush and gush, the slavering superlatives and 'lotus feet' rhetoric that accompanies a feudal guru-based culture. I grew up with a rationalist critique of religion, and although a love of art softened some of the dogmatic aspects of that rationality, I'm still a stout champion of commonsense on many matters.

Having got that out of the way, let me confess that he awes me. Not merely because he is wise, but because of how lightly he wears that wisdom. Not merely because he is compassionate—and he has been profligate with his time, his attention, his energies—but because he gives of himself without being patronizing, without ever allowing the recipient to feel diminished. Not merely because he has presence. But because that presence spells so much more than what contemporary culture eulogizes as charisma. Not because he is regarded as a master. But because his refusal to exude any sense of entitlement has actually helped banish my long-standing allergy to the term.

He is quite simply the most alive human being I have met. Also the most spacious, capable of turning from robust to refined, energetic to still, earthy to subtle in a moment. That also makes him the most remarkable person I know.

Poetry matters to me. I value its language of texture and inflection. That makes me wary of many of the foot-in-the-door strategies of advertising. But in this case, it wouldn't be far from the truth to say that I can divide my life into two distinct phases: pre- and post-Sadhguru. Before and after. To give an idea of why I value the 'after', it would make sense to share something about the 'before'.

Like so many others, I've spent much of my life wanting to know. And that's meant a pretty basic quest—a search for a teacher. I don't think I've asked for much either. Omniscience? No. In fact, I sensed early that those who seemed to have all the answers were shamming. Corruption is a strong word, but my earliest experience of it was among teachers. Several teachers I knew in school and university—and this made the exceptions blaze in comparison—were into barely-concealed power trips. In short, they were the first bullies I met. Of course, I learnt the game too. I learnt to play clever, but not contrary; bright but not bratty. But even as I feigned docility, I'd encountered enough Big Sisters by age ten to develop a deep appreciation of the subtler nuances of democracy.

My first job—college teaching from which I fled in two months—helped me realize the challenges of running that democracy. How easy it is to infect a classroom with one's bigotries—however liberal their content. The only survival strategy for the student, I realize, is to retaliate with her own brand of rigidity, only too discover later, much later, that she must spend the rest of her life unlearning it.

The finest teachers I've known—and they were few and far between—impressed me (though I didn't know it then) with the absence of personality. They weren't seeking to be guides and mentors. Instead, they created a clear, flexible unsentimental space in which one could try, flail, flounder—and finally, hopefully, float.

But what did I want to know exactly? Well, the regular stuff. Death, birth, suffering, the universe—all those mysteries, all those terrors. Questions that the Buddha and every young person before and since have started off with until the distractions of formal and worldly education take over. Nothing I learnt in school or university ever seemed to address those questions. But education raised plenty of others. It offered enough fodder to keep me busy and occupied for a long time.

But somewhere the old questions stayed, and gnawed. And it is those questions that probably led me, as they have so many others, to the study of the humanities, and later, more specifically, to literature. Art was the only place in which it seemed kosher to wonder about the meaning of life. Everywhere else the existential questions seemed more taboo than sex. Strangely, while the mention of the latter was now a marker of liberalism, the former had turned near sacrilegious. The existential journey seemed synonymous either with ash-smeared sadhus at the Kumbh Mela (endlessly archived by coffee-table books) or Rolex-watch-flashing godmen in limos. Not entirely without reason, spirituality had become the new heresy.

By the time I was through with my Masters, I realized that while I found 'lit crit' cerebrally seductive, I still had questions that couldn't be answered by academics alone. I realized that for me creative writing had always come much closer to grappling with the real stuff. My instinct told me I was right to distrust the glamorous glibness that I was fast learning to adopt as an aspiring young academic. At least, poetry implicated something more than the intellect. It seemed to be about the larger life of the mind. And above all, it made room for stammering, for doubts, for pauses. For silence.

For a long while it felt like this passion offered enduring sustenance. I saw the magic, the way metaphor transfigured, made whole; the way it brought together the abstract and the sensual, idea and passion, the ephemeral and the crunchy, and made them inseparable. That and an avid interest in philosophy seemed sufficient. Life was challenging. As a writer living in an intense city, surrounded by creative friends, making my living off writing on the arts, I knew I had the life I had always wanted—exciting, precarious, counter-cultural. The way it should be. But it wasn't enough.

In 1997, something decisive occurred—something quiet but in its own way momentous. I was returning by train from Delhi after a particularly relaxed week's holiday in Nepal. All was well with the world—or at least nothing seemed more depraved than usual. And then a process started that lasted for several days. I started dying.

Not physically. I wasn't recovering from an illness or sickening for one. Not psychologically either. I wasn't depressed—and I've had my share of the blues to know that this wasn't the familiar geography of the doldrums. But I knew I was dying. The process was tangible. Back home, desperately clutching at familiar anchors, I watched my partner and my cats turn into shadowy, insubstantial figures. I watched all the moments I had considered valuable—the triumphs, the elations, even the rages—turn hollow. I watched the slow squeezing out of hope. I longed for my daily dose of drama—even the old stab of buried traumas. But it felt like some essential glue was drying up. I went to bed each night hoping things would be different the next morning, and would wake up to see my body stiffen into carcass-like inertness. And yet, I was alive like never before, watching what was happening with horrified mystification.

The worst was being deserted by language. I groped for words to talk about what was going on, but they slipped out of my grasp. All I could do was pray for the return of normalcy. But even as

I did, I was dimly aware that what was happening was more real than anything I had ever known. Watching my breath seemed no longer to be some dreary spiritual penance; it was the only way to make it from one moment to the next.

The experience didn't last. As I started coming out of that phase, there was calm of a kind. It was the calm of returning to health after a long illness, of having lost everything and knowing there was nothing more to lose. But even as I watched the experience recede with relief, I knew that it was vital that I remembered. This strange encounter with death had brought with it an unambiguous picture of what really counted. Books, love, travel and art were all very well, but what really mattered, I now knew, could be only this: making sense of death and, in the process, hopefully making sense of life as well.

I did forget, of course. The experience has flattened into memory, and I have domesticated the intensity to a manageable level of discomfort. It prods me every now and then but it hasn't unravelled my life like before. I have continued to blunder along, consumed by my regular quota of resentment and envy, inadequacy and grief. But along the way, a certain shift did occur. My primary self-definition now was seeker, not poet.

And so my reading took on a new feverishness. Metaphysics was no longer enough. It was the voices of mystics that I sought. From St John of the Cross to Ramakrishna, Krishnamurti to Ramana Maharishi, Nisargadatta Maharaj to Meister Eckhart, and more. I found narratives difficult, so novels were on the backburner. Poetry remained important, but seemed limited. If it was a deep way of knowing myself, it wasn't deep enough, I decided. Rilke and Stevens and Neruda could take you up to a point, but for all their virtuosity, they were still *sahridayas*, compatriot questors. I didn't want the blind certainty of the believer. But neither did I want the comfortable uncertainty of the committed agnostic. I wanted the clarity of one who knew. I wanted nothing less than a stalwart—weatherbeaten, unfaltering.

After a time, reading wasn't enough either. What I was seeking, I realized, was a living guide: someone who knew what it was like to make the journey—not accidentally, but consciously—to places beyond the ken of the rational daytime mind. It had to be someone who knew more about the inner realms than the artist or the scientist. I knew there were a dozen different rational explanations of my experience. But I also knew that neither logic nor art could touch the mystery of that event, or enter that cold penumbral space of emptiness it uncovered. The only people who seemed to address that shadowy province in ways that made sense to me were the mystics. But did they even exist in my world?

I became a regular visitor to the home of a local Vedantin, a retired banker, in south Mumbai. He made no extravagant claims, just that he had stumbled upon the simple experiential discovery that 'I am not the doer'. The visits helped. I respected the man tremendously. His clarity of vision was more than apparent. But what of my own journey? Everything he said made sense intellectually, but I was beginning to realize that there were vast areas of myself that were far from intellectual.

Like so many modern seekers, I have felt a long-standing affinity with Buddhism, and decided to give the Vipassana meditation course a try. I fled from the ten-day silence course in three days flat. While the concept of a no-nonsense breath-focused programme of self-observation appealed, I realized I wasn't yet ready for this level of austerity. I returned chastened, aware that the problem was with me rather than the course. What had grabbed the mind still hadn't grabbed the gut.

A tryst with a popular Kriya yoga course followed. That helped too. It activated a new level of energy and wellbeing. But I soon reached an impasse. I didn't find the guidance I was seeking. It was paradoxical. I knew my deep mistrust of hierarchy, my stubborn intellectual arrogance. At the same time, I wanted guidance from someone I could trust.

It was a double bind. At some point, I decided that enough was enough. I was tying myself into knots with my contrary desires. The answers, if any—and I knew this as well as the next person—were to be found within myself. Yes, it would be nice if this self were less fraught and fissured, if it were a more peaceable place to be. But there was no point looking for elevator music and air-freshener in my innards. I wasn't going to be harmonious. I wasn't a round peg in a round hole and never would be. I was a trapezium and that was that. It was time to settle down and accept my angles.

Then in May 2004 I attended a talk by someone called Sadhguru.

When I entered the auditorium in south Mumbai that evening, I had no particular expectations. But I was curious. I took my place in the very first row with a couple of colleagues from the arts centre I worked in.

I had seen posters of the man plastered all over Chennai some years ago. They showed a man with a flowing grey beard, staring beatifically heavenward. He looked too copy-book to be true. My mother attended a talk by him soon after and had told me she was impressed. But when I read a book by him that she recommended, *Encounter the Enlightened*, I decided he was too brusque and arrogant for my liking. A picture of him on a motorcycle in a Sunday newspaper supplement convinced me that he was also far too macho. My kind of spiritual teacher, I told myself, would have something unmistakably feminine about him (even if he'd committed the unfortunate oversight of being born male).

I don't remember much of the content of that evening's talk. But I was riveted. It made immediate and enormous sense. It spoke to where I was directly. What appealed even more was how it was delivered. Not mannered, not self-conscious, refreshingly devoid of scriptural flourishes, it was incisive, wry, funny, unsentimental. It was clear that the speaker wasn't sectarian. And he wasn't asking for faith—or recruits.

I was struck by this man, seated with easy grace before a mike, by his uncompromising forthrightness, the mix of dry humour and warm human sympathy that emanated from him. Something about him seemed familiar. I can relate to him, I remember thinking. I know where he's coming from. He could even be a friend. A friend from whom I could learn a great deal. And perhaps that makes him a teacher as well. My kind of teacher. One who understands egalitarianism. One who doesn't look smug. And most importantly, who looks like a person I can trust.

I particularly liked the democratic tenor of his talk, his refusal to mystify the mystical, his refusal to see any divide between the material and the spiritual, the profane and the sacred. 'Every human being is spiritual. The only choice you have is between being spiritual consciously or unconsciously. Do you want to walk with your eyes closed or open? That is the question.'

And there was the way he drew our attention to the miraculous alchemy of our daily lives: the process by which a human being was capable of eating a banana, for instance, and transforming it into a part of himself. But this miracle, he pointed out, was still unconscious. 'If you consciously transform the banana into the human being, you become the Creator Himself.' The path to which he was inviting us was a path from compulsion to choice, from the habitual to the conscious, from unawareness to awareness. It appealed. More vitally, he seemed to know what he was talking about.

Later I recalled Sister Nivedita's line about her early encounter with Swami Vivekananda: '. . . I saw that although he had a system of thought to offer, nothing in that system would claim him for a moment, if he found that truth led elsewhere.'

I knew what she meant. For all my scepticism, I thought I knew the smell of integrity when it came my way. I enrolled for a two-day Inner Engineering Programme that weekend.

By the end of the two-day programme, I found myself walking up to this strange figure (who looked like he'd stepped out from the swirling mists of time with his turban, shawl and flowing beard) and asking him, somewhat incongruously, if we could meet over a cup of coffee. He looked at me with characteristic intentness and suggested that I come and meet him in the ashram that September.

That evening I called my mother and said, 'Perhaps I have found a "guru".' The word was still inflected, my approach still guarded.

Four months later I visited the ashram. Coffee didn't happen (though he did tell me he favoured decaf). A conversation did. Over the next few months, that conversation deepened. Five years and several programmes later, it has deepened further.

I still have trouble calling him Sadhguru. Ceremonial nomenclature makes me uncomfortable. But there's no doubt in my mind that he is a guru. What's more, the word doesn't bother me quite so much. It seems like no more than a description—albeit an inadequate one—of a certain kind of person; a person who has a profound understanding of the workings of the inner life and knows how and when to make responsible surgical interventions in the inner lives of others as well. The knowledge is not theoretical. Sadhguru has no qualms about admitting that he is a spiritually 'uneducated' master who has read none of the seminal texts on yoga in their entirety. He needs no textual verification of his insights. His own inner experience, he says, has never failed him.

I have often been uncomfortable with the emotional pitch and fervour, the bowing and scraping that seem to be appurtenances of discipleship. But I have also realized that at least some of this is impelled by genuine feeling. As for the guru himself, he has never asked for weak-kneed devotion; he offers instead a path of self-empowerment, a time-honoured path that, he reiterates time and again, can make you master of your own destiny. When I once asked him why he tolerated certain acts of (what still seem to me to be excessive) self-abnegation—such as some meditators helping him on with his footwear—he replied simply, 'It's obscene to keep giving and not receiving. This is a typical cultural expression for some people. There's a very deep sense of gratitude that they want to express. It means something to the giver, and I don't want to take that away.'

At the same time sentimentalism is peripheral at Isha and I have seen the ways in which emotional resilience is encouraged. The love for the guru is always palpable—and remains, as always, a powerful source of spiritual alchemy—but it is not for nothing that Isha yoga practitioners are described primarily as meditators, not devotees. He himself has described the sometimes overwhelming feelings nursed by disciples for the guru in typically dispassionate terms. 'It is just like a plant, not longing for water emotionally or mentally—it is a deep energy longing. If there is a drop of water there, the roots will find their way to it. There is no emotion in it. There is no mind in it. It is a different kind of intelligence . . . It is just life's longing for itself.'

Yoga is the path of *sadhana*, of concerted and persevering practice. And yet, with no self-aggrandizement whatsoever, Sadhguru does acknowledge that much can happen in the presence of a live master. All it takes is the right level of receptivity. Having witnessed and experienced some of those 'transformations' that occur spontaneously in his presence, I no longer doubt his credentials. He once described a guru as a live road map. And that's the image to which I relate most. Not a patriarchal messiah. Not a card-holding member of the spiritual elect. But a map, a path, willing to be worn and abraded by the footprints of hundreds of thousands of travellers eager to make their journey home.

I still feel like a trapezium. But my angles bother me less. And a few of them have fallen away. It feels like there's more breathing space. And more room for trapeziums in this world. And I know that I have felt empowered enough to stir out of a comfortable—but limited—place in my head to start a journey to a more open, less judgmental residence somewhere in the vicinity of the heart (although Sadhguru himself dismisses my description of this cerebral-to-cardiac trajectory as 'too much of a cliché'). I'm nowhere near getting there. But it seems worthwhile to try. And while it's probably a dangerous address, it feels like a more authentic one. The head still remains a space I spend a good deal of my life in, but I hope there are fewer vested interests about inhabiting it.

I still have misgivings that rise, subside and rise again. Institutionalized spirituality, for instance, still makes me uncomfortable. Volunteers who exude the sanctimonious zeal of new converts make me uncomfortable. Marketing mechanisms, though these are more muted at Isha than elsewhere, make me uncomfortable.

But every time I meet the guru himself, my ambivalence invariably drops away. Even if Isha's many new ventures and meditators—myself included—are works in progress, he strikes me time and again as the genuine article. There's nothing phoney here, no comforting platitudes, no smarmy PR-savvy spiritualism. There is a dynamism and stillness about his presence that I instinctively trust.

'It's a totally wrong perception that you have to be fired up to do something,' he once told me. 'Only small things get hot to do things. I'm a cool fire. That's how existence functions. It's cool, but creative. The really big things in existence never get hot. Take the Creator, for instance. You're born, you die—He's fine either way.'

There has always been a far-from-cool urgency about my interactions with him, however. I know others feel it too. It seems like his intensity is contagious. 'He's a fast-forward guru', someone once said. To me, it feels like he represents a live connection with a power source into which it makes some gut-level sense to plug. And quick.

Do I believe gurus have an exclusive hotline with divinity? Absolutely not. It seems ludicrous to suppose the spiritual life is the preserve of a chosen few. Nor has Sadhguru ever made such a claim. Quite the reverse, in fact. What then is the need to 'plug in' about? I've often tried to analyse the 'Sadhguru contagion'. What is responsible for that heightened sense of aliveness that I and so many others feel when he is around?

Is it his personality, I've wondered? But then, the 'personalities' I have known have emitted a stench of self that has left me feeling exhausted after a time. Is it his intelligence? But I've met better informed, more intellectual heavyweights, and have invariably wanted more. I have finally concluded that it is simply his presence: a spontaneous, intense and unencumbered all-there-ness. One recognizes it as the presence that would surface if we were all to drop our camouflages, our agendas, our ancient terror of our own vulnerability.

A body 'from which God was radiating terrifically,' was how Frank Humphreys, a Western disciple, once described Ramana Maharishi. I wasn't sure what it meant, but it rang true when I read it years ago. I had a hunch I'd recognize the phenomenon if I came across it. And then I did. That's where the gut-level sense comes in, I think. You know you've found the real thing, even before you know what it means.

This book is an attempt to share some of that sense of wonder that these years of knowing Sadhguru have been about. More fundamentally, it is an attempt to tell the story of an exceptional man.

There is much that makes him exceptional. There's his confounding life story, for instance, that so often stretches the limits of one's credulity. (If one believes it, it is only because the man himself is so nonchalant about it. As he often says: 'It would be foolish to believe it, but it would be even more foolish to disbelieve it.') There's the strange and powerful energy form he has created—the Dhyanalinga—which draws thousands of international seekers on a daily basis. There's the transformational meditation curriculum that he has authored, that stirs, unsettles but invariably deepens and profoundly alters the lives of practitioners from all over the globe.

For me, as for many others, he is a guru. But for all those, also like me, who have nursed an entirely pardonable scepticism about the word, I hope this book will offer the portrait of a fascinating contemporary mystic, and more importantly, a deeply human being.

Someone asked me the other day: what exactly does it mean to have found a guru? I'm still finding out, I told her. But it's a bit like finding out that the silence of the world in response to the human cry for meaning—which Camus spoke of—isn't entirely unreasonable.

I also made another discovery: that the guru doesn't have to be an authoritarian figure in one's life. Many people I know assume that the relationship between guru and shishya is hierarchical in an almost medieval sense of the term. While a deep respect and love for the guru naturally induces a certain trust (vital to any process of learning), it was also refreshing for me to find that one could have an unstuffy relationship with the master, without that respect diminishing in the slightest.

Do I agree with everything he says? On matters spiritual, I wouldn't quibble. But on other issues, I quite enjoy the sparring. He's often termed me 'a typical Mumbai intellectual' and 'an idealist from the art world', by which, I know he really means 'wishy-washy liberal'. At times, he hasn't been that euphemistic either. I think I have been less rude, although I have often informed him that he is inconsistent and despotic. But I relish the arguments. And I'm thankful to have a guide who's secure enough to allow for dissent. Uncritical obedience doesn't come easy to me, and I'd never have been able to join the ranks of the perpetually rapturous, however hard I tried.

I once asked Sadhguru about that enigmatic Biblical line: 'But many are called and few chosen.' It seems unfair and undemocratic, I argued. Why should the mysterious knowledge of the self be limited to a few? Why can't everyone be chosen? I remember his answer clearly. He replied: 'It would be more accurate to say, "Many are called, but few choose".'

And for all those who still can't help thinking of gurus as manipulators of gullible millions, it may be useful to remind oneself that this man, like so many mystics before him, does not ask you to follow. He does not ask you to wait. He does not ask you to forsake your rationality. He does not ask for obedience. He does not ask for belief. He simply suggests that you choose.

The live road map is still available. And the choice still exists.

'Pure Awareness and Madness'
The Beginning of the Journey

If you were to collect your luggage from Baggage Claim at Coimbatore airport and head for the exit, you would find a taxi counter to your right marked 'Isha'. You could hire a car for the thirty-kilometre journey. It would take you an hour and a half to reach your destination, though some of the more intrepid Coimbatore cabbies could get you there sooner.

The first part of the drive takes you through crowded city streets, bustling with shops and cyclists, luxury cars and ambling cows. Coimbatore is a wealthy city, a major industrial centre of the South, and the static of commerce is very much in the air. Situated on the Noyyal River, flanked on the north and west by mountains, blessed by a mild climate, it still remains—despite increasing levels of congestion—a city of some charm.

But gradually, you find your taxi swerving away from city streets. You are heading west. Rural south India, never far from the surface, starts emerging from the crevices. You are hurtling through villages now. The roads grow narrower, the terrain greener, and suddenly up ahead, you see the mountains—the Velliangiri Mountains, the 'white' or 'silver' mountains, as they are known, forested, mysterious, cloud-crested. Abruptly, silence falls.

It makes the roar of the car engine seem louder than before. You can still hear the cry of a village child on his way back from school, the bleating of a goat, the honk of a passing motorist. But the silence is tangible, as is the wild lonely scent of mountain air. You pass a board that tells you that you're only a few kilometres away from your destination.

The car enters a dirt track. Its progress is now slow and epileptic. The monsoons have ravaged the earth, leaving a trail of craters and stiff furrows of mud. You lurch. The cabbie whistles softly, but doesn't look particularly perturbed. The devotional Tamil film songs warbling forth from his music system lose none of their piercing ardour. At last you're there.

A security guard asks you the purpose of your visit, hands you a visitor's tag. If you've been to other ashrams in India, you might be struck by the difference in appearance. There's austerity here, but not an unimaginative functionality. The aesthetic is one of uncluttered stone and wood, spare and yet crafted with an exquisite attention to detail. You see it in the way each rock, shrub and tree is positioned. Nothing tamed, nothing manicured. But there's clearly much guile in this guilelessness. And at every turn, there are the mountains, a forbidding reminder of how little separates you from a seething, lawless wilderness.

You may be inclined to go first to your cottage, if you've booked one, deposit your bags and recover from your journey. But perhaps you are impatient. The purpose of your visit, like that of so many others, is that mysterious shrine you've heard so much about. Perhaps friends have told you about it. Perhaps you stumbled upon it on the web. Perhaps like so many others, you dreamt about it even before you saw it. But you know that you need to get there, and preferably, soon.

There is a *parikrama*, a ritual circular journey, before you reach your goal. You leave your footwear in a stall and then meet a volunteer who tells you something about the significance of what you are about to experience. You start walking around the precincts of the shrine, stopping, if you are inclined, to take a ritual dip in a temple tank before you enter. But this is not just a ceremonial cleansing, you are told. The *teerthakund* is a subterranean tank—thirty-five feet below the ground—whose waters are energized by a *linga* made of solidified mercury (a feat made possible apparently by a yogic process of alchemy called *rasavaidya*). The result: exceptional psychological and physical benefits as well as a heightened state of receptivity. You are tingling and invigorated as you emerge. But if you're sceptical about this kind of thing, you may attribute it to no more than the aftereffects of a cold bath. And yet, the place is atmospheric. The enormous murals, painted with natural dyes, which adorn the roof and walls of the surrounding vault, create an effect of dignity and muted grandeur. The sense of expectancy mounts.

Your next stop is the recently established shrine of the Linga Bhairavi. She is the resident goddess, you learn, fiery, compassionate and wild. She inhabits a small and vibrant space, nestled to the south-west of the parikrama. Her abode is intimate, her colours flaming crimson and smouldering coal-black. The place is managed entirely by priestesses in vermilion saris; male attendants are conspicuous by their absence. You may find yourself uncomfortable with the flagrant display of idolatry. There is certainly a fair amount of chanting and coconut-breaking going on. But you can't help noticing that there is a spareness and elegance about the ritual. There is evidence of taste everywhere—in the textured walls, the fabric, the simple symmetry of the idol—and it is possible to appreciate its restraint and beauty, even if you cannot summon up any real fervour. You could secretly find yourself making a wish (she is, after all, known to be a boon-granting goddess, and you might consider it a sound idea to stay in the good books of goddesses, notoriously temperamental women in all spiritual traditions). As you leave, the Devi's lingering diamond-studded gaze follows you.

You walk further and find yourself approaching the gateway to the main shrine. Visually, it is a dramatic moment. You see the elliptical dome outlined clearly against the softly rolling Velliangiri Mountains, frosted with mist. The dome, you learn later, is made entirely of brick and mud mortar, untarnished by cement, steel or concrete. A Sarva Dharma Stambha or pillar stands at the entrance, emblazoned with sculptural symbols of various faiths. It is yet another reminder—apart from the abiding silence—that this is not a regular Hindu temple you are about to visit. You climb the three steep cobbled steps. You now walk a stretch of open space, flanked by rock panels on either side that reveal scenes from the lives of south Indian mystics. The walkway is clearly designed, in the manner of traditional sacred architecture, to heighten the mood of suspense. It works.

Then it is upon you. The space seems larger than it appears from the outside, illuminated by the wavering glow of lamplight. Before you towers a massive dense granite column of over thirteen feet, its implacable black surface punctuated symmetrically with seven copper rings. The base takes the form of a gigantic seven-coiled stone serpent. Around it is a simple water border, on which flowers, surrounded by oil lamps, float serenely. If you have been to other places of modern Indian worship, you will be struck by the unfussiness here. The space is stark, unostentatious, distinctly womblike; the impact primal.

You make your way to one of the shadowy alcoves and sit down to receive the Dhyanalinga.

The Dhyanalinga means different things to different people. For some it is nothing short of an epiphany. They emerge, stupefied and ecstatic. For others, it is a process rather than a place—a deepener, a clarifier, an intensifier. They emerge distinctly different from the way they entered. There is a quiet about them, a greater awareness about the movements of mind and body. A few say they experienced nothing out of the ordinary. And yet, minutes turn imperceptibly to hours before they emerge. Almost all acknowledge that they experienced a sense of having been sifted and sorted. Distilled.

'It came to me like a gift from God at a time when I really needed it,' says classical vocalist, Sudha Raghunathan. 'I was actually meditating effortlessly—something I've wanted to do for years, but never knew how,' writes a visitor from Michigan. 'It's the strangest experience I've ever had. I've been to many *shakti sthals* in this country, but never one that reverberates with this kind of raw energy,' says a retired businessman from Punjab. 'I went in, my mind racing with worries. But when I was in there, those anxieties just lifted; it felt like someone was holding them inches away from me and I could breathe again,' says a German visitor. 'It felt like I had found my teacher, one who would always be there for me, one who gives freely, unstintingly and impartially,' says a Lebanese meditator. 'Often I enter the place with doubts about what I'm doing, whether I'm just escaping my worldly responsibilities by coming here. But each time I sit in the presence of the Dhyanalinga, those doubts evaporate. I know just why I'm here,' writes a schoolteacher from Canada. Another young woman puts it even more succinctly, 'It's become the truest friend I've known.'

There are those who testify that the process starts even before they arrive. For them it is just accidentally encountering a picture of the Dhyanalinga that produces a frisson, an insistent curiosity. This seems to have happened on occasion to those who have had no prior interest whatsoever in the spiritual life.

Does the image kindle something atavistic, some deep response in the unconscious mind to an elemental form? Or is it just the carefully-orchestrated drama of the entire experience that does the trick? And what is the Dhyanalinga anyway?

The answers you'd elicit would be varied, depending on the seeker in question. 'An instrument for meditation,' would be an answer from the rational end of the Isha spectrum; 'Shiva' would be an answer from the more devotional end.

Eventually, you'd gather something to this effect. You'd learn that the Dhyanalinga is the only one of its kind on the planet. You'd learn that sitting in its intense energy field is equivalent to sitting in the presence of a live master. You'd learn that it is a perennial energy form, indestructible, immortal, destined to live on even if the planet were to perish.

The Dhyanalinga, then, is a living, pulsating presence, not merely a stone edifice. It would be possible (a volunteer at the entrance tells you) to do away with the granite form entirely without affecting the efficacy of the linga. But if the structure is retained, it is because most seekers need some tangible form to which they can relate.

There is a medieval counterpart in Bhojpur in the state of Madhya Pradesh, you'd find out, but one that was tragically distorted before it reached completion. And that makes this Dhyanalinga a triumph, an achievement that is not easily recognizable for those unaware of the history of this spiritual science.

And why a linga, you might wonder. Surely a linga is a symbol immediately associated with phallus worship and a brand of Hinduism? It is that, and the volunteer isn't apologetic about those associations. But it is also much more than that, he tells you. The ellipsoid is actually a fundamental form. Modern science holds that the core of every galaxy is an ellipsoid. Spiritual seers from various traditions have always known that it is the first form to emerge from formlessness (or the void, or whatever you choose to call that primordial state). It is also the last form before dissolution.

And so the technology of linga-making is an ancient one, found at varied levels of refinement in several cultures of the world. It is one that requires high levels of spiritual mastery and understanding. But the science of creating a Dhyanalinga requires a level of prowess that is even more considerable. It takes more than virtuosity. It takes, you are told, a fierce commitment and a brand of near-insane courage. It took, in this case, a willingness to lay down one's life—not just once but several times over.

There are many ways to tell the life story of the Dhyanalinga. But none of them can be separated from the life of its author. There are many ways to tell his life story as well. One is a strenuously unvarnished account stripped of any detail that might cause

Aum Sarvebhyo Devebhyo Namaha
Aum Pancha Bhutaya Namaha
Shri Sathgurave Namaha
Aum Shri Prithvyai Namaha
Aum Adiyogishwaraya Namaha
Aum, Aum, Aum

When you
FOCUS
ON WHAT YOU WANT,

everything else
falls away.

discomfort to a sceptic. The other is a more generous chronicle that straddles fact as well as unverifiable but illuminating detail.

The author of the Dhyanalinga is a lover of metaphor. When a child once asked him whether life was true or a dream, he replied with a mystic's classic ease with paradox: 'Life is a dream, but the dream is true.' He reads and writes verse, but the Dhyanalinga alone would be sufficient testimony to the fact that he is a poet. He frequently draws attention to the distinction between 'fact' and 'truth'. It is the distinction every lover of art knows only too well; the finest fiction and poetry are so clearly the realm of the latter. This makes it seem like an act of violence to exclude the non-rational from this story.

At the same time, the creator of the Dhyanalinga is a sceptic too. His rationality can be scathing, and his dismissal of the deceptions on the spiritual path, unequivocal and severe. This makes it easier to believe the more incredible aspects of his tale. If the reader could hear the matter-of-fact tone with which many of these incidents were narrated, it would probably make it easier to accept them.

Let's start this story with an option. The next chapter is a possible beginning to this story. Not the only one, however. Those who find it difficult to stomach could simply move on to the one after that and pick up the narrative from there.

Truth or fact. The real or the historical. The choice is yours. But a word of warning: at several junctures in the story, the two aren't quite so inseparable. An insight into this enigmatic combination—also a key to what a reader can expect from this story—is to be found in the way the creator of the Dhyanalinga once described his creation. 'It's a cocktail,' he said, 'of pure awareness and madness.'

And that is probably as accurate a description as you can get of Sadhguru himself.

'Falling Upwards'
Lifetimes Three

The following is a story Sadhguru has often related.

Around four hundred years ago in the Raigad district, now in Madhya Pradesh, there lived a man named Bilva. He was a tall, strapping young man, fearless and intensely in love with life. He was regarded by his tribe of snake charmers as a strange and unconventional character. He was a Shiva devotee, a rebel, a chronic rule-breaker. When he walked, it was with the arrogance of one who regarded the earth as his inheritance. It offended many. They found his intensity disturbing, the majesty of his bearing at odds with his station in life. An archetypal figure, he seemed genetically programmed to be at odds with the world he lived in.

He transgressed caste rules by falling in love with a Brahmin girl named Shambhavi. It was a doomed situation. The caste hierarchy of his day was rigid and unforgiving. But Bilva was a man of passion, rather than reason. To protect his clan from the repercussions of this forbidden love, he decided to move them to Sambalpur in modern-day Orissa. Apart from reasons of safety, there was also his deep devotion towards the deity of the Mukteshwar temple near that town.

The lovers continued their clandestine meetings in the fields and forests that Bilva knew so well. But their liaison could not be kept secret for long. Shambhavi's community soon discovered the truth and all hell broke loose. The curses and threats did not deter Bilva, however. He started devising strategies of elopement with the woman he loved. He was just twenty-seven years old, a man in the prime of his life, and he knew no fear.

Eventually, a group of men from Shambavi's family, spearheaded by an enraged uncle, and aided by the local ruler, laid a trap for the young man. It was a full moon night. The lovers had planned a secret rendezvous in the jungle. Bilva walked unsuspectingly into the trap. Before he knew it, he was surrounded and taken captive.

He was tied to a tree and one of his own snakes let loose on him. The snake venom coursed through the young man's veins. His blood thickened. The pain mounted. His lungs constricted. But determined not to give his tormentors the pleasure of watching him die an ignominious death, Bilva started watching his breath. He watched as it grew laboured, as it came to a final rasping halt. But what should have been a brutal end became a graceful exit. He had left his body in full awareness.

That awareness brought him back in his next birth as a spiritual aspirant. His spiritual sadhana was infused with a touch of venom. That venom gave a fierce edge to his spiritual practice, a near-insane urgency, which was never to leave him. Shivayogi reached high levels of yogic mastery through unrelenting penance. He came from a Telugu-speaking family, and travelled widely in his lifetime as an itinerant sadhu. In the time-honoured tradition of committed seekers in the country, he lived a life of acute hunger and hardship. Much of his time was spent on the mountains of Velliangiri, the abode of many legendary seers of the South. His yogic legerdemain won him a devoted following. He had at his command a formidable array of psychic powers or siddhis. But he was painfully aware of his own shortcomings. That he was not what people presumed him to be shamed him. He knew he was no more than an impostor until he attained his ultimate goal. Sadhguru describes it as a lifetime of painful, heartbreaking penance.

One day, as the yogi sat in meditation in the mountains, a wandering sadhu stopped by his side. This was Sri Palani Swami, a great sage from the hills south of Coimbatore. He owed his name to the fact that he had spent two and a half years in a state of samadhi in the town of Palani. Since then he had spent his life wandering the Tamil countryside, bestowing his guidance on many spiritual seekers. Palani Swami immediately recognized the ferocity and anguish of Shivayogi's yearning. All that was needed for the next step was the intervention of a guru. The next step, he knew, would be the conclusive one: 'falling upwards' into the unbounded realm of freedom.

But Shivayogi was a Shiva devotee and a proud man. Knowing he would be unwilling to accept spiritual intervention at the hands of anyone but Shiva, Palani Swami, in his compassion, appeared to him as the Adi Yogi himself. Shivayogi surrendered. Palani Swami then raised his staff and placed it on the seeker's forehead. In that moment, Shivayogi reached the state he had been in quest of all his life. Enlightenment dawned.

The guru went quietly on his way. Not a word had been uttered between master and disciple. No oaths were taken, no pledges of undying loyalty sworn. They were never to meet after that brief meeting. But Shivayogi would never forget the legacy of that encounter. The touch of Palani Swami's staff had freed him. But in its own strange way, it had also bound him. It had brought him to his final destination as a seeker. But it had sown within him a seed that would mark the beginning of his journey as a guru. It conferred upon him a responsibility that would take him lifetimes to fulfil.

That seed was the dream of countless yogis before him. It was the recipe to create a sacred form that would liberate not just a spiritual elite, but vast sections of humanity. It was the formula to make freedom available to all. The tale of the Dhyanalinga starts here.

While it was an honour to be chosen for this heroic undertaking, it was also a daunting prospect. Others had tried and failed. The Dhyanalinga was a yogic enterprise that seemed historically doomed. Its creation involved the participation of men and women in prolonged and intense spiritual practice—a situation that was always far too unconventional to meet with social comprehension. Tragedy had marked the lives of those who had had the temerity to attempt it. But Shivayogi's indebtedness to Palani Swami made failure out of the question. He knew that if he did not succeed, he would simply have to start over. Abandoning the mission was not an option.

Shivayogi's determination to realize his guru's dream failed in his lifetime. He died at the age of fifty-seven. The mission, however, endured.

In the early part of the twentieth century, Shivayogi returned. He was now Sadhguru Sri Brahma, a south Indian mystic, also from a Telugu-speaking family, famed for his abrasive manner and extravagant compassion. Numerous ashrams across southern India still stand as testimony to the devotion of the common man for this irascible but strangely lovable mystic.

At one point, when he lived at the ashram in Coonoor (still to be found in front of a well-known cordite factory), Sadhguru insisted on flouting British Raj restrictions that prohibited people from crossing the tracks at the nearby railway station. The rules were particularly stringent during the Second World War. But that did not deter him. When he was arrested for his offence, he simply walked out through the prison gates and strode back to his ashram. Nothing much could be done after that. Word spread and the Nilgiris region was soon filled with his staunchest disciples.

On another occasion, a crowd that had gathered to hear him speak near the Ooty Lake was agitated by some of his outspoken comments. Generous with his abuse, which was directed as freely at the gods as at those around him, Sadhguru Sri Brahma was often perceived as an arrogant and ungodly man. When the situation seemed on the verge of erupting into violence, Sadhguru paused and asked an eleven-year-old boy in the crowd to step forward. He placed a hand on the boy's head, and bade him walk on the lake. The boy proceeded to do just that. The simmering crowd fell suddenly quiet. Sadhguru was known to perform this kind of flamboyant miracle, however, only in extreme situations.

Sadhguru Sri Brahma did his best to establish the Dhyanalinga. But social opposition to this spiritual process was considerable. What was this peculiar yogic practice that involved the involvement of men and women in conditions of intense proximity? The notion offended some of the most fiercely-guarded norms of south Indian orthodoxy. Sadhguru was hounded out of Coimbatore.

In a fury, the yogi walked for days on end. For his faithful disciple, Vibhuthi, keeping pace with him was not easy. What made things even more difficult was procuring provisions from the locals of the villages they passed, cooking a meal and hastening to his master's side before he moved on. It meant waiting until his master was deep in meditation and then surreptitiously placing the meal in front of him. The disciple would then go into hiding and from a safe distance, watch his master eat his food. More overt intervention would have further incensed Sadhguru who was already in an inflamed state.

The guru and the disciple walked on at a relentless pace. Eventually they reached Cuddappah in modern-day Andhra Pradesh. Here they settled down in the small temple of Someshwar, dedicated to the intoxicating form of Shiva. The temple priest and other officials beat a hasty retreat, unable to bear the scorching intensity of their presence. There was a reason for choosing this temple: Sri Palani Swami had been here in his lifetime.

For the next six months, in this nondescript little temple in the dusty town of Cuddappah, a plot was hatched by guru and disciple. It was a plot that decided the future destiny of more than two dozen people, right down to the family and the specific womb in which they were to be born, the skills they would acquire, the kind of lives they would lead. It was an attempt to create a future environment that would be congenial to the creation of the Dhyanalinga. The hurdle that had prevented the Dhyanalinga from reaching fruition right through history was social. Yogis of virtuosity had been thwarted by the rigidity of prevalent norms. In a shrewd tactical move, Sadhguru decided to place some of his trusted disciples in the families from which he anticipated the most hostility. The rationale: being implicated, they would find it difficult to foil his plans. But one thing was clear. Opposition was inevitable. The creation of the Dhyanalinga would always meet with bitter adversaries.

The stage was now set for the final act. Scripted with attention to infinitesimal detail, the next performance had to be the clincher. But before the great plot was swung into action, Sadhguru made one more attempt to accomplish his aim. He chose the body of a *balayogi* or child saint, Sadananda, in an ashram at Vajreshwari in western India. Having attained enlightenment at the age of eleven, Sadananda had spent three-odd years in a *samadhi* state and had shed his body at the age of twenty-six. Though he now had a plan in place, when Sadhguru saw this alternative opportunity in the form of a carefully prepared body, he grabbed it.

For a few months, he inhabited two bodies. He knew his lifespan was limited and he worked intensely to create a few disciples who could fulfil his mission. But he was disappointed. The situation he found in Vajreshwari was no more conducive to the creation of the Dhyanalinga than the one in Coimbatore. He shed the balayogi's body, reverted to his own and prepared for his own departure. Another lifetime had failed. It looked like Palani Swami's dream was to remain just that: an enormous possibility that the world was just not ready to embrace.

Sadhguru now returned to the Velliangiri Mountains. He ascended the seventh hill, the wild and windswept landscape of which still says much about the man who chose it as the site of his final departure. Here he left his body through all seven chakras—the mark of a Chakreshwara, a yogi of rare accomplishment, his precursor being none other than Shiva, the first recorded yogi in the history of mankind.

But before his spectacular exit at the age of forty-two, Sadhguru Sri Brahma made a declaration: 'I will be back.'

'This One Will Graze Human Beings'
The Black Sheep Who Turned Shepherd

'Others graze sheep; this one will graze human beings.' This was the cryptic remark made by a visiting clairvoyant who was asked to cast the horoscope of the newborn in the Vasudev household. He wrote with a flourish across the child's horoscope: 'He is blessed with a fortunate life.'

Jagadish had been born on 3 September 1957, at eleven fifty-four, six minutes before midnight, to Susheela and her husband, Vasudev. He was born in Mysore, a city redolent with historic and cultural associations, an erstwhile royal capital, synonymous in the popular imagination with palaces and landscaped gardens. It had been a tardy arrival. The anxiously awaited child made his appearance twenty-three days late. Perhaps he had some idea of the postnatal challenges in store for him.

The youngest child in the family, Jagadish's birth was preceded by that of a boy and two girls. There was customary tension in the Vasudev family over the choice of the children's names. The grandparents preferred traditional names, while the parents' tastes ran to more contemporary alternatives. In each case, they eventually arrived at a truce. When the former suggested Papamma as a name for one of the newborn girls, the latter settled on Pushpalata. When Raghavendra was deemed the appropriate name for the first son in the family, the parents opted for Ravindra.

In this case, however, the visiting fortune-teller clinched the matter. He simply conferred his own name upon the infant. Jagadish—or 'the lord of the universe'—would be his name, he decided. Jaggi was later to become the child's inevitable nickname.

A year before Jaggi was born, the Vasudevs had had a male child who died in the early stages of infancy. He was a beautiful child, endowed with all the astrological signs of future greatness. The infant did not live beyond a few days, however. As Jaggi—now Sadhguru—remarks in typically impersonal terms, 'This one made an attempt to return in 1956. But since he didn't meet with success the first time, he tried again a year later. The second time it worked.'

The Vasudevs were a Telugu-speaking family, based in Karnataka. Dr Vasudev, a noted ophthalmologist, came from an affluent family of Bangalore. His mother had died of tuberculosis when he was a child, and he grew up determined to fulfil her dying wish that he become a doctor. This was, however, against the wishes of his father who preferred that he shoulder responsibility for his share of the family business. Encouraged by his maternal uncle, the young boy studied medicine at Mysore Medical College, choosing to specialize in ophthalmology. A fiercely principled and self-respecting young man, he managed to fund much of his education through scholarships, often studying late into the night by the light of streetlamps.

In due course, his family arranged his marriage to Susheela, the daughter of a wealthy and aristocratic family that traced its lineage to Krishnadeva Raya the famed ruler of the Vijayanagara Empire. Susheela was a gentle and soft-spoken woman who enjoyed the traditional role of family caregiver and nurturer. But she was no pushover either. As all her children—particularly Jaggi, the habitual scamp—discovered, she was capable of being firm when the situation demanded.

Since he had been born with his mother's umbilical cord coiled around his shoulder, Jaggi was regarded, according to traditional superstition, as a potential threat to family wellbeing. 'There was a belief that the maternal uncle's life would be at risk,' he says. Among the various precautions taken to ward off the danger was the refusal to submit the child to a haircut until the age of five. 'This meant that my hair grew wild and curly, and was tied in two pigails. Every day in school, I'd beat up someone who made any comment about my hair,' he recollects.

Dr Vasudev's profession as ophthalmologist with the Indian Railways meant a life of frequent transfers. As a result, Jaggi changed schools several times over, as the family moved between Shimoga, Chikkaballapur and Guntakal before returning to Mysore in 1969.

Gifted with a lively imagination, insatiable curiosity, high energy levels and a cheerful disregard of authority, Jaggi was the kind of child every adult learns to regard with dread. 'Sitting in class was impossible for me because when teachers were talking, I could see that they were talking about something that didn't mean anything to their lives,' he says. 'It was just a job they were doing, so I did not want to listen. I knew that whatever they were saying, I could read in a book, and get for myself very easily.'

Clearly, some of the changes of school were due, at least in part, to the fact that he was the quintessential rogue—irrepressible, feckless, devil-may-care. Life was unpredictable with him around. Nothing seemed to daunt him. He was willing to implement the most hair-raising stunts without the slightest thought of personal safety. 'Does nothing scare you whatsoever?' his parents would often ask despairingly. They seldom received a reply. Jaggi's demeanour was taciturn. That made it even more difficult to fathom the next trick up his sleeve. And the answer was self-evident: if anything at all could tame the boy it wasn't going to be fear.

'Either you're the Divine or the Devil,' spluttered an incensed schoolteacher when Jaggi refused to respond to his order to leave the classroom as a punishment for writing something cheeky on the blackboard. Seeing the student's infuriatingly unrepentant countenance, the teacher hissed darkly, 'And I know you're the latter.'

Tales of his misdemeanours are legion. He learnt the delights of truancy at an early age. It seemed far more sensible to spend the day perched on the upper branches of a tree than pore over pages of math. Few teachers had any idea what they were talking about, he decided. They were mere dictaphones on autopilot; their drone could get you through exams or guarantee a cure for insomnia, but little else. At an early age, Jaggi showed evidence of a trait that was to last a long while: an inability to suffer fools gladly. He never took exams very seriously, but invariably managed to scrape through, despite his teachers' dire predictions. Earning the reputation of an enfant terrible had its uses. Once everyone had given you up as a lost case, it meant at least that you were left to your own devices.

His lunch box and water bottle were the only companions he needed when he was on his tree. He spent the greater part of the time daydreaming, allowing the gentle rocking of the breeze to lull him into a state of quiet. He later described this as his first experience of the meditative state. He had no watch with him and was unaware of the passage of time. It was when he saw other students emerge from class that he knew that school was over. He would then scramble down and cycle home. 'I would climb to the topmost branch of a big tree and just sit there. It would sway and sway. After some time, it would transport me to a completely different kind of experience within myself, a trance-like situation, where I would lose all sense of time. I would just sit there on the tree from nine o'clock in the morning to four-thirty in the evening when the school let off. Much later when I started meditating, I realized that unknowingly I had been becoming meditative. Of course, I hadn't even heard of the word at the time. I just liked the feeling that sitting on top of a tree gave me.'

But truancy was not limited to day excursions on treetops. Jaggi was also given to secretly packing a picnic hamper (largely comprising boiled eggs and bread), leaving a note for his parents and disappearing for days on end. What did he do on these expeditions? Roam the forest, catch snakes, fish, trek, climb trees. He loved the outdoor life and the laws of nature seemed a lot less duplicitous than those back at home or school. When his food ran out, he returned home. His parents, he figured, had no reason to fret. He always left a note informing them of his departure (though not his whereabouts) and he always returned—eventually. A voracious eater, there was absolutely no question of his starving himself. The lure of Susheela's kitchen ensured that his vagrancy was always within bounds.

School had its moments, however. Jaggi was a force to reckon with in various class and school teams: hockey, kabaddi, football, volleyball, boxing, soccer, cricket and badminton. On those occasions when he graced the classroom, he enjoyed geography lessons. He was fascinated by the glimpses it offered into other lands, climates, cultures. An avid reader of the *National Geographic* in the school library, he loved the smell of its crisp pages and the distant worlds that its glossy pictures conjured. He often yearned for his own copy, though it wasn't until much later that he could afford the subscription. 'It took twenty-five years for me to get one,' he laughs. 'Even today, I get my *National Geographic*.'

His love of geography was linked to a deep curiosity about the physical features of the land around him. His capacity for observation was keen. 'What interested me was the way the world is made, the terrain, the way people live. I used to take my cycle along the mud roads in the countryside, riding a minimum of thirty to thirty-five kilometres a day. By the time I came home, I'd be all muddy and dusty. I particularly enjoyed mapping the terrain I'd passed through in my mind. I could just close my eyes when I was sitting alone and redraw the whole landscape that I'd seen that afternoon—every single rock, every outcrop, every single tree. I was fascinated by the different seasons, the way the land changes when it's ploughed, when the crops start coming up. That's how I started reading Thomas Hardy, because he describes the English landscape for pages on end. I was doing the same in my head with the landscape around me. Even today it's like a video in my mind. If I want I can replay the whole thing, those years and years of what I have noticed. These last three or four years of my life are not so clear. But before that everywhere that I've been—especially the terrain, the shapes, the forms—is so very vivid in my mind.'

His reading habits were omnivorous. Like the average Indian middle-class child, he read his share of Enid Blyton, but never found it adventurous enough for his taste. He devoured a fair amount of Russian literature, which in India of the 1970s was available at throwaway prices. After the age of twelve, it was the usual glut of racy suspense thrillers: from Alistair MacLean, Louis L'Amour and Frederick Forsythe to Leon Uris, Wilbur Smith and James Hadley Chase. His brother and he also devoured comics: from *Phantom* and *Tarzan* to *Archie* and *Mandrake*. 'But his favourite was *Asterix*, which I never enjoyed,' says his brother Ravindra.

Since they were only a year apart, the brothers often shared clothes. 'I remember a thief once stole all our shirts at night through the window,' recalls Ravindra. 'We woke up with no shirts to put on our backs and no shirts we could call our own! We eventually borrowed shirts from the neighbours and marched off to the cop station.' The thief, however, was never caught and the brothers were compelled to replenish their wardrobes.

A trip to the cinema on Saturday evenings was a weekly ritual for the Vasudev family. While the parents watched Hindi films, the children opted for English. *Ben Hur, Roman Holiday, Mackenna's Gold* and *Casablanca* were among Jaggi's special favourites. He still remembers going to see *Psycho* at the age of seven. While his terrified sisters soon fled the theatre, the implacable seven-year-old stayed glued to his seat until the bitter end. 'I had a ticket and saw no reason why I should leave,' he shrugs. 'My sisters waited for me outside.'

There were two English movie theatres in Mysore city and for a couple of years Jaggi watched two films a week. On holidays at his grandparents' home, he and his cousins would sometimes go and watch Telugu cinema. 'The theatres were all ours and we could go in and come out at any time we wanted. There were no tickets, nothing. We watched many N.T. Rama Rao movies at the time.'

Jaggi's experience of cinema had little to do with a cathartic involvement in the storyline. 'I was far more interested in the way it was shot. The scenes, I realized early on, are just about acting. I could see and appreciate that. I could shed tears in a movie if I wanted, but not for some sob story. If something really beautiful happened—moments of great love or joy—I shed tears. I still can and do. But if I wished, I could just sit there and watch the whole thing critically. I was capable of both.'

A close classmate, who was to remain a firm friend in later years, was Somanna, a boy from Coorg. Both discovered similar reading habits. They also happened to be on the school hockey team: while Somanna was a 'centre forward', Jaggi was a 'left out'. Their other great affinity was their ability to get into scrapes and their ingenious ways of bailing each other out. Once when a classmate was hauled up for calling the teacher 'Sleeping Lady' (the secret name by which the class referred to their somnolent social studies teacher), the outraged teacher asked the class to suggest an appropriate punishment for the boy. 'Pardon him,' piped up Jaggi. That did it. He was promptly dragged by his shirt to the headmaster's office. 'Of course, that wasn't a new place for me,' he says dryly. His teacher pronounced him the 'ringleader' of 'a bunch of rogues' and he was suspended for fifteen days.

The suspension was never a cause for gloom. It meant a happy fortnight wandering the countryside. 'The best student in school always gets extra vacation!' he grins. 'And I never complained.' These 'vacations' were not infrequent. Arranging a dead snake or frog on one of the blades of the classroom fan was not exactly the kind of deed teachers found amusing. Nor was it considered particularly appropriate to inform a teacher who caught him playing hooky that exams came twice a year while mangoes came only once. The argument was certainly logical—mango-picking being a strictly seasonal activity unlike exams that reappeared with monotonous regularity—but teachers seemed to live by a humourless logic of their own.

A slightly trickier issue was the 'vacation letter' despatched by the headmaster to Jaggi's parents. But a friend like Somanna, the son of the local postmaster, proved to be a blessing. The letter was intercepted at the post office and never reached the Vasudev household. 'It meant being friendly with the school peon and finding out when the letter was being posted,' he says. 'Once we knew that, I'd go to Somanna's house at night, shin up a gulmohur tree into his bedroom. Somanna's brother hated me because we were as thick as thieves. So I had to wait for him to go to sleep and then slip into the bedroom. After that, we spent the night sorting out the letters—and helping out the postmaster.' On the couple of occasions, when such letters actually found their way to Jaggi's father, he only threw up his hands in grim despair, declaring, 'Let them throw you out.'

While teachers were generally an odious species, Jaggi was at least on one occasion pleasantly surprised. He remembers a teacher entering his ninth standard classroom. She was the new English teacher, young and full of enthusiasm for her first assignment. 'I remember her walking around the classroom,' he says. 'She was a tall woman. She was wearing a starched white sari. At one point, she came and stood near my desk. When she wasn't looking, I squirted blue ink on her sari with my pen. The fabric absorbed the ink like blotting paper.' That day at lunch break, he was summoned to her office. 'I entered. She asked for my pen. I handed it over. She didn't say a word. She simply pulled out an inkpot, filled up the pen and returned it to me. I said thank you and left. It was such a fabulous response, I never forgot it. After that she became my favourite teacher. The incident became a big bond between us. Much later, she became the principal of the school.'

Recently, after a talk in Mysore, he met another old English teacher. Excited by this encounter with her former pupil, she hugged him and remarked that she hadn't forgotten his schoolboy distaste for Robert Frost. Sadhguru couldn't remember it. She reminded him, 'You hated the line "The woods are lovely, dark and deep". You'd say, "Why 'woods'?" There's so much more to a tree than wood.' Laughing, Sadhguru now adds, 'It's true. I've always thought seeing a tree as wood is a bit vulgar; like looking at an animal and thinking only of meat or looking at a woman and thinking only of sex.'

Jaggi's fascination with wheels started early. Ravindra recalls how both of them coveted the Robin Hood bicycle, their father's prize possession. 'Then came the Vespa Piaggio scooter which, again, was the source of everyone's envy,' he says. 'We used to take turns riding on that scooter. My father used to lock it away and hide the key. He also noted down the number of kilometres on the speedometer. But I had made a duplicate key without his knowledge and used to ride it when he was in the bathroom or sleeping. We were careful to disconnect the speedometer cable and then run it, so he had no idea it was being used. After he found out about our stealth riding, he used to touch the engine every now and then to feel the heat, to check whether we had been up to our tricks! But we were careful to pour cold water on the engine and cool it down before he came on the scene. It was great fun while it lasted.'

Yoga entered Jaggi's life unobtrusively. It was the summer vacation. He was thirteen years old. He was part of a clamorous mob of thirty-five-odd grandchildren, all of whom had congregated for their holidays in their grandfather's ancestral home. In the backyard stood a well, over a hundred-and-fifty-feet deep, that was a source of great fascination for the boys. While the girls played hide-and-seek, the boys' regular pastime was to jump into the well and then claw their way up its steep sides, grabbing at improvised footholds and heaving themselves up. Once they reached the top, the idea was to jump in again and repeat the procedure. 'It was usually summertime when we were there, so the water was normally about sixty to seventy feet below ground level,' he says. 'Both jumping down and climbing up were a challenge. If you didn't jump properly, your brains could become a smear on the wall. And then, while climbing up, there were no steps, no ladder, nothing; you just had to hold the rock surface and come up. By the time you came up, your fingernails would be bleeding, out of sheer pressure. Just a few of the boys could do this. I could do it and I was pretty good at it.'

One day, an old man, well over seventy, appeared on the scene. He seemed an innocuous bystander. The boys paid little attention to him. Their expectations of the geriatric gentleman were clearly not very high. Their mouths fell agape when the old man nimbly leapt into the well without uttering a word, and clambered out quicker than any of them. A chastened Jaggi had just one question for him: How? 'Come,' replied the old man, 'and learn yoga.'

There were no second thoughts. Physical fitness and agility were Jaggi's highest priorities. And if yoga provided this level of strength and vitality, he was a willing student. Jaggi proceeded to become a student of Malladihalli Swami (the popular name, he discovered, of Sri Raghavendra Rao, the well-climbing wizard). 'And that's how I got into yoga,' he says. 'I just followed this man like a puppy. And I am telling you this so you know—even if you get into it for the wrong reasons, it still works!'

He learnt a simple set of yoga *asanas* that he practised daily. The regularity of his yoga regimen surprised even him for discipline had never been one of his virtues. But somehow the everyday yoga just seemed to 'happen' for years on end. 'When I got up every morning yoga would simply happen, no matter where I was and in what situation I was, through the next twelve or thirteen years, without a single day's break. This simple yoga that was taught to me kept happening and led to a much deeper experience later. Till that experience, I had no idea that I was doing a spiritual process. I only knew that this yoga definitely set me apart physically and mentally from many people. But that's about all, I thought.'

It was a long time later that he discovered that his master was actually a yoga practitioner of exceptional calibre. Malladihalli

Swami's achievements would probably fill pages. Though he never shifted base from his tiny village of Malladihalli (in the Chitradurga district of Karnataka), he was a formidable teacher and practitioner of yoga and Ayurveda, and taught these disciplines to thousands of students in his lifetime. He ran an Ayurvedic hospital, a World Yoga Trust and several educational institutions on a non-profit basis. He declined the many state and central government awards that came his way on the grounds that it was his aim to collect not awards, but funds for his projects for the needy and underprivileged.

He seldom talked about his own yogic prowess, firmly believing that yoga was not meant to be exhibited and turned into a competitive sport. But Jaggi discovered that his amazing teacher actually did four thousand and eight *surya namaskars* a day. He was also a body-builder and an expert on traditional martial arts. Many years later, even after Jaggi had put in eight years at the gymnasium, he was still unable to beat his teacher at wrestling. 'He was an excellent wrestler. I was good at that time, and I was known to be very, very quick. And there were other boys who were stronger than me. If we got into the wrestling ring with him, it was always the three of us against him. But we never lasted even a single minute! He always had all three of us pinned down within a minute's time, this eighty-three-year-old man.'

A story he often relates is how his teacher once happened to be waiting at a railway station with a couple of friends. It was a Sunday evening and the Swami was in a hurry to return to his ashram where he had several patients to attend to the next morning. After a while, they discovered, to their dismay, that there was a railway strike. There was nothing to do but wait. The Swami, however, decided to take matters into his own hands. His friends watched open-mouthed as he leapt down on the railway tracks and began running homeward.

He ran the entire distance of seventy kilometres in the course of a night, and was at his clinic at the crack of dawn, well in time to attend to his first patient. No one in the ashram had a clue of his nocturnal journey. It was much later that his two companions reached the place and disclosed what had happened.

'He was almost superhuman,' says Sadhguru. 'You couldn't believe a man could be like that. When he was in his eighties, we used to visit him and make fun of him. We'd joke and say, "Okay, when will you go, old man? It looks like we will go before you." He used to very confidently answer, "I have another forty years of work. I will finish that and then go." The way he was going, it looked like he was easily going to fulfill that.'

Malladihalli Swami taught yoga, says Sadhguru, to his last days. At the age of a hundred and six, he collapsed while delivering a lecture in Mysore city. He was admitted to hospital and diagnosed with a minor heart attack. He regained consciousness at night to find himself in an ICU, surrounded by a maze of needles and tubes. The impatient master simply wrenched them out, jumped out of the first floor window and ran home. He died peacefully three months later in his ashram, having led an active life until the very end.

Much later, Sadhguru was to reveal that Malladihalli Swami was none other than a student of his own master in another lifetime, Sri Palani Swami. When I first heard this, the implications fascinated me. Does that mean your master actually engineered your tryst with your yoga teacher in this lifetime, I asked him. Sadhguru shrugged. His manner grew remote, as it often does when he talks of his guru. 'A guru's compassion and a guru's conspiracy work in so many ways,' he said quietly. 'A guru doesn't even know the difference between the two. Whatever is his whim will just find its way in the world. Maybe I was a small part of his plan. At least that's how I look at it.'

There was little to show that Jaggi himself was anything other than a schoolkid in a perennial state of energy overdrive—more stubborn than most, maybe, but basically a boisterous young prankster. There were other signs, however, that did not go unnoticed by those close to him. His mother was often disconcerted by his ability to remember incidents and conversations that had occurred at home when he was only days or months old. The details he recalled were often so trifling—such as the colour of his mother's sari, or what someone said on a particular occasion—that his memory of them was all the more baffling. Then there was his ability to size up a person at first glance. It is a trait that has not left him: his capacity to instantly assess a newcomer, the personality as well as the general life trajectory.

These latent abilities lent him an air of maturity far beyond his years. 'Probably this was the reason why no one in the family could cuddle me, like they did other kids,' he says. 'My presence was like that. It just didn't allow me to be like a normal child. So, because of this, nobody could take me on their lap; nobody could fondle me; nobody could carry me.' Even as a toddler, he disliked being carried. When he went out with his family, he would choose to walk, while his elder brother was invariably carried by either of his parents. 'Somehow it was difficult to hold or hug me,' he laughs. 'I am still difficult, see . . .?'

The ability, which no one knew about, was his sudden perception, at the age of five, of people as unclothed physical forms. The visions were far from lustful. It was simply the ability to see those around him as naked bodies. A while later, he saw them simply as puffs of air (which he learnt much later to identify as the 'energy or karmic bodies', *pranamayakosha* in yogic terminology). There was nothing odd about these visions as far as he was concerned. He simply assumed that everyone else saw the world the same way. It was only in his adulthood that he recognized these early flashes of altered perception for what they were.

'This happened when I was five–six years of age, or even later,' he recalls. 'This was a common thing for me. If I just sat down in the family sitting room and looked at people—you know, my mother, father, brother, sisters—I would just see them as hazy beings. They were just like ghosts, moving here, there. I always wondered, what the hell are they doing? If I was moving around or talking, then I would see them as people. But if I simply sat down, I would just see them as smoky people walking around. And once you see them as semi-solid, smoky people, the whole drama becomes meaningless, you know? Suddenly my dad comes and asks, "What happened to your mathematics? When is your quarterly exam?" It was like out of the blue. I wouldn't know what he was talking about. It's like watching television after you press the mute button. Suddenly, the whole drama becomes absolutely ridiculous.'

His vacant expression wasn't regarded as a sign of any kind of profound wisdom at the time. If anything, it annoyed his family. 'To the extent that my father started thinking I needed psychiatric help!' he says. 'It's just that I realized very eaıly that I did not know anything. Because of that, I had to pay enormous attention to everything around me. I could stare at a leaf or a glass of water endlessly. I could stare at the darkness all night. If I saw a pebble, it would rotate endlessly in my head. It's not that I was thinking about it. It's just that the image would keep turning in my head a million times. I would know its every grain, its every angle. If someone spoke, I realized they were only making sounds and I was making up the meanings. So I stopped making up meanings, and the sounds became just funny. I could see patterns spewing out of their mouths. If I kept on staring, the person would disintegrate and become just a ghostlike form. Then all that was left was patterns.'

This ability to see things he shouldn't presented its awkward, if hilarious, moments. When he was in Class I, he innocently asked his teacher why she was wearing red underwear. 'She freaked out,' he recalls simply. And that, no doubt, is an understatement.

Later in his adolescence, this heightened sense of perception prompted him to ask on entering a male friend's room: 'Hey man, who's the girl in here?' The question was spontaneous. He had actually been able to 'sniff out' a female presence, despite the fact that there were no obvious traces of anyone else in the room. There was no perfume in the air either. His friend informed Jaggi somewhat huffily that his sister happened to be visiting and was in the bathroom. 'He got all worked up just because I had smelt his sister!' laughs Sadhguru.

He adds that this sense of smell has saved his life on many occasions in the forest when he was able to scent danger before it actually appeared. 'And it's enriched my experience of life in so many ways as well. I experience the world much more fully because I can decipher its smells.'

His early capacity for visualization was also considerable. When his cousin visited him at the age of ten, he introduced the boy to his own private fantasy world on the terrace of his home. It was a world that had been worked out to the minutest detail. 'I would always climb to the third-floor terrace where there was no staircase, so nobody could reach me. Only I had access to the place. Nobody else could climb there. I just built a home, a world of my own, another world, in the smallest detail. It is very difficult for people to understand this. Suppose I want to create a flower, I went cell by cell. You know how much time it will take to mentally create this flower? Point by point—like this I created a whole world of my own. I just sat like this for five or six hours, unmoving, building it, piece by piece, piece by piece. It became such a reality. Nobody else had entry into my world, but I sometimes took my cousin on a tour. And the boy went so crazy, he wanted to go there every day. If I didn't take him, he would start crying!'

What was the world exactly? 'A Xanadu without the palaces,' he says. 'A wild place with wild animals. There was a leopard there, and a rhinoceros. The rhino was my favourite animal.'

This anecdote seems to offer early evidence of a visionary ability—the capacity to think big and think small, simultaneously. It is something every human being is capable of, says Sadhguru, if one could just learn to dream dreams of which one doesn't feel compelled to be the protagonist. 'If you have the necessary stability to remove yourself from the activity you are doing, if you can completely eliminate your person from whatever you do, suddenly you can raise the pitch of your activity to a completely different dimension. But people do not know generally how to act towards something that doesn't concern them, or something they are not identified with, and that is the limitation. That is the terrible crippling limitation that the human being has imposed upon himself. He cannot act upon what is not him or his.'

The terrace was Jaggi's private lair, the site of his crazy schemes. Since it could only be accessed by someone athletic and persevering enough to use a pipe, a tree or a window grill, no one in the family entered it. This was just as well, for Jaggi's other disturbing idiosyncrasy—for which the terrace was the inevitable locus—was a passion for snakes. Not surprisingly, it was a passion that met with unanimous disfavour in the Vasudev household. Jaggi's knowledge of birds and reptiles was instinctive. From the time he was a four-year-old preschooler, he had always preferred the rich roiling gutter outside his school to the sanitized lifelessness of the classroom. 'My maidservant would take me every morning and leave me at school and then again pick me up in the afternoon. I always made a deal that she should leave me at the gate and not come inside the school. As soon as she went, I would come out and sit beside this gutter. I was never interested in the classroom.'

There was nothing stagnant about the gutter, he knew. To someone of his size, it was nothing less than the 'Grand Canyon' itself, rife and swarming with unexplored possibilities, home to a dazzling variety of snakes—water snakes, garden snakes, little snakes, big snakes, venomous snakes and non-venomous snakes. 'It never occurred to me to be afraid of snakes. I don't know why. Maybe I looked a little freakish to other people because of this. But just as I was comfortable with everything else, I was comfortable with snakes as well. They never alarmed me.'

He frequently collected frogs and tadpoles in empty medicine bottles garnered from his father. Unfortunately, the snakes couldn't be so easily accommodated. That didn't deter him for long, however. Ravindra was among the first in the family to discover the mini reptile farm on the terrace. 'I found Jaggi had put snakes inside glass jars. I thought it was weird, but I didn't let my parents know about it. I knew my father would raise hell.'

In time, Jaggi developed a considerable reputation as a neighbourhood snake catcher and was paid handsomely for his services. 'Generally, people fear snakes because they move very quickly. But that was never an issue for me because I had learnt that a human being can move much quicker. When I went to catch snakes, I didn't go with a stick, wait for them to settle down, then hold them down before picking them up, which is what snake catchers generally do. I could go even to a provoked cobra and catch it directly. I did this for many years. I don't know if I have the speed or coordination to do it today. But it was something I did with great confidence then.'

He was also able to intuitively discern the presence of snakes. 'I developed a certain keen sense, which has gone out of my system these days because of a lack of application. I could easily track a snake in the wild. I would smell it and just go and catch it. If I went to some spot on Chamundi Hill, I would know under exactly which rock the snake would be at that moment. These days I have lost that sense. Too many people and too much city stuff around me these days.'

It proved to be a lucrative knack to have. 'Ever since my childhood I have not taken a single rupee of pocket money from my parents. I was earning my own money even when I was in the sixth and seventh standards. There was a large Central Institute nearby, which had a very large campus with many snakes. There was a norm there: if anybody caught a small snake there, they would pay twenty-five rupees. For a large snake—over three feet long—they would pay fifty rupees. Fifty rupees was a lot of money in those days. So on Saturday afternoons if I went there, I would catch three or four snakes in an afternoon, which would leave me with a hundred and fifty or two hundred rupees. That was one of the ways I earned my pocket money.'

One day he caught a snake that had made its way into a local tube light factory—to the great relief of the factory workers. He couldn't bear to be parted from his prize catch, however, and decided to smuggle it home and hide it under his bed. It soon became a close companion.

Inevitably, his strange 'under-the-bedfellow' was discovered in the course of time by his father, who decided to investigate the source of a fierce hiss. 'When he heard that strange sound, my father went down on his knees and looked to see what it was,' recalls Sadhguru. 'I had my snake in a big glass case. That tube light factory had given me a big laboratory jar, free of cost, which I could close partially. That allowed me to keep the snake in it. I'd keep him in the jar all day, and in the evenings, when I came back from school, I'd take him out somewhere and give him exercise before putting him back again. So my father looked at the snake, and he just freaked out! He was hopping mad when I came home. Of course, he was also terrified. Everyone at home was literally standing on chairs and sofas!'

Jaggi couldn't understand what the outrage was about. It was true that his snake was a twelve-foot-long cobra. But it was a beauty—not to mention, a friend. He grudgingly relocated the reptile—flouting his family's strict instruction that the snake be cast out of the house. He built a large cage and housed it on his terrace. It lived with him for three years. Thankfully, no one in the family ever visited the terrace in that period.

He was later to discover the source of his deep connection with snakes. It was, he realized, the legacy of an earlier lifetime. But there was more. The traditional veneration of snakes and cows in India, he often explains, is not a mere matter of superstition. All human beings, says Sadhguru, have lived out lifetimes as snakes and cows at some point in their journey of existential evolution. 'One aspect is the symbolism of the *kundalini* energy and its nature—its similarity with the snake in terms of movement and stillness. But another important aspect is that the snake is a compulsory and significant step in the evolution of a being. As the monkey is a significant step in the evolutionary process of the body, the snake is a significant step in the evolutionary process of the being. So is the cow. That's why in this culture, you are not supposed to kill either. If you find a dead snake or happen to kill one in India, you must give it a proper funeral and burial. A snake always gets a proper burial, because in terms of its being, it is very close to a human being. Killing a snake has always been seen as murder.'

Jaggi's encounter with reptiles was not always so amicable. On one occasion, when he gently pulled out a cobra from a rock crevice on a visit to a nearby hillock, he was taken aback to find two entwined snakes emerge instead of one. Before he knew it, the second cobra struck. Its fangs sank into his foot three times. The third time was particularly dangerous, for it struck the fleshy region between the toes. 'Once the venom enters you,' he says, 'you can feel a different kind of pain. It's like an injection. I knew it had entered my system. I didn't know how much. What I did know is that when a cobra bites, your blood starts coagulating, your heart's ability to pump blood grows difficult, and usually the anal outlet bursts because of this difficulty. One thing that could help slow down the process, I knew, is black tea.'

He had no time to lose. He dropped the first snake, managed to disengage the second, mounted his bike and started pedalling furiously homeward. He stopped at the first house he saw on the way, explained his predicament to a somewhat bemused lady and asked for five to six cups of black tea. It was a strange request, and it sent the woman into a flurry of nerves, but thankfully she acceded. Jaggi gulped down a pot of tea and managed to find his way home.

In characteristic fashion, he informed no one in the family. 'Initially, I thought I'd tell my father. As a doctor, he could have taken me to hospital or done something. Then I thought, what the hell. My eyelids were a bit heavy and droopy. But otherwise I was all right. I thought, let me see what happens.' He did a few yoga asanas, ate a quick meal and went to bed. Twelve hours later, he woke up. The black tea hadn't failed him.

There was one person in the family from whom Jaggi seemed to have inherited his wild and wilful ways. Family holidays were often spent in the home of his maternal great grandmother. Regarded as 'a devil of a woman', she was the original family rebel—a woman who flouted the convention of her day with impunity. Her wealthy husband owned acres of land, but she perversely chose to build a small temple on someone else's property. 'She believed no one could own land,' says Sadhguru. 'There is a Telugu saying that the only piece of land that rightfully belongs to you is "six by three"—the space you occupy when you're buried.'

Her behaviour was a source of considerable embarrassment to the family, but she remained blithely unconcerned. 'She was the family's disgrace, a thorn in everybody's flesh,' he says. 'You could not ignore or forget her, because people gathered around her. At least if people forgot her, if she had gone away, we could have said that she'd died. But she was right there and she ran a kingdom of her own.'

Her cussedness extended to other areas as well: she lived to the age of one hundred and thirteen, witnessing the deaths of her children, and even some of her grandchildren. An earlier exit would probably have been more convenient for her as well as the family. But with her intense love of life, she couldn't be induced to give up the ghost quite so easily. 'She chewed tobacco from the age of fourteen,' says Sadhguru. 'She chewed for ninety-nine years and at the age of one hundred and eleven, she got throat cancer. She refused to be treated. So two years later she died without any treatment. Most people did not know her name. When she grew old, because of a certain sciatica problem, she used to limp a little bit, so people just called her "Kuntamma"—that means "limping woman". Nobody knew her name because after a hundred and thirteen years, who'd remember your name?'

His reminiscences about this eccentric and flamboyant family figure are vivid: 'I have never seen my great grandfather; he died long ago. But my grandfather was the richest man in town. Somebody must have told him, "If you feed the poor you will go to heaven". So every morning he took out his attendance book. All the beggars in town—a little over two hundred people—could come there and be fed one full meal. They had to be registered in the book; otherwise they would not be fed! Every morning, my grandfather sat at the front of the house and watched, because he wanted to keep accounts of how many people had been fed. It was all being recorded. And people kept coming to him, because almost everybody in the town owed him some money. They'd come to settle their interests or loans. I'm sure if he did not have money people wouldn't have come. They came almost crawling in front of him because he had money and power. This was at the front door of the house. After they were done with the ugly business, they would all generally go to the back door. There, my great grandmother would reign. She had a certain way of sitting there; it made people think she was arrogant. She never uttered one arrogant word to anybody. But she just struck that kind of posture.'

If caste and creed were important at the front door, the rules of membership at the backdoor were quite different. 'At the front, if you were of the right caste, money would be given to you like this with a magnanimous gesture; if you were of the wrong caste it would be thrown at you. But when people came to the back door, all of them were embraced by this old woman.'

He remembers how her 'great hoot of laughter' reverberated down the length and breadth of the street she lived on. 'It was nothing short of scandalous at a time when women didn't have the licence to speak, let alone laugh. And she laughed because she saw life with much more depth than anybody could have imagined. Everybody around her looked like utter idiots to her.'

For Jaggi, holidays at her place spelt excitement. He remembers her as a great storyteller. 'When we went for summer vacations, if we stayed for thirty or forty days, she could stretch one story for the entire duration of our visit. Every evening we assembled for the story. "One day a princess came . . ." she would say, and start combing her hair slowly. That one story would spread across a whole month or more.'

Her most flagrant break with convention was, however, her mode of worship. In her pooja room, she dispensed with ritual and worshipped with an abandon that would have been conventionally regarded as nothing short of sacrilegious. Jaggi sometimes sat in the sanctum of her shrine, but was never rebuked for this transgression. He often watched her weep and laugh, sing and dance, address her deities with backslapping familiarity and kick flowers in their direction.

'I have seen her in absolutely exuberant and ecstatic states,' he says. 'She would go into the pooja room where, in Indian households, as the family gets richer and richer, the number of gods goes on increasing. This was a very rich family, so we had dozens of gods—silver ones, golden ones, every kind. She had very long hair, well below her hips, and she let her hair loose. And she would be singing and dancing, tears flowing down her face, but laughing like crazy; and she would pick up flowers with her toes and throw them to the gods. I did not know why she was doing all of this, but everybody liked to hang around her, because she was exciting. And, above all, she laughed. She laughed a lot.'

It was when he looked back upon her that Sadhguru realized what a remarkable woman she had been. 'She looked very unreasonable—not the kind of person you would want to have in your family. She was trouble. But because she looked inward, she knew things that nobody could ever figure out. She could not articulate this to anybody because there was not one person she could speak to. So she just laughed it out. Everybody looked like an utter idiot to her because what she could see, they could not see.' He asked her once, 'What on earth are you doing?' 'Never mind,' cackled the old woman. 'One day you will understand.'

It was to be a long time before he did. But even at a young age he was more amused than shocked by her behaviour. He shared some of her iconoclastic spirit already. He was impatient with ceremony. A diehard sceptic, he refused to accompany his family to the local temple and was often left with the footwear-stall attendant outside. These stints convinced him that something was seriously amiss with the whole business of conventional worship. 'I don't believe in anything that I cannot see. This was not an adolescent problem; this was a childhood problem. Right from my infancy I didn't believe anything that was happening around me unless I could see it and understand it. So, even when I was four or five years of age, I refused to go with my parents to the temple. They were not very religious. They went once or twice a year. But even then, I refused. I had questions. They never got around to answering my questions, so I never entered the temple. I was always in the custody of the chappal-*wallah*. As they handed over their footwear they handed me over also. They'd say, "Take care of him because he may run away somewhere." So the chappal-wallah always held me with one arm and did his business with the other. He knew that if he looked the other way I'd be gone! So that's where I learnt a lot about Indian footwear problem. And one of the first things I did years later at Isha is to organize how everybody should park their footwear.'

With a chuckle he adds, 'Today we can proudly say that around eight to ten lakh people come to our functions but not a single slipper ever goes missing. I always say, "This is something I learnt in my childhood." I understood the serious problem of footwear very early.'

As he sat at the footwear stall, Jaggi began observing other details. 'When I turned eight or nine years old, it intrigued me that people were all going into the temple to talk to God. I wanted to see how they would be after they met him. So I planted myself in front of a major temple, closely watching everyone. When they came out I usually found people were gossiping about something that they had seen in the temple. Or they found that their footwear had walked away with somebody else! And when they saw it was gone, they cursed creation and the Creator. Nobody ever once thought, "God could have taken my footwear because maybe he needs it!" No, people cursed the whole world. I always found people coming out of restaurants had more peaceful and joyful faces than people coming out of temples. In the divine-versus-dosa contest, dosa is a clear winner.'

Jaggi also abhorred caste distinctions. This made him particularly caustic about the visit of the pundit to his home to officiate at family poojas. He was to wonder later whether some of his denunciations were needlessly hurtful. But at the time he couldn't help himself. Caste hierarchies, overt or subtle, made his blood boil. It was also apparent to him that these rituals had more to do with human insecurity than spiritual yearning. 'I saw that it was either fear or greed that was the basis of everything that was happening. I knew even then that that couldn't be called spirituality. This was just survival routed through heaven, and it didn't even work! This is a nation that is living proof that it's not worked. We have over three hundred thousand gods, and every kind of ritual, and every kind of prayer that nobody else knows on this planet, but still half the people can't eat. Only those who have handled their lives sensibly have survived. So I saw that for survival you just need to learn to use these four limbs and a few brain cells. You don't need God to survive; you don't need the divine to enter your life to handle your business or your money or your children.'

Another early trait was a level of dispassion which marked even his closest relationships. Jaggi seemed curiously untouched by intense family feeling or fierce attachments of any kind. While he loved his family, there was a clarity about the nature of such relationships that once took even his mother by surprise. 'My mother was a very devout woman. For her, her whole life was her husband and four children. She never thought anything about herself; she just gave her life to us. So there was no need for her ever to say, "I love you", or anything. Such a thing was never expected. . . . I developed a kind of relationship with her where, though I was the youngest in the family, I was like her elder brother in many ways. She would share things with me that she would not share with anybody else. And when I took advantage of that and joked, she would always say, "Why am I sharing this with you?" So, on a certain day, because of some interaction, somehow she grew a little tender and expressed her love to me. She was not really saying, "I love you", but somehow [expressed her deepest feelings]. For me it was just very matter of fact. I just asked her, "If I had been born in the next house, would you still feel like this about me?" It hurt her very much. She broke down and went away. I didn't intend to hurt her. I just asked a simple question. These questions were constantly going on in me about everything.'

Jaggi hadn't intended to make a point. But her fourteen-year-old son's question had provoked an important moment of insight for Susheela. After a while, she returned. 'She came, tears still in her eyes, bowed at my feet and went away,' he says. 'Some kind of realization happened within her. And it was good for her. Our ways of thinking and feeling are so deeply identified with things we are associated with—our body, our parentage, our children, our wives, our husbands, our home, with just about anything.'

Perhaps the strangest thing about Jaggi—still unknown to his family and friends—was his early preoccupation with death. In the dead of night, he frequently slipped out of his home and visited the local graveyards of Mysore. At other times, he used the pretext of walking his dog (Ruby, a water spaniel, and later Caesar, a German shepherd) to make those long secret sojourns. There was a schoolboy excitement about spirits and the tantalizing prospect of conjuring up one oneself. But deeper than that was a fascination with the business of dying. The young boy spent hours looking at charred human remains, skulls, disembodied limbs—the grisly debris of cremation rituals. Sometimes he would pick up some disengaged part of the human anatomy and hurl it back into the smouldering pyre. Long after the funeral mourners had dispersed, Jaggi would linger on and watch, observing details unsentimentally.

When he was in Class IX, a fellow student named Sucharita died of pneumonia during the school holidays. Initially, her classmates had no idea of what had happened. Sucharita didn't return from the Dussehra vacation, and Jaggi and his friends had fun impersonating her voice when the teacher called out her name from the attendance roster. Twenty days later, they discovered that she had died. Jaggi was mystified. What he felt was not grief, for he hadn't shared a particularly close relationship with her (although he had raided her lunch box on occasion). But there was an intense curiosity about what had become of someone who had sat in class with him for years. He learnt from Sucharita's brother that in her last days of delirium she had often mentioned the name 'Jaggi'. That fuelled his curiosity. What exactly had happened to Sucharita? Where had she disappeared? Where was she now?

There was only one way to find out. One day he stole ninety-eight Gardinal Sodium tablets from his father's medicine cabinet. He prepared carefully for the event. He left no notes. He saw no need for such sentimental flourishes. But he distributed all his treasured possessions in advance to his friends. For a schoolboy, he was a person of considerable means. His property was coveted by his peers. But this was his grand moment of renunciation. He gave away his prized copper catapults and his earnings as a snake catcher (a princely sum of one hundred and twelve rupees). His pet cobra and other snakes were released in the Chamundi Hills, and his pet turtle into the local Kukkarahalli water tank. Divested of all worldly belongings, he now heroically skipped his evening meal. Then he swallowed the contents of the bottle, lay down and waited to see what happened.

Three days later he woke up in his father's hospital. He had slept through the collective alarm, the emergency rush to the hospital, the stomach wash. When his parents asked him what he had been thinking of, he muttered something about having mistakenly eaten cactus fruit. No one ever found out the truth. The annoying thing for Jaggi was that he hadn't found out anything about death either. The only noteworthy discovery he made was that for the next three months whenever he laughed, the mirth was uncontrollable. He decided that this had to be the peculiar aftereffect of a bottleful of barbiturates. The other chastening aftereffect was that he was considerably poorer. His friends refused to part with all that he had bequeathed to them in his earlier spirit of magnanimity. He did recover half the money, however, after issuing some threats and following up on a few.

Recently, more than three decades after the event, after his life has taken various dramatic turns, Sadhguru met his schoolfriend again. 'She looks much the same,' he says matter-of-factly. 'Same height, same build. She's been to the ashram. She even uses some of the words she used in her previous lifetime.' The new 'Sucharita' is now half his age. How did he recognize her? The karmic body again, evidently. Karmic bodies, he says, are as easy to identify as one's own luggage at Baggage Claim in airports. Each one is too idiosyncratic to be confused with any other.

When he was fourteen a new fascination dawned. Jaggi turned political. From this point on, his flashes of heightened extrasensory perception diminished. They were not to return until he was twenty-five. Now what mattered was the outside world. Social justice became a paramount concern. Revolution was his credo. It appealed to his innately nonconformist spirit and unleashed what he later termed 'a fiery thought process', a fierce commitment to address issues of poverty and discrimination.

His sympathies were initially stirred by the speeches of Professor Ramalingam, the father of a schoolmate who was a year his junior. A couple of his friends shared his leanings. The group was later inspired by the larger-than-life presence of Devanur Mahadeva, a charismatic intellectual, writer and revolutionary at the Mysore

University. It was Mahadeva who was responsible for starting the small but influential militant newspaper, *Bandaaya* (Revolution), later renamed *Nara Bandaaya* (Human Revolution).

For two years, Jaggi threw his support behind Naxalite groups. He became a subscriber to various agit-prop journals and read widely. When a student agitation broke out on the university campus over a professor's misconduct with a female student, it was grist to his mill. Student violence erupted and the police was called in. Jaggi volunteered to stick virulent anti-establishment posters all over the city, even daring to paste a few on police vans. It took nerve and Jaggi was never short of that. It won him a bet with his comrades. Sticking a poster meant twenty rupees, and Jaggi earned a tidy hundred. 'The police were inside the van—dozing a little, talking, smoking. It was sometime between eight and ten in the evening. The trick was to quietly go and stick one poster, and then walk away and wait for some time. Later, from another direction, you come again, stick another poster and go away. I was able to stick five posters on the police van. Half of them on the windshield, half of them down on the bonnet. I wanted to stick them all on the windshield, but I couldn't reach. Anyway, I stuck five posters and made a hundred rupees out of the Revolution.'

But disenchantment set in by the time he was sixteen. He found himself uncomfortable with the level of self-deception among his confrères, many of whom seemed wilfully blind to the chasm between their radical politics and their positions of personal security. Jaggi continued to read Marx and admire Che Guevara, but decided to dissociate himself from the extreme Left. There was too much rage and hatred, he felt, without any constructive alternative in sight. Many years later, it was a significant moment for him when a considerably older Devanur Mahadeva—the hero of his radical years—joined one of his meditation programmes along with his family.

'I couldn't help seeing the loopholes,' he says, looking back on this political phase of his life. 'This phase helped me pick up some things of value, but it couldn't inspire me for long. I had enough zest and life in me to keep me active and going at everything. But nothing—no individual, no particular event, either historical or otherwise—was an inspiration. Maybe I was just too arrogant. I don't know.'

On reflection, he attributes it to an ability to look at things with a certain directness, unclouded by vested interests. 'Suspicion has never been my quality. I think my most significant aspect is clarity, utter clarity about things. So I saw loopholes because there were loopholes. I was not looking for them. I have never looked for anything in my life. I just look. And that's what I am trying to teach people now: if you really want to know spirituality, don't look for anything. People think it's about looking for God. I tell them, don't look for anything. Just learn to look in an unprejudiced way; then you will see what is there. A seeker is not looking for anything; he is just looking. If this quality of simply looking doesn't come into you, you will see all kinds of things, but not reality.'

A wandering astrologer passed by his home around this time. Interested in finding out about her first daughter's marriage prospects, Jaggi's mother invited him in. But wary of allowing the girls to interact directly with the stranger, she persuaded her son, Jaggi, to meet him. Jaggi grudgingly agreed, though he had no patience with this kind of thing. To his amazement, the man rattled off a litany of intimate family details. He refused to say anything about Jaggi's eldest sister, but predicted that the second one would be married by next May. As for Jaggi, the astrologer looked the boy up and down expertly, and prophesied that he would start building a temple by the age of thirty-seven.

The atheist of the clan and a temple? Clearly, the man's powers of divination were seriously impaired. The family laughed it off. Jaggi probably laughed the loudest. And yet, his sister did get married the very next year on 25 May. The other sister took a spiritual path and joined the Sarada Math of the Ramakrishna Mission. Jaggi, however, continued to remain faithfully allergic to temples.

His eldest sister's decision to embrace the monastic life did not go down too well with the family. Manju had always been a carefree, somewhat fashion-conscious young woman. Ironically, in an attempt to discourage her more materialistic inclinations, Dr Vasudev had started taking her with him on visits to the local Ramakrishna Mission. The situation changed rapidly. Soon Manju's extensive wardrobe was whittled down to four well-worn saris. The trips to the Mission became frequent. Anxious at this unexpected turn of events, Dr Vasudev and his wife started looking out for marriage alliances for their eldest daughter. Manju was now adamant, however, that marriage was not for her. Her priorities lay elsewhere.

Once, when his parents were visiting Bangalore, Jaggi saw Manju go secretly to the family cupboard and withdraw her school-leaving certificates and mark sheets. He knew instantly that something was afoot. As someone who frequently plotted escapades of his own, he knew that these were vital identification documents to have with you if you were leaving home. After Manju had left home that morning—ostensibly to go to a typing class—Jaggi took a look at her cupboard. The four saris were gone.

While he felt no particular affinity for her cause (he would much rather she had joined the Revolution than Ramakrishna), he retained his essential empathy for those who wanted to run away. He gave her time to make good her escape. Then at five o'clock that evening, he called his parents in Bangalore and broke the news. Panic ensued. The Vasudevs hastened home. After feverish investigations, an indignant family search party traced Manju to the Sarada Math in Trichur. It was now a matter of salvaging the family honour and rescuing the 'misled' girl before it was too late. They were refused admission into the premises, however, and returned, truculent but defeated. Jaggi remembers his father crying for three days after that, a broken man.

A month later, when tempers had subsided, and rage had been replaced by resignation, the Vasudevs did meet Manju. She was now a brahmacharini, content with her new life, and her parents had no alternative but to reconcile themselves to this state of affairs. After all, there had always been a spiritual streak in the family, they rationalized, thinking back to her great grandmother before her. Besides, there were still three other children who would hopefully do them proud in more worldly ways. Little did they know what was in store for them.

A new phase dawned. Career options were being discussed at home. Jaggi decided one morning that he would join the army. He had still to finish his Class XII when he did the National Defence Academy exams. The incentive was simple. It seemed to offer a life devoted to all that he loved: hang gliding, mountain climbing, trekking, hockey. As he said later, 'I simply thought I'd be funded for my adventures.'

He cleared all the physical and aptitude tests with ease and was called in due course to Bhopal for an interview. He entered the room to find three seated brigadiers, all gleaming badges and bristling moustaches. He took a seat only to be reminded that he hadn't been instructed to sit down. The interview had started off on a wrong note. Things got rapidly worse. On hearing that he enjoyed geography, one of his interviewers asked him to name the place in Scotland famous for angling. Jaggi replied that he didn't know, but added with typical flippancy that in three months' time he'd be in a position to teach them a thing or two about geography. Not surprisingly, the reply did not go down well with his interlocutors. Jaggi abandoned his military dreams without too much regret.

Back home Dr Vasudev was beginning to despair of his endlessly dissident ways. He would have ideally liked his son to become a doctor. 'He was so keen on this that whenever possible when talking to us, he would pull out all his old notes,' says Sadhguru. 'He had stood first in college in his time. And not only did he preserve his textbooks, he had kept all his personal notes, the case histories of all his patients. Everything was written down in his small neat handwriting. He would tell us, "I've kept these because one of you is going to study medicine"'.

When medicine was clearly out of the question, engineering seemed the next best alternative. But Jaggi was averse to that as well. When face-saving degrees in commerce and science were also rejected, his father was at his wits' end. Would this boy never see reason, never mend his ways?

Jaggi's next decision was not designed to allay parental anxieties. He decided to abandon formal education and embark on a self-study programme at the Mysore University library. He would set out from the house every morning at nine and make sure he did not return until eight in the evening. There seemed little point spending time in a home where he was so obviously the black sheep. Always fond of food, his injured pride made him go hungry much of that year. Between breakfast and dinner, his only sustenance was books. He read widely, if randomly, dipping into literature as varied as Homer, Thomas Moore, Western philosophy and popular mechanics. He was inspired enough by his reading of the latter to embark on the building of a hang glider. 'I built it out of bamboo and parachute silk which I got from somewhere. Then I tried taking off from Nandi Hill.' He did take off, but he also descended sooner than he had expected. He broke both ankles in the process. Years later, he took a hang-gliding class with a British pilot and finally succeeded.

Money was not a problem. Jaggi had always been resourceful. He had never relied on his parents to provide him with pocket money to fund any of his whims. His varied unorthodox skills—pigeon farming, climbing water tanks backwards, selling cows that he ingeniously transported from Ooty—had earned him a substantial sum. There was a time when he had sixty-five thousand rupees in cash—a fortune for an adolescent. The money was invariably invested in funding collective cycling expeditions and maintaining his cycle in top trim. Additional money was kept aside for a more ambitious future plan—a cycling expedition to Moscow.

After a year of blissful bookworming, Jaggi condescended to go to college. It was his mother's tears that won him over eventually, rather than the paternal lament about everyone else in the family being a graduate. But he was adamant about what he would do. It would be English Literature and nothing else. How on earth will reading poetry help you earn a living, asked his ever-pragmatic father. But as someone who had never been short of schemes to make money, livelihood issues were far from Jaggi's mind. 'It's either literature or back to the library,' he said, and his father evidently considered the former the lesser evil.

He spent the next three years ostensibly as a student of Mysore University. He was clear that he would only go to evening college. 'It started at six and closed at nine thirty every day. But I was clear that the day was for me; the evening was for my parents.' Once again much of his time was spent outside the classroom rather than in it. He did not endear himself to one of his lecturers when he stood up in class and asked her to give him her notes so he could photocopy them. It would save her the trouble of dictation and him the trouble of attending, he said. 'I found that all that was happening in class was dictation. And I was definitely not planning to be a stenographer. I had a million questions all the time. I was always looking for those who could answer them. So I said, "I am not willing to write notes. But I have questions; can you answer them?"'

Not surprisingly, his professors were happy to grant him free attendance for the next three years. He was far too disruptive a presence in the classroom. 'So I made a deal with all the teachers. On each day of the month, they would mark me; on the last day of the month, the attendance was registered. That day I would enter and just make sure they were keeping up their end of the deal!'

All that was required from his end, apart from token attendance at lectures, was to turn up for examinations. He made sure that happened, whenever possible. On occasion, however, it was clearly not possible. 'I was in my second undergraduate year. The inter-university football match was going on. I thought I would watch the match for half an hour or so, and then go for the exam. I was all prepared for it. I just sat there and began watching. And soon I got so involved that I stayed till the match was over. That's when I realized that the examination was also over!'

There were a couple of teachers whose classes he found inspiring. While he attended their lectures, the rest were scrupulously avoided. 'When I took English Literature, it was because I thought it would be the least intrusive,' he laughs. 'I thought any other subject would be too much of an intrusion on my life. I thought literature meant I could read stories and poetry. But along with literature I had to study geography and sociology. Geography was fine with me—it was about the planet you walk upon. But sociology was all about people's opinions and seemed so absolutely stupid that I just refused to stay in this class. You know the way attendance is marked? Since my name starts with J, it was usually called out in the first three minutes. I had to stay in the class only three minutes. I was already impatient; even three minutes were too much! After that, I walked out of the window. The windows were large, bigger than the doors. The sociology teacher told me that this was 'deviant' behaviour and said I was a juvenile delinquent. She was using sociological terms, you know. Walking out of the window was not a simple thing; it was "deviant"! To me the window wasn't deviant; just convenient. But after that day, I started using the door.'

Gleefully, Jaggi took to the garden. It was at this time that he also found himself in demand as a problem solver, an informal psychotherapist. He found it came easy. He was a good listener and his unfailing clarity of perspective helped him offer sound advice on various matters. 'Fellow-students came to me with all sorts of issues,' he recollects. 'Education problems, union problems, boyfriend/girlfriend problems, and family problems. How many problems young people have is just incredible. It is not that old people are authorized to have problems, but when you're young, you expect the old to be stupid, and the young to be alert to life. But they kept coming with their problems. So I just sat there, watching these hazy beings coming and spilling their problems. I was the only freak who didn't have a problem. I just offered my own wild solutions to everything.'

And yet, some of those wild solutions had a distinctly human side. 'Till that point, I just got angry with people's stupidity. But when I heard the variety of problems that these hazy beings, these spooks, brought with them, slowly I became compassionate. I started reaching out to them. I knew it was stupid. All I had to do was knock them on their heads and tell them, you're just stupid. But somehow my anger began to turn into compassion.'

It was also at this time that Jaggi discovered a similarly fanatical bunch of motorcycle enthusiasts. 'We lived on our motorcycles. We were mad about them. We were literally physically attached to them at every moment. We spent all our time fiddling with the engine, thinking of how we could make the machine go a little faster.'

A spontaneous forum arose under a huge banyan tree on the campus grounds. Someone named it the Banyan Tree Club and the label stuck. Someone else proposed a journal and this soon turned into a monthly publication. The club had a simple credo: 'We do it for the fun of it.' It attracted those willing to engage in a variety of discussions: from Jawa motorcycles to how to make the world a better place. 'We would all assemble under this tree, sitting on our motorcycles,' says Sadhguru. 'And we'd talk for hours. Of course, we'd never get off our motorcyles at any point. That would have been sacrilege.'

This informal assembly seemed to make a lot more sense than the classroom. 'I wasn't really arrogant,' he says of those undergrad days. 'Perhaps I was in my attitude, but not in my behaviour. It's just the idea of having someone else certify me for life made no sense to me. I knew I didn't need a certificate to ride my motorcycle or to make money. If nothing else had worked, I might even have started a motorcycle garage.' Recently, he made the point again at a satsangh: 'I've always believed doors should open for you not because of your qualifications, but because of who you are.'

Jaggi's approach to life was not quite as offhand as the flippant motto of his Banyan Tree Club suggests. On one occasion, a friend was hit by a truck and was badly injured. His head had cracked open and pieces of his skull lay scattered across the road. Jaggi picked up the fragments and rushed his friend to hospital. 'You know, his head just opened up and pieces of his skull were all over the place. I picked them all up, put them in my pocket, picked up this guy and took him to the casualty ward. There was a big commotion there.'

Jaggi found he had to deal with the inevitable red tape attendant on any accident. He had to bluff his way through several bureaucratic questions, in an attempt to speed up the process. He then ran from pillar to post to arrange for blood for the emergency operation. His friend survived the night and seemed to be in a critical but stable condition. 'Next morning, I came home dead tired and I was just going for a bath. Then I touched my pocket, and I found I had all his skull pieces in my pocket. I'd forgotten to give them to the doctor. I then went back and told the doctor, "I've got his skull with me." He said, "It doesn't matter. We've just bandaged him. Let him stabilize, we will see." Anyway, he took what I had. I had three pieces in my pocket. They tried to move the boy to a hospital in Bangalore and he died on the way.'

This experience motivated Jaggi and a group of young friends to set up a casualty ward management team. It entailed the constant presence of at least one volunteer at the casualty ward of the major general hospital in the city. As soon as an accident victim was admitted, the volunteer's role was to assume responsibility for the patient, claim to be acquainted with him and contact his family based on any information found on his person. The team operated for over a year and a half. Jaggi remembers admitting five accident victims himself. Three died; two survived.

And so his college years were crammed with a curious mix of anarchy and social engagement. In Jaggi's view, there was no real distinction between the two. (To this day, he does not believe a moral code is a prerequisite for compassion.) The days were full.

He was never short of friends. There were his trekking friends, his college buddies, his motorcycling companions. 'I had different types of companions for different kinds of activities. If I went out on wild trips, trekking, and this kind of thing, I had one set of friends. If I went motorcycling in the city, I had another kind of friends. I was a different person in every one of these groups. Generally, you know, in many places people saw me as a very taciturn guy who barely speaks. But in some groups they saw me as a very boisterous person, someone who talks a lot, does a lot. In some places, people saw me as a very withdrawn person; in other places people saw me as overly active. It depended on which kind of group I was in.'

But he was aware that these friendships were based from his end on a certain enjoyment of their company rather than any deep emotional need for it. Solitude and company, he recalls, were both fine with him. He knew some of his friends had keener intellects than he did. But he realized pretty early that he had more clarity than any of them. There was no sense of superiority about this, and he points out that there has never been anything of the detached Vedantin about him. It is just that while he was involved with those around him, he had no particular expectations of them. The same held true of his interactions with his family. 'I had lots of people around me, many of them dear to me, but I never sought any friend for emotional support. Such a thing never occurred to me. There have probably been two levels to my life always. On one level, I was trying to live according to my age. On another level, I was so old, so old . . .' he trails off, obviously reluctant to sound patronizing. After a pause, he adds, 'Most of the time, I was seeing them as hazy, half-light, half-shadow kind of figures moving around. I don't want to say there was no attachment, because that sounds spiritual and I was not spiritual in any way. They belonged to me, but I didn't belong to them. That's the closest I can get to describing the situation.'

Perhaps not surprisingly, as a reader, he was drawn to the

European existentialists. 'I remember reading Camus' *The Outsider* at fourteen, and it seemed so familiar. The way the hero responds to his mother's death, for instance, made immediate sense to me. If mothers do die—which they always do—it's not the end of the world. Most people suffer from an excess of guilt rather than grief anyway. That's why the Hindu way of giving the bereaved lots of activity to engage in immediately after the death has always seemed to me to be a clever way of handling things.' Even when he was a seven-year-old, he had shocked the mourners who had congregated after the death of his grandfather with his cheerful observation: 'But he's an old man. He must die.' Was that an insensitive or exceptionally wise remark? No one could decide. An uneasy silence descended.

Despite his innate sensitivity, there was nothing lily-livered about Jaggi's approach to the business of living. While peace made sense to him, he had little use for passivity. Once when he was busy fiddling with his father's old Murphy radio in the evening in the hope of tuning into some Western music on Radio Australia, he heard a sudden rattle of curtain rings. A thief who had crept into the house stood less than twelve feet away. 'The curtains had been removed for a wash and when the burglar held the door frame, the coil wires made a noise. He was a big guy, I remember, his trousers rolled to his knees.' Jaggi's reflexes were quicker than his guest's. He reached out, grabbed a steel vase nearby and knocked the man hard on the head. The thief sat down for a moment stunned, then rose and scooted, leaving a pool of blood in his wake. Jaggi called his mother from the neighbour's house and calmly informed her of their unexpected visitor. While the news was, not surprisingly, enough to make his mother fly into a state of panic, the imperturbable eleven-year-old was simply satisfied at a job well done. 'My cricketing practice did the trick.'

The lessons he learnt from life were invariably based on practical experience, rather than garnered secondhand. He recalls killing a monkey with his bare hands at the age of seventeen on his terrace.

The provocation? The fact that the monkey had attacked him. 'It was in my mother's family home in Chikkaballapur. I was on the terrace and this monkey was sitting on a lamp post. He made a face at me. I made a face back. The next thing I knew the creature was in the air, coming straight at me. It was a direct attack. I caught him by the throat and held him tight until my thumb went right in. I stayed like that until he lost all resistance. Later I buried him in the garden.' There were murmurs in the family about the boy having killed Hanuman. But for Jaggi there was no ethical dilemma. He had merely done what needed to be done.

Even as a young boy of eight, when he was told to go kill a chicken for lunch at his grandfather's house, he had no qualms about obeying. 'In my father's home, chicken was bought in the market. But in my grandfather's home, the boys of the family were expected to do the killing. So I was sent out to kill one. The way it was done was simple: you waited till the animal was comfortable and then broke its neck. You did it so swiftly that the chicken probably didn't even know it was dead!' It's just that the procedure proved to be a little more demanding than he had anticipated. He remembers being overwhelmed by the sudden spurt of energy released at the moment of slaughter. He went away and sat down for a while, feeling sick. It become apparent to him then that there was far more to the act of taking another life than he had supposed. 'It wasn't a moral response,' he says. 'It's just that I was unprepared for that huge explosion of life. It left me dizzy. If you have to kill an animal and then eat it, I suspect very few people would remain non-vegetarian.'

The unsentimental approach coexists with a very real compassion towards animals, as those who have seen him with his dogs will testify. When his childhood dog, Ruby ('who was mine, unlike Nancy, the dachshund, whom all four of us were equally involved with') developed an acute skin ailment, Jaggi refused to give in to his father's suggestion that she be put down. He learnt of a possible herbal remedy and each day plucked the herbs from a nearby hillock, ground them to a paste and smeared it over her body. The dog eventually died, but not from want of painstaking care and attention. Many years later when he owned a farm, he had a pair of bullocks that helped to plough his land. 'I decided not to shoe the bullocks. I hated the indignity of it: turning them over to put on the shoes.' But the compassion cost him dear. He found that his bullocks' heels wore out and they were in extreme pain. 'I had two lame bulls that couldn't work. But I got them shod and kept them. Eventually, I sold the farm along with the bulls. I've never sent my bulls to the slaughterhouse. I kept them even when they were old and unfit.'

Jaggi's growing years were not without their share of romance. At the age of nineteen, he fell in love with a young Muslim girl in the neighbourhood. They enjoyed their share of stolen magical hours, reading poetry and holding hands. The relationship grew in intensity and lasted a few years. But it remained surreptitious and like so many other teenage relationships, did not last. When her marriage was arranged elsewhere, things came to an abrupt close.

It was more of a turning point than he knew. While the event helped catalyse his journey inward, at that time it was simply heartbreak with all the cataclysmic sense of despair and loss. 'I wasn't just hurt; I was devastated. Everything fell apart. It left me in a completely new space within myself. If you're only partly broken, it hurts. Remnants can hurt. But if you're completely pulverized, it leaves you in a vacuum. Then you realize it's not a vacuum; it's your own thoughts, your imagination that have broken.'

He withdrew into a shell after the break-up, not talking to anyone in the family for a week—a source of considerable concern to his mother. Later, he romanced several other young women (many of whom were his girlfriend's friends) in quick succession. A typical vengeful rebound dynamic, I remarked. He disagreed. 'There was no vengeance. I just chose to be frivolous. I wondered, why am I denying myself in every way? Why am I denying myself for something that doesn't exist? Probably this is how I'd have been if I hadn't had this relationship going. It had been intense and it passed quickly. When it was over, it left me numb and immobile. Everything was demolished. Maybe somewhere I began to realize then that living your life around someone else or even yourself is meaningless. Both you and the other are just a figment of your imagination. I'd always thought it was worthless to build a life around myself, and it seemed wonderful for a time to build life around someone else. But I now saw that it just wasn't the way life is meant to be. Life is for living, not for building. There was no disappointment or frustration in this realization. I saw that life is just on; you participate in it as much as you can. But this idea of *my* life and *your* life makes you build structures around things that don't exist.'

When Jaggi emerged from this spate of romances, it was with a far deeper and more mature understanding of love—one that was neither irresponsible nor puritanical. He was even able to see his failed love affair as a blessing in disguise. 'Thank God she broke it as soon as she did. Or else I'd have spent my whole life like this. Later I approached my relationships with love, involvement and commitment, but never built my life around them.'

In a particularly relaxed late-night conversation, he once mentioned that his first girlfriend's appearance bore an uncanny resemblance to someone he had known intimately three lifetimes ago. She was, he realized much later, remarkably similar in height and build to Shambhavi, the woman in the snake charmer Bilva's life. I asked him if, on some level, this coincidence had confused him on an energy level. Was that why he was so drawn to her in this lifetime? He paused for a moment and then cautioned me against seeing it as a 'sappy' reincarnation romance. 'At the time, this relationship meant everything to me,' he said gently. 'I don't want to take away from that. Let's not bring in a past-life angle and trivialize it.'

He confesses that he now finds it strange to meet some of his old friends from his Mysore college days. Some have been successful in their careers, while some have fared less well. But what strikes him now is just how world-weary and lifeless they all seem. He remembers them as vibrant young men—a few with an eye for pretty girls. But burdened now by work, family responsibilities and the accoutrements of adulthood, they seem to have lost their zest for life. For their part, they regard him with a certain wariness. Unsure of the social protocol involved in interacting with a friend-turned-spiritual-master, they are even more unsettled by his joie de vivre. Somehow that doesn't seem quite in keeping with their notion of a guru. In the process, they seem unable to revive the easy camaraderie of the past. The irony, says Sadhguru, is that it is not I who have changed, but they.

'When we meet they are very uncomfortable,' he says. 'I'm just fine, much more alive than I was at that time. But they have usually become dead serious. They have families, children, jobs, and you know, whatever they thought was joy has become a burden.' He laughs. 'And they can't believe I still laugh and joke and talk. Then they pull out their cigarettes and ask, "Do you smoke?"

'I say, "No."

'"Oh, you don't smoke? Okay."

'Then they are a little apprehensive about whether to smoke or not to smoke. And I say, "You go ahead. It's okay with me."

'"You don't smoke and you don't drink?"

'"No, it never occurred to me."

'"Oh, so you've given up everything."'

He laughs again. 'Just look at that perception: people actually believe that if you don't smoke, if you don't drink, you've given up everything!'

Despite his erratic attendance and breezily irreverent approach to education, Jaggi graduated. He even managed to stand second in English Literature in Mysore University—something that shocked all who knew him, including himself. The inevitable 'What next?'

reared its head in the family. There was talk of a Masters in the air. But Jaggi would have none of it. He informed his parents he had already read all the books prescribed in that syllabus. He would now earn a living and realize that long-cherished dream of travelling the world on a motorcycle. But how do you plan to make a living, asked his parents cautiously. They were long accustomed to Jaggi's bombshells. But nothing prepared them for this one. Poultry farming, their son replied laconically.

And he meant it. 'By then I had ridden all over the country. It was when I went to the Nepal border that I realized I actually needed papers to ride further. Until then I thought my motorcycle could take me anywhere. But those guys at the border said, "No, you can't go unless you have these papers." I didn't know what papers they wanted. I had my motorcycle registration and my licence, but that was not good enough. That's when I thought, okay, I need something else to go where I want. Since then I'd been dreaming about it. I said, once I have enough money I am just going to ride off somewhere, where people can't stop me. I was just longing to earn some quick money and leave. At that time there was a big boom in poultry farming and so I just got into it. My father said, "What am I going to tell people? That my son is rearing chicken?" I said, "That's your problem." I built my poultry farm with my own hands, single-handedly.'

The two-and-a-half-acre farm was some twelve kilometres from his home in a remote part of Mysore. Jaggi's day started at the crack of dawn and ended late at night. There were times when his late arrival compelled him to spend the night outside the house for he was reluctant to disturb his family. The first six months were going to be hard work and he was prepared for it. He single-handedly, built the cages for 3,200 birds, his hands bleeding from the effort. He lived on bananas for days on end to save money. He also devised ingenious ways to supplement his income. He picked up the wood of fallen wayside trees around the city in the early hours of the morning, and started making bricks. This turned him at one point in time into a pretty successful brickmaker in Mysore city. It seemed a simple moneymaking strategy. He wondered why no one else thought of similar schemes. It only confirmed a hunch he had long nursed that the rest of the human population was somewhat dim, if not downright dull.

Soon the business took off. The profits started rolling in. The Vasudevs looked on in disbelief as their problem child turned overnight into a successful businessman. Life was suddenly smooth sailing. Jaggi devoted four hours every morning to his poultry business. The rest of the day was spent reading and writing poetry, swimming in the well, daydreaming on trees, enjoying the pastoral idyll that he had created for himself on the farm. 'From the age of thirteen, I had been doing *asanas* and *pranayama*. Now meditation also entered my life. So I would either meditate or write or read. The eggs kept coming, the money kept coming. After I finished my morning work, I would just go sit on top of a huge banyan tree. With my eyes closed, if I sat there, I didn't know what happened. For hours I would just hang around on the tree. My poultry farm days were very beautiful. I could read as much as I wanted. I was writing a lot of poetry. Nobody came and bothered me. For days I did not see any human face except one or two labourers who were working there. It was a good life.'

The destination was remote and few visited him. That made it an ideal space for a menagerie of reptiles. Soon, he had a flourishing serpent colony. Getting up every morning was a particularly slow affair. He had to take care not to disturb any of the two dozen cobras and vipers that slept in and around his bed. He discovered a lot about yoga by being with them, he maintains. Their presence meant learning how to stay motionless and totally aware.

'I had over twenty to twenty-five snakes in my bedroom,' he says. 'It was a large room, where I slept, did some minor cooking, and kept some of my books. That one room in the farm was my entire living space. And I used to have these snakes all over the place. All of them were poisonous snakes, generally cobras, sometimes vipers. I was always more wary of the vipers than cobras because the cobra gives you sufficient time, even if it bites you. It gives you about six hours. Vipers give you about two and a half to three hours. And with cobras, you can still function for sometime; with vipers you can easily get paralysed. I had both, but mostly cobras, because the cobra is also a more attractive snake. It has a certain pride, a certain majesty about itself. So when you have so many snakes in the room, you don't know where they will be. A snake can get into the most impossibly small crevices. Often, when I slept, they would get under the blanket. And if I got up early morning or in the middle of the night, I'd notice a snake moving in my blanket. That meant I had to move very carefully; one wrong movement and it could bite. You don't know where the head is, where the tail is; it's all covered with cloth. So it was a great exercise in awareness for me; I had to learn to move in extreme awareness, conscious that even a twitch from my side could be fatal.'

The wild streak persisted. It was, as he often says, 'the era of blue jeans and the Beatles'. Jaggi now owned his own motorcycle on which his exploits were nothing short of hair-raising. Always quick to take up a challenge, he rode dangerously between the wheels of the timber trucks on the Mysore–Hunsur highway. 'These timber trucks don't have side bodies. There is just timber, and between the two wheels rolling in front and in the rear, there is space. So, I'd take the motorcycle between the two wheels and come out. If you just made one mistake, you'd be plastered on the road. But my friends and I went effortlessly in and out any number of times.'

The nearby Chamundi Hill was a favourite haunt. 'Riding motorcycles on Chamundi was a religion for us. In the night we would go up, and through the night we were riding up and down the hill, trying to get at those corners better and better, faster and faster. One day I thought just why ride on the road? I'll just ride off the mountain.' It was, he decided, the quickest and most exhilarating route down Chamundi Hill. That meant staying clear of the road. And it meant hurtling dramatically and at full throttle through a morass of tree, bush, rock and hectic undergrowth. At one point, his journey came to a violent and abrupt halt when his cycle jammed into a branch, but he extricated himself and completed his mission. When he emerged, he was blood smeared but victorious. A broken ring finger seemed a trifling price to pay for such euphoria.

There was a time when some of his motorcycling friends—with much gung-ho idealism—were seized with the idea of setting up a commune. They even went so far as to locate a hundred-acre plot of land for the dream project. 'We identified some forest land which was owned by a friend of ours who was a timber merchant. It was available at two or three hundred rupees per acre. We thought we'd start a community—all young people just going and living there together.'

The blueprint was determinedly anarchic. There were to be no rules, no regulations, no externally enforced discipline whatsoever. It was a noble and high-minded venture in its own way. But like all ventures born of lofty intentions and zero pragmatism, it never materialized. Given the later lives of many of its members—some of whose lives were wrecked by substance abuse of various kinds—'it's a blessing,' says Sadhguru wryly, 'that some dreams don't come true.'

'About one in ten was drunk all the time,' he recalls. 'Another five or ten per cent was smoking ganja or something. Nice people, but somehow they had all fallen into these kinds of habits. I have been in their company plenty, but it didn't occur to me that I needed to do anything like that. I didn't avoid it, nor did I go after it. It's not like I was holding myself back because of some moral fear. Nor did I want to do it. It's just that maybe I was too much on my own buzz to need to do any of those things. If I had formed a community with all these people I can imagine where they would have taken it.'

Success in his field made Jaggi more adventurous. He decided to diversify. He admits that it was around this time that he allowed his life choice to be somewhat determined by social expectation. 'This is the only time that I reacted to the social situation and got a little caught up with life. My father was always lamenting that everyone else's sons had become engineers, industrialists, joined the IAS, gone to America. And everywhere, everyone I met—my friends, relatives, my old school and college teachers—said, 'Oh, we thought you'd make something of your life but you are just wasting it." Slowly this began to prick me. I said, okay, let me do something.'

In partnership with a civil engineer friend, he entered into a construction business. The family looked on in disbelief. Now what? Would this new scheme work? It flourished. 'In about five years we became a major construction company, among the leading private contractors in Mysore. We had a small-scale industry going. We were just two young boys and everybody was thrilled with us. Now, there was big money. My father was very happy. It doesn't matter whether you are a doctor or not; you are "doing well", that's what counts. And doing well means you are making enough money.'

It looked like Jaggi's dreams of travelling the world on a motorcycle were not far off. Life was running so smoothly, he often says in jest, that he sometimes felt the planet revolved around him, not the sun. It seemed like nothing could conceivably go wrong.

And then, things did. One fine day, Jaggi's plans flew right out of the window.

The Man Who 'Went Up and Never Came Down'

From Motorcyclist to Mystic

The day dawned like any other. There were no portents, no prophetic dreams. Twenty-third September 1982, it was a busy weekday in Jaggi's life. He had a regular breakfast ('of *uppuma*', he recalls, when I ask him if he remembers such trivia about an otherwise momentous day) and made his way to a work meeting. A major contract had been signed a few days ago, and he and his business partner had much to discuss. In the afternoon, he dropped off his partner for a brief siesta. Jaggi then went home for lunch. He still remembers the main dish that afternoon: *bassida-saru*, a Karnataka speciality which has an Andhra variant (at which his mother excelled). It was now two thirty. There was time to kill before the next meeting.

A motorcycle ride was Jaggi's inevitable choice. He had acquired his first motorcycle a couple of years ago. After riding a bicycle in his schooldays and stealthily appropriating his father's scooter and brother's motorcycle in his high school and college years, the Yezdi motorcycle was now his prize possession. He maintained it with fanatical zeal and kept it in prime condition. He now had several friends who were motorcycle fiends and shared some of his passion for wild adventure. But no one else was quite as determined about seeing the adventures through to their end. If Jaggi decided one night he wanted to go to Goa, he would set out at once. There was no question of waiting for others to join him. Planning, as Jaggi knew, meant endless procrastination, and he had no patience with that. 'People are willing to walk with you only as far as it's convenient,' he says. 'When their comfort zone is crossed, they drop off. Very few go all the way. But I've always been one of those who go all the way once I commit myself.'

His snake-and-motorbike fetish, coupled with his daredevil temperament, had earned him the tag of 'Deadly Jaggi' among his friends. 'It's not that I was impulsive; I was just life-oriented,' he says. 'I measured the consequences of my actions. It's just that the more dangerous they were, the more they attracted me. Someone once told me my guardian angel must be very good and perpetually working overtime! There was always in me a longing to test the border, to cross the edge. *What* and *why* were never questions for me. *How* was the only question. When I look back now, I realize that I never thought about what I wanted to become in life. I only thought about how I wanted to live my life. And I knew that the how could be determined within yourself and by yourself.'

The favourite destination for young Mysoreans was Chamundi Hill, a mandatory halt on every tourist's itinerary, famous for its panoramic view of the city and its picturesque Shakti temple of Chamundeshwari (the tutelary deity of the Mysore maharajas). Jaggi knew the hill intimately. He had been there on jaunts since he was a child. It was here that he had been bitten by a venomous snake many years ago. It was down these slopes that he had careened wildly on his motorcycle, eventually plunging to the bottom, bruised and bleeding. In recent times, he had even conducted business meetings on the hill. Nocturnal drives and parties up there were a regular feature. For some inexplicable reason, mountains had always fascinated Jaggi. From an early age, there had always been mountains in his eyes. One particular mountain dominated his vision. He didn't give it much thought. He simply assumed others too, saw a similar landscape.

Now, with an hour to spare before his next meeting, Jaggi turned toward Chamundi again. 'In Mysore, there is a tradition. If you have something to do, you go to Chamundi Hill. If you have nothing to do, you go to Chamundi Hill. If you fall in love, you go to Chamundi Hill. If you fall out of love, you go to Chamundi Hill. I had recently fallen out of love and I had nothing to do, so I went to Chamundi Hill.'

He sums up what happened next simply: 'I went up and didn't come down.' When he eventually did return, it was five hours later. He had gone up, a young happy-go-lucky motorcyclist. He returned, a mystic.

'I was just sitting on this particular rock,' he was to say years later. 'I had my eyes open, not even closed. I thought it was about ten minutes, but something began to happen to me. All my life I had thought, *this* is me [pointing to himself]. Suddenly, I did not know which was me and which was not me. The air that I was breathing, the rock on which I was sitting, the atmosphere around me, everything had become me. The more I say, the crazier it will sound, because what was happening was indescribable. What was me had become so enormous, it was everywhere. I thought this lasted a few minutes, but when I came back to my normal senses, it was about seven thirty in the evening. My eyes were open, the sun had set and it was dark. I was fully aware, but what I had considered as myself until that moment had just disappeared. When I was eight years of age—I remember this incident very well—something happened and I cried. That day I made up my mind that I would never cry again; I should never cry. I held myself like *this* [showing a closed fist] and whatever situations came, I did not shed a single tear, from eight until twenty-five. And here I'm sitting, tears are flowing to the point where my shirt is wet, and I'm ecstatically crazy! I do not know what is happening. I have always been peaceful and happy, that's never been an issue. I've lived life the way I wanted. But here I am, drenched with a completely new kind of blissfulness. When I apply my logical mind, the only thing it can tell me is that I'm losing my balance. That's all my mind can tell me. But it is so beautiful that I don't want to lose it.'

Sadhguru rarely says any more than this about that afternoon on Chamundi Hill. There were no words to describe the experience. There are still none. On being pressed, however, he has alluded to the experience in oblique ways. 'It's like being drunk all the time without ingesting a drop of alcohol,' he once remarked. On another occasion, he said, 'Life is all there is. There is no mountain, no flower, no cloud, nothing. It's just energy—a raw pulsating mass of energy. You can call that the Creator, or creation, or you can call it yourself. It doesn't matter.' Another time he declared, 'Enlightenment is not an achievement. It's more like a homecoming. An absolute *coming home*—that's enlightenment.'

Yet another time, he reflected, 'It means you just see life as it is. You take away everything—all the poetry, all the investments—and you see life just the way it is. You realize it is multidimensional. You realize that if you don't enjoy the whole scope of life, it's a foolish way to live. There is no "this is it" or "that is it". There is no this or that. And that's that! There is no yes and no; just yes and yes.'

On still another occasion, when asked about his inner state since that historic afternoon, he replied, 'I'm now a total fake. You're only half-fake. My personality is totally self-created. It's just an act.' And is there a liar behind the lie? No, he replied, just a lie, no liar. Then what lies behind the act, I once persisted. His reply was cryptic: 'Wild emptiness.'

Like all those before him who have crossed that mysterious threshold between the temporal and the transcendent, finding a logical idiom to describe the experience seems to have been impossible. Besides, at the time of his awakening, Jaggi was unsure of how to explain it even to himself. Only one thing was clear to the young man who descended the mountain: life would never be the same again.

It was past eight at night when Jaggi reached his office. He paused. Through the window he could see his business partner seated at his desk. His partner looked up expectantly, waiting for him to come in and explain his five-hour absence and catch up with the proceedings of the day.

The Yezdi engine was kept running. Jaggi sat on his motorcycle for close to ten minutes without dismounting. Then he turned and left, much to his colleague's bewilderment. He drove slowly around the streets of the city he knew so well. Everything seemed the same. Mysore by night was unchanged. And yet. He reached home by ten thirty that night. He spoke little, ate a perfunctory dinner. That night he stayed up in bed until 3 a.m.

A week later, the experience recurred. He was at the dining table with his family when it happened. All of a sudden, he was 'blowing' his head off. He thought it was for a couple of minutes. Seven hours had elapsed. On another occasion, thirteen days passed. 'I just sat down for thirteen full days,' he says. 'I neither ate nor slept nor used the toilet for these thirteen days. I simply sat down. Actually in my experience, it felt like only fifteen or twenty minutes. So time was just disappearing in my experience. It took about six weeks' time for me to stabilize this and make this into like a living reality all the time. And it took some more time for me to stabilize that experience within myself.' There was no explanation for what was happening. His family was as baffled as he was. He confided in a few friends who were equally clueless. Some asked if he was on hallucinogens.

Things changed rapidly. A visiting nurse from his father's railway hospital suddenly fell at his feet. Others, inexplicably, started doing the same. As someone who had never touched anyone's feet in his life, this was a bizarre experience for Jaggi. Even more awkward was when people started asking him to make predictions about their future; someone even implored him to divine the date of his daughter's marriage! And yet, Jaggi was also aware that he was no longer the same. For one, his appearance had actually begun changing. It wasn't just the general climate of the face; it was, strangely enough, the actual physical features, the shape of the eyes, the voice, even the structure of the body. Others began noticing the changes too. 'My voice changed; my eyes were bigger, brighter,' he says.

What accounted for this physical transformation? What had occurred, he says, was a realignment of his entire inner constitution. 'The thirteen-odd years of yoga bore fruit at this time. Yoga is essentially a way of recreating the body so that it serves a higher purpose. That's why the system works. The *chakras* are not static physical manifestations; they are mobile and one can move them within and outside the system. The science of making a deity is just this. There is a whole technology for transforming the human into the divine. The human body can function as a piece of flesh and blood or as the very source of creation. The human spine isn't just a bad arrangement of bones; it's the very axis of the universe. It just depends on how you reorganize your system. In my case, from being a physically intense person, I learnt to carry my body as if it was not there at all. My physicality became very relaxed. Earlier, all that intensity was in my body. People could feel that: if I entered a room, it meant action. But now I learnt to carry my body differently. The reorganization of my chakras also meant that I could be different from one situation to another. To this day, that remains. I can be a totally different person, almost unrecognizable to some people, depending on the needs of the situation.'

And there was the irrefutable testimony of his inner experience. Life had always been exciting. But now it was rich, intense, simply blazing with a level of high-voltage inner discovery he had never known before. From this point onward, Jaggi's inner life was always more eventful than his outer. 'I was now aware of a million different things happening inside me at the same moment. That's how it is with me even now. Even while I'm conducting a conversation with someone, I'm aware of innumerable things happening within simultaneously. It's like a kaleidoscope. And that boggles people's minds. They don't know how to make sense of you.' His father continued to be perplexed by his strange son whose life alternated hectically between meditation and motorcycling. For his mother, Jaggi had already been more of an elder brother than a son for a while.

Yet another fallout of this experience was his heightened sensitivity to the feelings of people around him. It seemed inconceivable to Jaggi that people around him should be in such states of discontent when his own life was simply exploding with ecstasy. There were times when just the sight of an unknown person on the street in a state of misery was enough to make him weep. Later, he was to learn to harness that reaction. An emotional response to suffering is something he now allows himself only on occasion. 'When I see a broken branch of a tree, for instance, my energy responds to it, but my emotions do not. Once in a while I allow myself the luxury of responding emotionally, but it's a luxury for me. One is still very much open to suffering but it is no more a psychological and emotional response.'

Six weeks after the afternoon on Chamundi Hill, Jaggi pulled out of his business. It seemed unfair to be part of something that his newfound perception would help him to manipulate to his advantage. It wasn't a moral issue that impelled the decision, just what he called 'life sense'. Moral codes, he now knew through experience, were merely an imitation of the way life was. It was clearer to him than ever before that he never needed to operate out of morality, merely out of his own humanity. 'It was easy for me now to read minds and make someone do exactly what I wanted him to. I still can. But what's the point? It's like playing golf with a five-year-old. I choose not to. It isn't about ethics. More a matter of aesthetics,' he says simply. Even today, with the expansion of Isha into various business ventures, he makes it a point to send representatives to meetings, rather than attend them himself.

After he began stabilizing, he realized that what had happened to him was quite simply 'the most beautiful thing that can happen to a human being'. 'Right now, people glorify childhood because a child can laugh, can jump around, can be happy for no reason at all. But I saw that it is possible to be naturally ecstatic without any reason at all in adulthood as well. And when I saw that this is possible for everybody, naturally I wanted to share it. My whole effort since then has been to somehow rub this experience off on other people.'

It was now beginning to dawn on him that what had happened so unexpectedly that afternoon on Chamundi Hill was something 'mystical'. Not having read any spiritual literature himself, he had no precedent with which to compare his own experience. Later, however, he would often ruefully remark that his own awakening was accompanied by none of the legendary lyricism associated with Gautama Buddha's enlightenment centuries ago. There was no luminous full moon, no hospitable shade of a peepul tree. All he had had around him, instead, was scorching noon heat and craggy Deccan rock. The result, however, was the same—just as personally momentous, just as life-changing.

If the Buddha had spent the following weeks enjoying his state of clarified insight and preparing for his years of mission, Jaggi did the same. 'I could just close my eyes, sit on a rock or under a tree, and that's it. My life was done. After a few days, I really thought, "This is it. There's nothing more to do. It's over." It was just a question of planning my exit. I thought I'd just be around for a little while, enjoy the whole beauty of it and then make an exit in style. People who knew me at that time would always hear me planning and talking about when I would leave. They couldn't understand. They said, "You don't seem like somebody who would commit suicide." I said, "Definitely not suicide. I'll walk out. I won't trouble four people to carry me to my grave; I will walk into it."'

And yet, like the sage of the Shakyas before him, he began to realize that his was not a personal discovery alone. Tempting as it was, the role of the reclusive mystic could not be his. His life so far had only been a preparation for this moment. Realization had happened, but it was more of a reminder than anything else. It had happened before. But something far more enormous—the Dhyanalinga—had still to happen. It came back to him in a rush—the gnawing ache of an unfulfilled promise. What had occurred was only the prologue. The larger, more significant narrative lay ahead.

There was a reason, he now realized, why he had been born into his particular family as well. There were no specific karmic connections, but this was a family that spelt minimal interference with his life mission. 'For a lot of people, their parents play a big role in shaping them . . . I had chosen to be born here because it was the family of least interference. My mother had a certain spiritual aspiration: she had been initiated by a yogi on Nandi Hills at the age of nine. And she never interfered in my life in any way. And as long as I passed my exams, there were no questions from my father either.'

He also realized now why the reminder had occurred at this precise moment in his life. The Dhyanalinga required a certain level of mastery over energy. It was not about physical or intellectual mastery, but an understanding of energy and its possibilities. At the age of twenty-five, Jaggi was at the peak of life, and his ability to manage his energies were finely honed. Without this ability, the capacity to retain the physical body would be severely impaired. 'Without ignorance, you cannot exist in the body,' he was to say later. 'An enlightened being has to know those tricks, or else he cannot remain in the physical. From this point of view, there are no enlightened beings on this planet. Most people are compulsively ignorant, and a few are consciously ignorant, that's all.'

As for the Dhyanalinga, how was it to be achieved? The technology didn't concern him just then. He knew it was there, that the details would fall into place once he put his mind to it. 'That's the way it has been with me,' he was to confirm many years afterward. 'Everything I know happens to me in a moment. When I'm walking on the street, I'm not carrying the burden of this knowledge. People usually become heavy and serious with knowledge. But when knowledge is transmitted in the form of energy, not as memory, the burden of knowledge is not on you. When my guru, Palani Swami, touched me with his walking stick, what cannot be learned in lifetimes was transmitted in one moment.' It is this instant retrieval system which has turned him into what has been observed by so many: a unique living archive, vast and yet curiously lightweight all at once.

The urgent need of the hour, Jaggi knew, was goodwill. Memories of all the yogis who had tried and failed before him came flooding back. Memories of his own fierce and futile efforts over three lifetimes returned to haunt him. He knew nothing was possible without social acceptance. He first needed to keep the appointment with his chosen band of loyalists, one that he had made a lifetime ago. After that his mission was to ensure that his guru's dream was not sabotaged yet again by human ignorance and suspicion. And no price was too high to pay this time. He was prepared, as he was to say later, 'to do anything that men should or should not'.

And so it looked like the wild agnostic Jaggi *was* going to build a temple, after all. But he knew there was no point divulging this to anyone just yet. Not that time was in abundant supply. For Jaggi knew something else as well. Something else that was to give his plans an additional impetus. He knew that he would leave the body by the age of forty-two. It meant burning the candle at both ends for the remaining seventeen years of his life. It also meant keeping all his entanglements down to the very minimum. He had to travel light.

And then in 1984 he met Vijji.

'My problem,' Sadhguru once said wryly in the course of a conversation, 'is that I'm far too democratic a mystic.'

He was alluding at the time to the way in which he allowed people around him to sometimes dictate the course of events in his life, even when his own perception revealed to him that the move was superfluous or undesirable.

The remark offers an insight into someone who has lived his life with a strange mix of control and carelessness, meticulous design and flamboyant improvisation. For all his farsighted planning for the Dhyanalinga a lifetime in advance, Jaggi, the chronic insurgent, who lived on the edge, has never quite been lost. Awareness and madness: that was how he once formulated the recipe for the Dhyanalinga. And it has entailed a volatile and unpredictable mix.

Seen in this light, perhaps the course of events after his enlightenment is not entirely surprising. First, after a year of withdrawal, meditation and travel, Jaggi decided to teach yoga. There was a thirst to share the fruits of his experience in some way. 'When I saw that you can be ecstatic for no reason at all—even in your adulthood—I naturally wanted to share it with people. That has been my effort ever since. I chose yoga because I had been practising it from a very young age, and saw it as a medium to somehow convey what was happening within me.' It also seemed like a logical way to get in touch with the people he needed to reconnect with for his mission.

It was not easy to win recruits for his first class. As a wild motorcyclist and successful businessman, he was reasonably well known in Mysore. But there were many who were suspicious of the fact that he had dropped out of his business and adopted a seemingly lotus-eating lifestyle. 'I just sat for a whole year, because simply sitting was the most phenomenal experience for me,' recalls Sadhguru. 'But that earned me the reputation of being a dangerous person. It took a lot of convincing and coaxing and coercing to finally get seven people into my programme.'

The first programme was intended to be two hours a day over four days. The second day, the class went on for five hours, and so also on the third. Eventually, on popular demand, it turned into a six-day programme. After that there was no looking back. Later, the programme was to be formatted, structured, edited and refined into its current Isha yoga avatar, but its genesis was with those seven students who placed their faith in an unknown teacher and took a plunge into the unknown. Jaggi was grateful to them for taking that risk. The fact that he could teach was as much a revelation to him as it was to them.

On one level, it could be seen as a mere shift of emphasis—from motorcycle maintenance to 'inner' maintenance—but it was to change his life and the lives of many others irrevocably. 'Since then there has been no looking back,' says Sadhguru. 'Millions of people have gone through these programmes now. It has gone through various stages of evolution, and we have now formatted it in such a way that it works for all kinds of people. At that time there was no format. I just taught as I liked. I was never spiritually exposed; nor had I read anything. Even now I am not spiritually educated, that's why people call me a Sadhguru. That means an uneducated guru.' He laughs. 'It literally means, 'someone who comes from within', who does not know the scriptures or the holy books or anything.'

Jaggi conducted his own class for a time, and then decided to work under the umbrella of other yoga organizations with similar objectives. Even if the aspirations were common, he was aware from the very start that none of those he worked with came from the same experience as he did. But working in collaboration had its uses. It enabled him to stay as unencumbered as he desired. 'I saw that everybody had all kinds of tricks and methods and techniques but they had no experience. I had had a huge experience but I did not have any methods or techniques. So observing others helped because at least it clearly taught me what I should not do. That was a valuable contribution—realizing what it is that should not be done, just by watching a few groups of people who are engaged in various levels of spiritual activity. Some of them have contributed to the Isha programmes in their own way. Knowingly or unknowingly they had picked up something, the value of which they did not know. The same things I picked up and later made into something totally different, altogether different. In many ways, what we do at Isha Yoga is unique; nowhere else on the planet is the presentation of yoga done the way it [is] done here. It may be the same content, but the way it is presented—the dimension and depth with which it is presented—is not being done anywhere else, as far as I know.'

He subsisted on his poultry farm rental, ate simply and lived pretty much in three pairs of jeans. He refused payment for his yoga instruction. His usual practice was to publicly hand over the proceeds of the class to an orphanage, old-age home or some other charity at the close of the final session of the class, mount his motorcycle and disappear for a month. Commitment to a cause could not curb his essentially free spirit.

And yet, two years after his spiritual awakening, he got married. Six years after that he would even have a child. What made the maverick mystic turn family man? Had he forgotten that he was to leave his body at the age of forty-two? Wasn't this brazenly inconsistent for a man who knew his life had a single-pointed mission?

So it would seem. But then again, perhaps not. For Sadhguru's love of life has always been far too intense, even epicurean, for him to reduce it to a mere game of chess. Most of the decisions in his life, major and minor, seem to have been born of an ability to strike an inspired balance—a wildly dynamic and precarious balance; one that sometimes seems to recall the dance of none other than the cosmic dancer of Indian myth and iconography, Shiva himself. It is an equilibrium between contradictions: creativity and calculation; passion and precision; recklessness and reason. There are a few times when the balance hasn't quite worked, when things have collapsed, misfired, and his own life has been derailed. But for the democratic mystic, perhaps that is all in a day's work.

He remembers the time he first met Vijji. It was after a yoga programme in Mysore. Vijji, a lively twenty-one-year-old (with an abusive marriage and divorce already behind her), had come from Bangalore to attend the programme. It was a programme with a strong psychological orientation, and participants' emotions were running high. Jaggi wasn't conducting the programme, but was invited to lunch. It was past four o'clock when lunch was served. He sat down to eat, looked casually across the room and his glance fell upon her. A distant memory was kindled.

After the momentous experience on Chamundi Hill, Jaggi's ability to retrieve memories from his unconscious had grown keener. This woman, he realized right away, had been his sister a lifetime ago. She had nursed a deep affection for her brother, but Sadhguru Sri Brahma had left home early and had lived out the rest of his life as a sadhu. Access to him, even as his sister, was awkward and difficult, and her love had never found its full expression. Perhaps it was not surprising then that she should have re-entered his life. 'Having a brother like Sadhguru was not easy. He left the house at the age of twelve. Off and on, he came into her life, but he would always leave. And he was mostly a naked sadhu. Sometimes he wore clothes, but most of the time, he wore nothing. So there were problems. There was this longing to be close to him, but she could not because she was a woman and his sister. So there were unfulfilled emotions; and those brought her back into my life again, but in a different way.' Jaggi realized something more now. He knew that he had to have her by his side this time around. She was vital to his life mission.

Vijji caught his gaze. For some inexplicable reason, she found herself walking over to his side. Even more inexplicably, she began weeping. It had been an emotionally high-voltage programme and no one thought this particularly unusual. Jaggi continued stolidly with his meal. He got up once he was through and left. However, that evening after the programme was formally closed, he did join a group of participants for a snack. That was their first interaction.

A day later, Vijji wrote to him from Bangalore. Ironically, she addressed him as her 'dear brother'. 'She wasn't even aware that she had written it,' says Sadhguru. 'It was her first letter to me and she wanted to write "dear Jaggi" but ended up writing "dear brother". I had just met her for a day; she was a young girl and

I hadn't said anything to her at that point. I kept that letter for a long time. Much later, I asked her, "Did you know you wrote this?' She said, 'Why would I address you as brother?" When I showed her the letter, she was shocked. She hadn't even realized she had written this.'

In the letter, Vijji confessed to an urgent desire to stay in touch. The attraction was immediate and mutual. If Vijji was drawn to Jaggi's dynamism, his contagious love of life and adventure, he was no doubt charmed by her childlike exuberance, her ability to segue in an instant between euphoria and gloom. 'There was never an in-between state for her. She was either up or down, laughing one moment, crying the next.'

'It's true that she came into my life somewhat early,' he now admits in a reflective moment. 'If it had been later, perhaps I wouldn't have felt the need to get married. There are many people in my life today with whom I work closely and share a deep spiritual connection. Marriage hasn't been necessary for that.' But at the time, marriage seemed to offer the only meaningful context for the two young people to spend time together. Nor was it something Jaggi regretted. The whirlwind romance surely owed more to a young man's ardour than to a future temple-builder's scheming calculation.

A week later, Jaggi surprised Vijji one afternoon at the bank in which she worked. 'Let's go,' he said with characteristic impetuosity. She hesitated. It was only half past three and the balance had still to be closed. The bank job meant a great deal to a single woman who had emerged from a difficult marriage; it spelt agency, autonomy, financial freedom and access to a world outside the home. She didn't even know Jaggi's full name at the time. She managed to wangle permission from the manager, however, and the two spent the evening together.

Other evenings followed. Vijji attended one of Jaggi's yoga programmes as a volunteer. The relationship deepened. One day, Jaggi called Vijji in Bangalore and told her to join him that very evening. This time Vijji did not hesitate. She went home, packed her bags and took the evening bus to Mysore. Her family was, not surprisingly, alarmed. Jaggi arranged for her to stay that night at a working women's hostel. The next day, she put her foot down and insisted on alternative accommodation. For the next few nights, the young couple camped on Chamundi Hill and then on B.R Hills.

Around this time, Jaggi was to conduct a programme in Gomatagiri. In the middle of the programme, the two decided to take a two-day break in Iruppu, the site of a picturesque waterfall around a hundred and fifty kilometres from Mysore. Jaggi had visited it often and had camped near the waterfall. It happened to be Mahashivaratri and a quaint village fair was on. At dusk, the two visited the local Rameshwara temple, a small and quiet shrine. The setting was ideal, the light mellow, the ambience made to order, and the two decided to be married. By the Hindu calendar, it couldn't have been a more auspicious time: it was on the same day that Shiva married Parvati. Even if they weren't aware of it at the time, Jaggi and Vijji were in august company. Shiva, as he says wryly, was also to be the only witness to their decision.

Soon after the event, Jaggi rented a home on the street adjacent to his family home. Three days later, they moved in. The place had a coconut tree and a sand heap. All that was needed to complete the picture was the sea. That was a minor lacuna. The young couple had imagination and romance enough between them to fill in that blank. Armed with two plastic buckets, a few utensils and the barest furniture, Jaggi and Vijji moved into their new home with the triumphant air of empire builders. The abundance of love made the frugal material conditions seem inconsequential.

I once asked him what marriage had meant to him. Did it fetter him in any way? Did his early failed romance change the way he approached this relationship? 'I approached this with a different level of maturity,' he replied. 'I never saw my wife as a peg. My marriage was built around me, but I never built my life around it. That doesn't mean I didn't love Vijji. I romanced her in every possible way. But I took her into my life as a flower, not a peg to hang on to.'

On another occasion, when I asked what role romance could play in the life of a mystic—someone who saw things 'just as they are'—he replied, 'I can look at a sunrise, dissect it and at the same time, enjoy it. If I look at a woman, I can dissect her, see kidney, liver, spleen, the insides, if I want to. But I can also look at her for what she is right now. Many spiritual teachers have said the body is filthy, that it is full of blood, phlegm, perishable organs. I know that's all it is. And it is still fine with me. It doesn't take away from its beauty. You're suggesting you have to be blind for the world to be beautiful. I don't see things that way.'

Jaggi's parents were initially wary of the relationship. His father raised the inevitable questions about pedigree, caste antecedents and Vijji's previous marriage. Jaggi replied that none of these concerned him. He was marrying neither her father nor her ex-husband, and issues of caste and social standing had never been of any consequence to him. In a matter of weeks, however, the equally inevitable thaw set in. Susheela grew increasingly fond of Vijji over time. The two developed a close bond that lasted till the end of Susheela's days. Vijji's parents, for their part, were relieved to know their daughter had married well the second time round. They also grew to respect Jaggi's vocation as a yoga teacher. This respect increased enormously after Vijji's father, who had suffered a paralytic stroke, was almost entirely cured after attending one of the yoga programmes.

Vijji had applied for a transfer to the Mysore branch of her bank. Once it came through, she resumed her job. Jaggi continued to teach yoga. The rent from his farm offered enough to keep his motorcycle operational. The petrol tank was full and likewise their hearts. Little else was needed. The most important thing, Jaggi had told Vijji at the very start of their relationship, was that she be prepared to hit the road at any given moment. She was willing. Her faith in Jaggi was unwavering. Her friends often observed that she seldom spoke a sentence in which his name did not feature at least three times! And so the two lived blithe gypsy lives, travelling for days on end on Jaggi's bike, with no fixed destination, frequently sleeping on the streetside, in a wayside forest or on a beach, or in the homes of hospitable strangers. There was a time when Jaggi's motorcycle logged fifty-six thousand kilometres in a single calendar year.

There was yet another detail Jaggi had divulged to Vijji at the very start of their relationship: the fact that he would not live beyond the age of forty-two. Their marriage came with a predestined expiry date. For Vijji, who loved Jaggi with a fervour that verged on the religious, this was no deterrent.

To a young collegian who visited Jaggi often at this time and regarded him as a mentor, Vijji's devotion to her husband seemed at times puzzling. He recalls how he once offered to help her make chapattis. Jaggi loved chapattis, and Vijji was particular about making them just the way he liked. The young man happened to scorch a chapatti in the process, and was bewildered when Vijji burst into tears. He had no clue what had provoked such an outburst. But that was Vijji. Volatile and highly strung, her love for her husband was fierce and all-consuming, perhaps even obsessive. But there was more. In her complete disregard for personal security and self-preservation, she was perhaps not so very different from Jaggi himself. Both were essentially creatures of reckless self-abandon. In Jaggi's case, the spontaneity was tempered by logic and foresight, a latent guru's ability to formulate and assess long-term goals. Vijji's emotional circuitry, however, seemed to come without a thermostat.

A year after his marriage, Jaggi decided he needed to make more money. 'Sitting in a city office and meeting people, thinking money all the time, calculating how you can get a little more out of them all the time, is something that I just couldn't live with. So I dropped my business and I thought I'll start another farm. Already I had one farm but I wanted something more. I was flying hang gliders. So I wanted a place where there was a slope. Anyway, this mountain madness was always there inside me.'

He bought a fourteen-acre plot of land around thirty-two kilometres from Mysore. It was situated on a hill slope, with a Shiva temple opposite, and a lake in front. It was rocky, uncultivable land, an unwise investment for agriculture—or so it was believed. 'People thought that this was crazy and it was a big laughing matter in the village. I was a joke in the village. Every day I would do something new, and they'd all think, "Oh, the idiot is doing one more stupid thing."' But Jaggi proceeded to plant coconut, cabbage, mango, and for some time, cotton. He cleared the surrounding bush; devised a simple but ingenious system of drip irrigation; used manure that he transported from the Mysore Zoo; and cut the abundantly available Parthenium grass and used it as mulch. The result: his crops flourished.

Jaggi's affinity with the natural world has been a long-standing one, and his life as a farmer was an extension of that instinctive sense of kinship. His approach to his work even today is invariably practical and hands-on. He has often spoken of the difference between faiths that 'look downward' and those that 'look heavenward'. The former, he points out, are far more respectful of the earth than the other-worldly ones. 'Those religions which see that God is in the earth, somewhere deep inside, they walk a little more gently upon this planet,' he says. 'Those who believe God's up there, they walk aggressively, because this planet is not so valuable to them; they think they're going to heaven anyway. If you walk through this life thinking too much of yourself, you're a vandal. If you take every step of your life in gratitude, if you see how small you are, you walk on this planet gently, like a pilgrim; this life could be your pilgrimage.'

One day he decided to start painting his farmhouse. This simple manual activity unleashed its own share of mystical insights. 'I was painting my farm building and, you know, I wanted to evolve easier ways of painting,' he recalls. 'I didn't have time because I was painting the whole farm single-handedly. So I would dip and just walk from one end to another; then I would dip again and walk from one end to another. So for the first smear, I dipped and walked. Here it came out thick; as it went on, it became thinner, thinner, thinner, and then disappeared. I sat there and it just blew my mind totally, because the whole existence was right there for me. This is all existence is. Something is gross; it becomes subtler, subtler, subtler, and it becomes non-material. When it becomes non-material, you call it divine. [When it is] very gross, you call it rock or matter. In between, there are many levels of subtleness or grossness. That's all existence is.'

He also dug a well on the land himself with the help of a few labourers. Here again he flouted popular wisdom by digging on the uppermost level of the gradient rather than on the lowest. The rock formation in the area convinced him that it would be the appropriate place. It was also more convenient than building a tank on low-level ground and then working out a system of water distribution to the rest of the farm. He found the process of well-digging—burrowing deep into the earth with nothing to sustain the digger except the uncertain promise of water and a distant patch of sky above—a deeply spiritual experience. The villagers watched with disbelief when he struck water at eighteen feet. It was considered nothing short of a miracle.

After some time, he began to toy with the idea of cooperative farming. It accorded with his larger vision for rural uplift. The idea was to give up individual ownership of property and create a collectively-owned modern farm on a thousand acres of land, and pool resources to cultivate cash crops that would bring in profitable returns. He interested several small farmers in the concept, and the project started to take shape in a modest piecemeal fashion.

'I thought we could make a thousand-acre farm with proper agricultural graduates, take bank loans, dig proper bore-wells, drip irrigate, grow about seven, eight different categories of crop (in the market if one fails, another one would make it), grade the land according to fertility and quality. The idea was that everybody gets an equal share of it. I tried to work on the concept. I even started writing a document on how to grow these crops in innovative ways. I wrote over eight hundred pages about each and every crop that grew there. Basically, I believed that if we integrated the farms, then whatever we did would be economically worthwhile. On two-acre and three-acre farms whatever you try to do just doesn't work. And if you grow just one crop, if it fails in the market, you are done. You are back into loans and suicides and the rest of it. But if there are eight crops growing, you can make some money off another crop if this one fails. And that money is anyway distributed among people.'

But he was also aware that economic reform was never going to be enough. The real transformation, he knew, had its source in the deepest, often seemingly arid, interiority of each human being, where even a distant patch of sky was often not visible. Mere material wellbeing was never going to be able to access that.

Things came to a natural halt when a mulberry farming experiment backfired. Jaggi's plan was to sell mulberry leaves to silkworm breeders and make a killing. The crop grew well. Harvest time was just a month away. One day Jaggi happened to mention to his one-man team that it was time to clear some of the dry wild bush around his farm by burning it, but with care. He proposed to do this on his return from Mysore. Some days later on his way back, he parked his motorcycle on top of the hill and paused, as he often did, to take in the panoramic view of his farm and the surrounding countryside. All he could see this time, however, was charred black land. As he rode on, puzzled, he saw the villagers turn to look at him, mute and ashen-faced. It was the expression one might cast in the direction of the damned. 'Everybody was looking at me like, that man is finished. That kind of look,' he says.

He returned to his land to find the entire farm gutted. His Man Friday had disappeared ten minutes before his arrival. But the terrified wife had been left behind to do some explaining. This was accompanied by much weeping and hand-wringing, but Jaggi was eventually able to gather a few facts. The enthusiastic employee had decided to set fire to the bush in his master's absence. In minutes, however, the fire had got out of hand. He had tried his best to salvage the situation, but the whole place was incinerated before his very eyes. Nothing remained to be said.

'The moment he heard the motorcycle, my assistant had just run into the mountains because he thought I was going to kill him. He had left his wife to tell me because I won't thrash his wife—at least he believed so. So she was standing there trembling, and she had taken defence behind her infant child.' He laughs. 'Probably she believed if she was alone I might strangle her or something. I looked around and it was totally burned up. All the bank loan that I had taken, all the money I was counting on, all the leaves, everything was just gone. I couldn't help bursting into laughter, but then I knew she would think I'd gone insane or something. I just looked at her as if to ask what happened. I didn't trust myself to open my mouth in case I laughed. She said, "No, no, we did not do anything here; he was just trying to set fire to the bush and we don't know what happened. Suddenly the whole thing caught fire."'

As he listened to her tale, it dawned on Jaggi that there was nothing more to be done. 'I had come prepared to stay for a couple of days,' he says. 'But now there was no work to be done on the farm. There *was* no farm. I was completely free. I just turned around and rode back to Mysore.'

He dropped in on Vijji during her lunch break at the bank and proposed taking her out to lunch. 'She asked, "How come you're back? You're not supposed to come back for two or three days."

'I said, "The whole farm is burned out and I am free." She gasped.

'I said, "I am asking you out for lunch. What are you complaining about?"

'She said, "But the farm!"

'I said, "It's burnt. We don't have to worry about it any more. Every day there were so many problems with the farm. Now all the troubles are over."

'She was disturbed and said, "But what are you going to do about the loan?"

'I said, "Right now, we are free. We'll see later what to do about the loan."

'She said, "How can you laugh in a situation like this?"

'I said, "Okay, if you want to cry, you cry. I'll take somebody else for lunch."

'Then she finally said, "Okay, if you're not bothered, what's my problem?"

'And I said, "Now you're getting somewhere!"'

The unflappable reaction to the crisis wasn't just to placate a partner in panic. Sadhguru quite genuinely holds that whatever the provocation, joy is always a very real choice. 'That farm burning up meant I could just travel for the next three or four months and teach. And you know, I did raise another crop. This mulberry would have been entangling for me for many years. I just put three-month cotton crops, made good money and cleared up my loans. Then, later, of course, I sold my farm, but I didn't sell because of any financial pressures. It's just I didn't have the time. See, you don't have to be joyful only when everything works out. If you are joyful, you will naturally function at your optimum level. So things work out far better for you than for anybody else because you're functioning at your best.'

The yoga classes were, in the meantime, going ahead full steam. Jaggi had felt intuitively that an important source of support for his life mission was likely to come from Telugu-speaking quarters. He had conducted classes in Hyderabad. These had been successful, but nothing fruitful in terms of his personal quest had come of it.

And then there were those mountains—the ones imprinted on his vision since his childhood. The fact that they had always been there—patient, majestic, indelible—convinced him that these were the site for his lifetime's work. He could see them clearly enough even now. But where were they? Did they really exist? For some reason, Jaggi was convinced they did. He travelled back and forth at least seven times on his motorcycle, up and down the Western Ghats, from Goa down to the very tip of the Malabar Coast in Kerala. In the course of his journey, he witnessed landscapes of great grandeur and majesty. But nowhere did he see those mountains, *his* mountains.

Then one day, he happened to visit friends in Coimbatore in the state of Tamil Nadu. The year was 1987. He alighted at the bus stand. The bus was early and he still had a couple of hours before his friends were due to meet him. He decided to wait at the depot. It was just four o'clock. The morning was dark, the air crisp and invigorating. Jaggi sat down on his suitcase. In moments, he entered a deep meditative state.

He had reclaimed his memories of previous lifetimes more than five years ago, soon after his Chamundi awakening. But mists still shrouded some areas of recollection. He had various hunches about the direction in which his mission lay, but they were still nascent, unformed. Now the last vestiges of forgetfulness were banished. As he got up to greet his friends two hours later, there were no more doubts.

He knew now where he needed to locate his life's work, and where he would find his loyalists. It had to be here. Here in this city of 'silver mountains'. Here in the land that Sadhguru Sri Brahma had travelled so extensively in his lifetime. It had to be Coimbatore.

'Compassion as Conspiracy'
Preparing for Harvest

'When you plant a crop, you know some weeding is necessary. But you never weed until a crop is strong enough to withstand it,' Sadhguru once told me. 'It's important to time it right.'

Despite having made his discovery about Coimbatore being the locus of his operations, Jaggi did not relocate right away. He spent much of the following year in relative seclusion on his farm. He cut down on his activities and devoted long hours to meditation. He was far from idle, however. From a mystic's point of view, it was a year of hectic activity. Jaggi was busy weeding.

What exactly was this spiritual horticulture about? Essentially, he says, paving the way for the next phase of his operations. It meant clearing the lives of those with whom he would interact of unnecessary debris. He was creating a situation conducive for all of them to collaborate towards a larger end. 'I knew there would be instinctive resistance from many quarters of Coimbatore to my plans. I saw it coming. And I was preparing for it, clearing the soil, pruning away as much as I could,' he says enigmatically.

In 1989, he conducted his first class in Coimbatore. It was attended by ten people. There was Raja, an engineer who was motivated by nothing more than curiosity and a vague desire to find a cure for his sinusitis. There was Swaminathan, a professor of zoology from Tiruppur, who hoped yoga would address his migraines. Ponnuswami, the owner of a rice mill, was afflicted with arthritis and desperate for a cure. Geetha, a young engineer, had been vaguely depressed for some time and didn't know why. These were just a few of the people who gravitated towards Jaggi, hesitantly at first, and with a mounting sense of gratitude and wellbeing later.

A Tiruppur meditator remembers parking his shoes outside the venue with an attendant at his first programme, only to find on entering the hall that the humble footwear attendant was the teacher himself, transformed now into a riveting speaker. Another meditator found it heartwarming that her yoga teacher didn't merely eat with the participants but was often to be seen quietly and methodically chopping vegetables for a meal.

This class wasn't just a course of yoga asanas, they discovered. Body-contorting hatha yoga was what Jaggi called 'Columbus yoga', a rebound from the West. The yoga he imparted was a mix of asanas, pranayama and consecrated meditation practices. The approach was simple and scientific, his instruction lucid, his discourses forthright and witty. But the initiations into meditation practices were explosive.

His presence was different too. This was no longer the taciturn Jaggi of old. Since 1982, Jaggi was a changed man in more ways than one. His presence radiated warmth and vitality; his intelligence was sharp and playful; his humour, infectious; his energy, inclusive and compassionate. He was fun to be around. He was a great listener. And he was charismatic, to say the least. When he drove his car through Coimbatore, it was at full throttle. When he trekked the mountains, it was impossible to keep pace with him. But there was more. There was a mysterious ability to draw people of varied temperaments and persuasions, ranging from the devout to the doubting, the emotional to the intellectual, the simple to the sophisticated, and the rustic to the urbane.

That radiance of presence is still in evidence. It continues to disarm some of the most committed guru-phobic cynics. There is a naturalness, an unstudied economy of word and gesture, and a palpable joie de vivre, that makes a strangely assorted bunch of people warm to him. Unpredictable, mercurial and yet endearingly human, he also seems to enjoy puncturing the stereotypic guru image whenever he has the chance. 'I refuse to be like those idiots on spirituality channels on television!' he remarked recently, as he contemplated joining the youth of Coimbatore on a dirt track motorcycle race advertised in the local newspapers. He didn't join the race eventually. But those who know him are aware that he very well could have. At the same time, the accessible manner is combined with a majesty that is difficult to ignore. There is nothing doctored about this grandeur. It is as natural as his rich belly laugh. And that commands immediate respect, even while his informal manner puts one instantly at ease.

There is an ability to relate deeply to people's emotional needs, and an equal ability for dispassionate and uncompromising analysis. This unusual combination is probably what makes him, as he has often said, a guru with whom both approaches are possible: *gnana* and *bhakti*; knowledge and devotion. People of both propensities are drawn to him.

The Isha (or Sahaja Sthiti, as it was known at the time) yoga class has always been based on a fundamental view of the individual as a cocktail of body, mind, emotion and energy. No one, as Jaggi said at the start of each programme, is all-emotion or all-mind. Each one is a mixed bag, and it is possible to create a yoga regimen that is suitable for every type of person. The course offers a mix of simple asanas, pranayama kriyas and meditation. Simple enough, seemingly. But many who have attended other yoga classes vouch for the difference.

What made it work then? What makes it work now? No one seems to know, not even the many Isha teachers who have carried it over the years to different parts of the world. But one thing seems certain: there is more going on in an Isha yoga programme than is apparent to the eye. The simplicity is deceptive. What becomes gradually evident to those who feel the need to marinate in the yoga but don't know why, is the fact that each programme is simply saturated with the guru's energy and presence. As someone who thought the word 'vibe' was used by a certain species of inarticulate new-age adolescent, I confess I've come a long way. Vibe is actually a pretty accurate word. The vibe is precisely what makes one return time and again to the programmes. Or indeed, to the ashram. Or to Sadhguru. The vibe is as tangible as a bell chime, as a deep inner throb, a steady, level pulsation. You recognize it as your guru's. You recognize it increasingly as your own.

In 1989, however, he wasn't Sadhguru yet. Just a young man in faded jeans and a T-shirt, with a beard, long hair and his fair share of charm. But things were happening around him, things no one quite understood. It wasn't just about ailments—physical and psychological—vanishing with the yoga he imparted. That helped, certainly, to give him credibility. But it was more about the way he drew people to him. In a short time, he seemed to have become indispensable to their lives. These were people of varying ages and from different walks of life, but they seemed equally devoted. They weren't quite sure how or why it had happened. But their trust in Jaggi was deep and instinctive. When meditators from Karnataka visited Coimbatore, they were amazed at the spell that Jaggi seemed to have cast over his Coimbatore flock. It seemed to recall the early prophesy by the soothsayer who had visited the Vasudev home all those years ago: 'He will graze human beings.'

Raja, who worked closely with him as a volunteer and later as a teacher, says that the qualities in Jaggi which he found most inspirational were his simplicity, his openness, his compassion and his infinite patience. 'It was from him that I learnt the knack of dealing with people. Even in the Teachers' Training programme, which is all about trampling on people's egos, I saw that he trampled with care, without hurting anyone. He seemed to know the trick of creating a spirit of willingness in everyone. After that, there was no question of anyone being hurt.' A clue to this approach is to be found in what Sadhguru said not so long ago: 'It helps to remember that nobody likes to be managed. But everybody longs to be included.'

Raja was also moved by the way in which Jaggi reacted to provocations of various kinds. 'He never lost his temper. Once I forgot to post some invitations to his family and friends in Mysore. He asked me time and again whether I'd done it, and I kept reassuring him that I had. I told him it must be a postal delay. Then about a week later, I found that the invitations were still with me. I hadn't posted them as I'd thought. I felt very bad about it. There were tears in my eyes when I apologized to him. But he was so gentle. He said that he did think I had forgotten, but he never reproached me. He said not to worry about it.'

In March 1990, Jaggi's personal life entered a new phase with the birth of his daughter. Voluntary parenthood seems an unusual decision for a man who knew he was unlikely to live beyond the decade. 'Yes, it probably was,' he admits. 'But Vijji was very keen on a child. She had friends who convinced her that motherhood was a crucial experience in every woman's life. And I gave in to her wish, because if I did leave by the age of forty-two, she would have someone in her life. It would be an incentive for her to live on.'

Acutely aware that time was now short, his life became even more hectic. He divided his time between Bangalore (where Vijji had been transferred) and various parts of Tamil Nadu other than Coimbatore, including Tiruppur, Erode and Karur, where he busied himself conducting programmes from morning to night. He took his daughter along with him on his travels and she spent a large part of her early life under the care of various meditators' families. Vijji and he managed to meet either in Coimbatore or Bangalore every other weekend.

The accounts of some of the senior Isha meditators offer an insight into just how Jaggi appeared to his nascent group of disciples in those days before he made the transition to Sadhguru. 'I went to a programme in 1991 against my will,' recounts Indira, now Maa

Karpoori. 'My husband insisted, and I reluctantly agreed to go for just the introductory talk. As Jaggi entered, I had a curious feeling. All my life I'd felt like I belonged nowhere. I'd searched everywhere—in temples, churches, and various spiritual traditions—and had always been put off by the fanaticism and hypocrisy. And here was this yoga teacher entering the class. All I could see of him were his feet. And I had these tears pouring down my face. I remember having this strange irrational thought: "How long you've made me wait." And a second later, came the thought, "If Jesus were on earth, this is how it would feel to watch him pass by."'

This was the year that Bharathi, a young mother of two (who had moved from Vishakapatnam to Coimbatore after her marriage), joined the class. A clear-thinking, level-headed woman, her response to Jaggi wasn't quite so emotional. 'It was some five or six years after I moved to Coimbatore that my sister-in-law told my husband about a new yoga class. She'd been told by someone that it would help her manage her stress (induced by the fact that she could never retain her domestic help!) and she thought it might address my husband's long-standing stomach ailment.'

Bharathi had no intention of doing the programme herself. 'I thought my life was reasonably comfortable—health and fitness weren't a problem; I had my kids, enough money, opportunities for travel, and I wasn't particularly stressed. So I didn't see why I should enrol. But on the day of the introductory talk, I dropped my sister-in-law off at the venue and she suggested I attend the lecture as well. I've never been into godmen or gurus. I've never fallen at any swamiji's feet. But I decided to stay on simply because I thought this would be a talk on the physical aspects of yoga. I went in and saw this bearded man in a white dhoti and kurta. He didn't look very impressive. He looked small to me; in some ways, a bit like Shankaran Pillai!' she laughs, alluding to Sadhguru's later iconic creation, the butt of his jokes.

While she wasn't particularly bowled over by the new yoga teacher's personality, she acknowledged that what he said seemed to make sense. 'He talked of how life could be so much more joyous than it currently was, if only we allowed it to be. It didn't sound too bad, so out of curiosity, I decided to join. By the end of the programme, I was totally sold on this yoga. The initiation into Shoonya meditation was the turning point. It was then that I understood for the very first time that there is another dimension to life—a deeper dimension, a dimension worth exploring, worth committing oneself to for a lifetime. I didn't know what it was. But I knew that this Sahaja Sthiti yoga class was just a front; that this man knew something and had something very huge to offer—and I wanted a taste of it.'

A couple of weeks after the programme, Bharathi happened to be at lunch with Sadhguru and a few members of her family. 'I was just sitting quietly, not paying attention to anything in particular, when slowly an involuntary tremor set into my being and body. The vibration in the body became so obvious that, not wanting to cause any embarrassment to myself, I went out of the room. But the tremor wouldn't cease for over a whole hour. I would say that this was my first real glimpse of Sadhguru's energy and reality.'

Suddenly, the simple yoga teacher seemed to be turning into something much larger than she had ever envisaged. 'He appears so very unassuming, but if you just allow it, his energies invade your inside and go on a rampage, to destroy that which is called "you" and reveal the actuality that you are. In my case, the invasion happened despite my resistance. Suddenly there was discontent and strife in my life, which had been absent earlier. What I thought was life was not life anymore. What I thought was wellbeing was not wellbeing anymore. What I thought as happiness was just an illusion. Ultimately, it became clear that what I had in life was not everything, nor was it the ultimate.'

Bharathi maintained her distance from the yoga teacher even while he became an increasingly important presence in her household. Her sisters-in-law frequently invited him over when he was in Coimbatore and the opportunities for interaction increased.

'Though my energies spoke a different language right from Day One, my logic wouldn't allow him to encroach on my privacy in any way,' she says.

Even though she continued to address him formally as 'Sir', she was aware of feeling 'helplessly drawn' towards him. At the same time, her meditative experiences in his presence grew in intensity. 'Life was exciting. He intrigued me enormously. And above all, I trusted him. I don't know why, but I knew I could trust my life to him.'

Indira found her life turning hollow and curiously thin in a matter of days. 'When I returned home after the introductory talk, even my home seemed strange to me. My husband and my job seemed alien. I was so disconnected. The only switch that was on was my connection with Jaggi. On the fourth day after the class, I went up to him. Before I could say a word, he said, "I know what's happening with you. Just relax." He knew me instinctively, and strangely, I trusted him right away.'

For all his gentleness and warmth, Jaggi's personality had another quality that these early meditators recognized right away: an intensity. 'He was a man in a hurry. That was clear,' says Indira. 'And though we were all mad about him, we also knew in our hearts that this man did not belong to us. I sensed intuitively that he'd come into my life to do something for me that no one else could, or would even dare try. I realized he wouldn't hold my hand. I sensed that he could be ruthless. But it was already too late to back out. I had no choice about it. My world was falling apart. I felt scared, suspended in a kind of limbo, and at the same time, I knew it was right. I started hearing my heartbeat, feeling my breath, in a way that I never had before.'

She recalls the time Jaggi gave Bharathi and her a photograph of himself. Careful not to rouse her husband's ire, she hid it in her cupboard among her saris. One day, she received a call from Jaggi in Mysore. 'Why is my photo lying upside down in your cupboard?' he asked crisply. She was too flummoxed to reply.

On another occasion, when she was in the middle of a flaming row with her husband, the phone rang. It was midnight. She answered it only to hear her yoga teacher's imperious tones. 'Why are you fighting? Shut up and go to sleep,' he said. She proceeded to do just that. 'Wrong number,' she told her husband and turned off the lights.

Somu (now Swami Gurubiksha), a young businessman who belonged to what he describes as 'a pukka moneylending Chettiar family', found himself in a dilemma immediately after attending the first programme. On the one hand, he felt instantly and compellingly drawn to Jaggi. On the other hand, there was his family allegiance to Yogi Ramsuratkumar, the well-known mystic of Tiruvannamalai. Surely it was sacrilegious to have two gurus? The only way to resolve this impasse was to regard Jaggi as a yoga teacher, inspiring but ancillary, and Ramsuratkumar as his primary guide. The dilemma lingered for several years even as his trust in Jaggi increased. 'The conflict was finally resolved once when I was planning to visit my hometown near Karaikudi in 1993. Jaggi told me then that two people in my hometown would inquire after him; he asked me to convey his regards to them. When I reached home, that's exactly what happened! I was stunned. I probably knew deep down by then that Jaggi was my master, but this incident confirmed it for me. I felt that Jaggi was conveying to me indirectly who my true guru was.'

The classes grew more frequent and rapidly more popular. In 1990, Jaggi conducted the Bhava Spandana programme (BSP) for the first time in Coimbatore. A course designed to arouse and transform deep and hidden feelings, and to clear psychological bottlenecks, it had a deep impact on the participants. Raja describes it as an 'emotional high'. When Indira did it in 1991, she found that she actually left her body during the death meditation. 'For the first time, I actually saw my body lying down there, dead, with flies hovering over my head. It cured me of my fear of death forever.'

The programme was far too emotionally charged and volatile for Bharathi's taste. She wasn't quite sure why intense emotion had to translate itself into such ear-splitting decibel levels, but she was able to sit through it as a spectator. 'It was far too emotional for me. Everyone was weeping and laughing, and I couldn't see why. At the end of Day Three, I had to squeeze out a tear to keep the others company! But the programme didn't disappoint me either.'

Already there was the sense of a rapidly unfolding journey of excitement and discovery. There were odd experiences that seemed to keep happening around the young yoga teacher. Bharathi had no explanation for any of these occurrences. But, determined to remain level-headed through it all, she refused to give in to any non-rational interpretation of these events. Sometimes Jaggi would tell her that he would 'be' with her at certain times of the day. At precisely those moments, although she was engaged in an entirely unrelated activity, Bharathi could suddenly smell the unmistakable scent of her master's presence mingled with the fragrance of ash. She refused to attach any significance to this, however.

There was the time he happened to ask her for a glass of water. When she brought it, he suggested that she drink it. 'I drank the water,' says Bharathi. 'But I had no sensation of drinking it. I was swallowing it, but my thirst wasn't quenched. It was a strange experience. That's when he said quite matter-of-factly, "It's going into me. I'm drinking it."' Indira recalls a similar experience as well.

On another occasion when Bharathi was besieged by doubt about the strange saga unfolding in her life, Jaggi took off a *saligram mala*—a chain of stone beads—from around his neck and placed it in her palm. All of a sudden, the beads slithered across her palm in a sinuous snake-like movement. She remembers crying out loud in sheer terror. Later she asked him what this meant. His reply was curt: 'Who wears a snake around his neck?' The answer was obvious: Shiva. But what on earth did Shiva—the first yogi, the first guru—have to do with this young yoga instructor from Mysore?

By this time, Bharathi had a sense of what later years were to confirm: the fact that her master had a mysterious and audacious game plan in which she and many others were to play a part. She had no clue what that plan was. (Years later, she understands that that plan is still unfolding.) But she realized that he was nothing less than a virtuoso conspirator. 'The fact that he's actually a brilliant manipulator amused me then, and it still does,' she says reflectively. 'I was aware even then that this was a chance to be manipulated by someone who really knows how to run the business of life.'

It was in May 1991 that Jaggi conducted a silence programme called Samyama for the first time. 'I had done it earlier for individuals. But this was the first time I was doing it for a group,' he recalls. 'There were around thirty-two participants, and it was like being in control of thirty-two tightrope-walkers.' Did the group situation make it potentially dangerous? 'Not for the participants,' he shrugs. 'It's important that everyone is focused on their priorities, that's all. If anyone falls, I'm the safety net.' Today the course draws over a thousand participants, and one can only imagine the levels of responsibility that entails for the guru. The safety net doesn't seem to show any signs of fraying, however.

Jaggi now realized he had to expand the largely health-centred 'Shakti chalana kriya' that he had taught so far, to include spiritual aspects as well. Having done this, he conducted Samyama for the same group again in December. He remembers the makeshift nature of the programme at the time. The music used in the programme was from his personal collection. And the mode of broadcast was novel to say the least: he played it on his Walkman, which, in turn, was placed strategically near a speaker. 'Now we have a state-of-the-art sound system—we've come a long way in these few years!' he smiles.

An advanced level programme, Samyama entailed seven days of silence and intense meditation. The results were volatile. As energy levels rose, participants discovered the strangest things happening. Some were overwhelmed by memories of incidents they had never actually lived out in their lives. Others found themselves laughing like hyenas, mewing like cats, hissing and slithering around the hall like snakes, leaping out of their seats, standing on their heads. One gentleman even found himself on Jaggi's lap! 'At the end of every meditation, I was always several feet away from where I started,' says Srinivas, an early meditator.

When they emerged from the programme, it was with a sense of having been laundered and utterly wrung out. Drained of their customary quota of life-drama, it seemed like all that was left was an abiding calm and a sense of wonder at the many trivial variables on which they had invested great quantities of time and psychological energy in the past. Many said that it seemed like the person they had been before the programme had been sloughed off like a snake's skin. From a teacher whose love of snakes was legendary, perhaps this ability to initiate a process of dramatic spiritual moulting was not so surprising. Gradually, the young yoga teacher was beginning to be perceived as someone to reckon with.

The programme, which takes participants through intense meditation, continues to arouse deep and life-changing responses. As energy levels rise, Sadhguru explains, areas of unconscious experience frequently start surfacing as well. In the early courses, the memories of past lifetimes that rose were often vivid and luminous. However, he weeded out this component in later programmes on the grounds that people could get sidetracked by these recollections. The crucial aim, he says, is to work out one's karma at an energy level. It is unnecessary for this to be worked out as conscious memory.

In her Samyama programme in May 1992, Bharathi suddenly found herself slipping out of her body while in meditation and had the distinct experience of travelling to another place and time. She saw herself in a rural landscape standing beside a prostrate figure. There was a great deal of commotion around her, and she felt herself consumed by grief. She knew she was the woman in the picture, and realized that the man before her had died of snakebite. In a flash, it struck her that the dead man was none other than her own master, Jaggi, in another lifetime. She also knew then that she had returned yet again to this lifetime to become his disciple.

Bharathi was simultaneously aware of herself as a woman weeping in anguish and as a woman lying unconscious in a meditation programme. She was a witness to the past and the present all at once. She was aware of participants crowding around her, of Jaggi tapping her forehead, working on her chakras, trying to bring her back to consciousness. She was vaguely amused by the mounting anxiety that had seized the group. It was forty minutes later that she opened her eyes and looked at her master. 'I knew it wasn't a hallucination. I knew when I emerged from this state that my association with this man had been from elsewhere, from an earlier place and time.' She knew now the reason for her deep sense of connection with him. But there was no emotion in her gaze. It was a strangely dispassionate clarity. Later she realized that reclaiming this memory had cured her of a long-standing fear of snakes.

In a later Samyama programme, she had another brief but vivid glimpse of two wiry naked sadhus striding along at a great pace. As she watched the scene, she knew intuitively that she was the younger of these two men, and that the other was none other than Jaggi. The master was walking rapidly, and seemed to be in the grip of a strong emotion. Those were hard times for the monks, she realized immediately. In a single moment, a past lifetime as Vibhuthi, Sadhguru Sri Brahma's close disciple and companion, came back to her.

When she came out of these experiences, Jaggi seemed to know what had happened. He asked her what sense she made of them. 'I've known you earlier,' she told him simply. 'But it's of no consequence to this life.' She maintains that to this day. 'The experiences didn't make me any more attached to him. In fact, I didn't attach much importance to them. I knew he'd offer these experiences to anyone who was available. Whenever people ask him if they've known him in any earlier lifetime, I wonder at their curiosity. My question is: What does it matter? He's here now. That's important. Having known him earlier doesn't really mean anything.'

But the experience did fuel one pressing question. 'I knew now that I'd been associated with him for at least two lifetimes. My question was: Why does life place two people together like this in lifetime after lifetime? To what end? What's this whole drama of life about? The question still remains.' She asked Sadhguru the question once. His reply was characteristically impersonal. 'See the drama through to its end.'

What she did know was that the programme left her with a growing sense of freedom and clarity. 'After Samyama, I felt I was living life in a different way altogether. I continued to do the same things, but I enjoyed it all a lot more. I still had strong likes and dislikes, but they didn't rule my life anymore. I still don't have any conscious burning thirst for enlightenment or samadhi. But my reverence for this man is purely because I know that he can really transform someone's life. It's happened to me. And it's happening still. The excitement's still there.'

It was soon after Samyama that Jaggi mentioned something to Bharathi that took her by surprise. 'He told me that I had a birthmark below my knee,' she remembers. 'He even described the size and shape. I told him he was right. He said that he had a similar mark on his shoulder.' It was the imprint of snakebite: the legacy of a lifetime in which they had both been scarred. 'A story suddenly fell into place,' says Bharathi. She points out that ever since the consecration of the Dhyanalinga, the mark has begun fading.

For Vijji, who did Samyama for the very first time in 1992, the programme reconfirmed her conviction that she could not meditate. 'I cannot leave Jaggi and meditate. If I close my eyes, I see Jaggi. If I open my eyes, I see Jaggi,' she confided to the rest of the class at the close of the programme. Tears coursed freely as she spoke. As her husband listened, they streamed down his face as well.

A twenty-one-day Teachers' Training course followed on the heels of the first Samyama programme. Eight participants enrolled for it. The Isha Foundation Trust was formed at this time. It was growing increasingly clear to the growing group of committed Coimbatore meditators that they needed a space where they could be with their master and pursue their common goals. Their lives had already been drastically transformed. Neither their professional nor their family lives seemed to make much sense anymore, and the prospect of life without their master seemed hollow. He was such an elusive presence that an ashram seemed a good way of anchoring him and ensuring that he did not leave them.

Besides, no one else in their lives quite understood what was happening. There were many in Coimbatore who viewed the new young yoga guru and his fast-burgeoning tribe of disciples with growing suspicion and hostility. The predictable rumourmongering had begun: Who was this young man who broke up homes and families? What was the spell he had cast over these people? Was there something more sinister and manipulative to the yoga he propounded than met the eye?

And yet, for the new Isha meditators none of this really mattered. It seemed impulsive and suicidal to those who knew them, but they were ready to throw in their lot with this young yogi from nowhere—a man without means or resources, but a man whom they unanimously recognized as their leader. It was a risk, but it already felt like there wasn't much choice in the matter any more.

For Raja (now in charge of Teachers' Training programmes), 1991 was probably the most eventful year of his life. It was the year he got married, had a daughter, enrolled for the very first Samyama and Teachers' Training programme and gave up his job to devote himself to Isha fulltime. 'One day in Tiruppur, Jaggi asked me what my plans were. I told him I didn't know. He asked me if I planned to get into business. I repeated that I didn't know. He said, "What about yoga? Would you like to take this to people?" I said, how? He said, "Now that you're trained, you can travel and teach." I asked him if I should resign from my job. He said that would probably make sense. A month later, I went to meet him in Mysore and told him I'd resigned. He was shocked at the speed with which I'd acted.' Raja still remembers how the soft-hearted Vijji burst into tears at his announcement. 'Now I'll have to take care of two families,' she said with typical generosity. Raja recalls that Vijji always made his wife, child and him feel like they were part of her inner family circle.

Looking back on his decision, he agrees that it was a kind of madness. 'There were no calculations. We never worried about the future. We did hear Jaggi say that he wouldn't live beyond the age of forty-two. But nothing mattered. We were convinced by what he said. And we loved him. After that, there was no room for fear.'

Apart from his admiration for Jaggi's charisma, Raja had also had his share of profound experiences with his master that had filled him with awe. On one occasion, Jaggi asked him to go and conduct a class in Tiruppur. Ninety participants had enrolled. Raja, who used to assist Jaggi but had never conducted a class independently, refused. Jaggi reminded him that he had been trained as a teacher, but Raja remained firm. Eventually, Jaggi suggested that he conduct the introductory talk, and promised to arrive soon after to conduct the programme himself. Raja boarded the bus to Tiruppur, expecting Jaggi to follow him in his car. 'I did the introduction that evening. The next morning there was no sign of Jaggi. I called the office in Coimbatore. I was told he'd gone to Mysore. I tried him there, but there was no trace of him. He'd just vanished.' Nervous and fuming, Raja conducted the entire programme himself. Days later, Jaggi appeared just before the initiation process, smiling infuriatingly.

On investigation, Raja found that Jaggi had been in Coimbatore all along. But he had deliberately avoided Raja's frantic phone calls. When some volunteers asked him why he didn't put poor Raja out of his misery, Jaggi replied that this was the only way to get him to conduct a class himself. He added, 'Raja thinks he's conducting the class. The fool doesn't know I'm with him daily.' Raja was shocked when days later, Jaggi pointed out a few specific instances in the programme when he had slipped up.

He remembers another occasion when he and Jaggi were having lunch during a Samyama programme. The night before, Raja had noticed a young female participant who seemed to be in an altered state of consciousness. Jaggi had noticed it too and had instructed him to keep a close watch over her. In the middle of lunch, Jaggi suddenly rose and rushed into the hall. The girl was slumped near the dais, unconscious. Jaggi, whose right hand seemed to have gone mysteriously limp, asked for some oil. When the oil was brought, he worked on the young girl's chakras for a length of time. Eventually, she regained consciousness. Later Jaggi told Raja that the girl had not merely left her body; she had actually appeared to him as a disembodied being in the middle of lunch, giggling wildly. That was the reason he had rushed abruptly into the hall. He had known that it was a life-or-death situation. 'Such things were always happening around him,' says Raja.

Then there was the time when Jaggi took a group on a trek up the Kumara Parvat in Karnataka. Just before the trek began, he looked up from a book he was reading and casually informed the group that Lord Kartikeya or Muruga (the six-headed Dravidian warrior deity, Shiva's first son and a yogi in his own right) had left his body up on this very hill. Less than a quarter of the way up, Jaggi was seized with tremors. He fell and writhed helplessly on the rough ground. It was clear that he was struggling to retain his hold on his body. The meditators had seen him in these samadhi states before, and they began rubbing his legs which invariably turned cold and numb at such times. He asked for a stone to be brought and rubbed it several times against his forehead at the *ajna chakra.* When he recovered, he seemed a changed person. He continued the journey with them, silent and forbidding.

That night when the party camped halfway up the mountain, he led them through certain meditations. 'The strangest things kept happening,' says Raja. 'Some were sobbing, others shaking. Srinivas kept standing up in the middle of the meditation, bringing the tent down.' The next day, Jaggi asked the group to go ahead up the mountain without him. When they returned after a particularly powerful meditation on the summit, they brought back a curiously shaped rock that they were told was a 'Shanmukha lingam'. Jaggi held the stone for a while, and then handed it over to the other members of the group. For Raja, it was hot to touch, while some of the others started rolling and shaking as soon as they came into contact with it. Later that night, Jaggi explained that a great yogi—very possibly Kartikeya himself—had left his body on this mountain. That was responsible for the incredibly powerful energy that permeated the place. For Raja, the incident only confirmed that life around his master could never be anything but unexpected.

Initially, despite his students' eagerness, Jaggi seemed opposed to the idea of any kind of institutionalization. 'I don't want to be tied to any one place. There are so many ashrams in the country already. Why do we want to start another?' But he gradually began to capitulate. 'I needed support and land for the Dhyanalinga,' he says, looking back on his decision. 'That necessitated the formation of a trust. I also realized I had to support a growing community of seekers, so an ashram seemed to make sense.'

Did his free spirit feel oppressed by the growing responsibility? 'Not really, because I've always seen it as play, not as work. Yes, it meant an increase in the levels of arbitration and mediation. I do get a little irritated by that every now and then.' After a long pause, he adds, 'There are times when I feel I would rather be walking the mountains than managing an ashram and yoga centre. But it doesn't really matter. Inside, I'm still a recluse. I am still in perpetual silence.' And are there ever any lapses in that inner silence? He smiles. 'Even those lapses happen in full awareness.'

And so in 1993, the seeds of the Isha Yoga Centre were sown. The site of the centre took everyone by surprise. The meditators had their own ideas about this. They shortlisted several possible places around Coimbatore for the purpose. Bharathi remembers how Jaggi was taken by local meditators to several scenic spots in Kerala and Karnataka. One day, in Trichy, three meditators animatedly told Jaggi about a place they had located in an area named Navamalai, which seemed an ideal spot to base the ashram. But despite their enthusiasm, they remember that Jaggi didn't seem satisfied.

Looking back, Sadhguru describes the search vividly. 'Right from my childhood, whatever I saw visually, always in the background, there were mountains. Until I was sixteen years of age, I thought in everybody's visual perception there were mountains too. Only when I discussed it with my friends, they said, "You're crazy. Where are the mountains?" But to me, they were always there in my eyes. So after sixteen, I knew I must seek this place, but then I dismissed the idea because it was always there in my vision. If something is always there, you get used to it . . . Then, when the time to start work on the Dhyanalinga came, I began looking for these mountains. I travelled everywhere, like a madman. I took my motorcycle and from Goa down to Kanyakumari, I rode up and down, looking for these mountains. I had said "mountains" and everywhere people were looking for the right mountains. But we just couldn't find them. People had almost reached the point of frustration. Then one day, we were driving to a place that someone had recommended, and on the way we came to a bend in the road. From there I could see the Seventh Hill. I just said, stop. And I burst into tears.'

It was a thirteen-acre site situated at the foothills of the Velliangiri Mountains on the outskirts of the city in an area called Poondi. Close to it was the well-known Thirumurugan temple, mentioned in ancient Tamil literature, and not far away, were the Siruvani waterfalls. Jaggi's instruction was terse: Buy it.

There were several reservations. The place seemed inaccessible and wild, notoriously frequented by elephants and bears, and human traffic in the area was known to cease after sunset. But Jaggi laughed off the anxieties. 'You are all meditators. Do you still have fear in your hearts?' he asked. He then reassured them that the place was ideal for the purpose and all would turn out well eventually. 'Just make up your minds to be with Isha, and see what happens,' he said enigmatically.

Less than eleven days after he had mentioned the place, the place was bought. Located deep in the heart of the forest, flanked by mountains, it was a wild but strikingly beautiful piece of property. Those who saw it at the time continue to marvel at the rapidity with which the place has grown in the past decade. All that it had at the start was a well, a shed and a wooden tree loft (possibly a machan for hunting purposes). Today the land has a meditation hall, a multi-religious shrine, a Devi temple, a temple tank, a school, a rejuvenation centre, a conference centre, offices and cottages that house three hundred residents and several guests. Many more acres have been bought and plans for expansion are still afoot. Amazingly, the fast-growing human settlement has not marred the beauty of the place. It remains one of the most architecturally tasteful ashrams in the country, its simple, elegant environmentally-friendly design gracefully complementing the context, rather than clashing with it.

And so by 1994, there was a rudimentary ashram, a cohesive and fiercely committed core group of meditators, and a young Isha yoga movement that was gradually beginning to make its presence felt in Tamil Nadu state. The stage was set. The guru knew it was time to act. He announced a ninety-day residential Wholeness Programme.

Coimbatore, Tiruppur and Erode are bustling commercial centres and many of the meditators had busy professional lives. Others had families and households to manage. The programme necessitated forty days of advance preparation on their part. The amenities at the ashram were barely functional. The only concrete structure was what is now known as the triangular block—still far from completion at the time. The participants would be required to eat, sleep and meditate in a single makeshift meditation hall with a thatched roof and mud floor. The toilets were rudimentary. The food was going to be basic: rasam, salad, rice gruel and pickle. There was to be no contact with the outside world whatsoever. On the day before the programme, the Coimbatore rains were so torrential that the road to the ashram was jammed and the water levels were rising steadily. It seemed insane and unrealistic to expect people to enrol for a programme this long and strenuous.

Fifty registered. All turned up. Forty-eight, as predicted by Jaggi, made it to the end.

'The programme was actually a blessing in disguise,' says Bharathi. 'All of us were already in the grip of a kind of collective madness. Our families, our friends, couldn't understand us. Some were convinced we were the victims of some kind of black magic. They even wondered if our *kanji* (gruel) was laced with some drug! So it was a relief to be able to leave our regular worlds behind for a while and immerse ourselves in what really mattered to us. We never thought of the outcome. Just being around the master was enough.'

She had directly approached her father-in-law—the head of the family—and told him that she proposed to do the programme and planned to leave her children with her visiting mother while she was away. He did raise an eyebrow when she mentioned that she'd be away for three months. But she convinced him that going for a yoga programme was no different from travelling to study or work.

Raja, who attended along with his wife, also left his three-year-old daughter with his parents. 'We didn't know what we had enrolled for. But we knew that in a single programme, Jaggi had been able to change us deeply. He often said that in a three-month programme, he would transform us entirely. That was a challenge.'

Kiran, now Swami Devasatwa, remembers how Jaggi insisted on driving his white Maruti 800 to the ashram through rapidly rising floodwaters the day before the programme, despite the warnings from everyone around him. It would have been perfectly reasonable to postpone the programme by a day, but Jaggi remained resolute to the point of being cussed. 'Even truck drivers weren't ready to try their luck. And immediately after he went through, one of them got stuck. But he just zoomed through.'

Later, in the course of the journey, however, his car was grounded as well. The volunteers pushed him through the first time. Raja remembers that the second time he got stuck, Jaggi simply left his car in the middle of the forest and walked to the ashram. 'The water had flooded the car,' recounts a meditator. 'It had risen right up to the steering wheel. We took Jaggi's daughter out of the car and a group of us actually had to lift the car out of the rut.' Eventually, a group of five meditators pushed the car to the ashram and Jaggi walked the rest of the distance.

By some equally strange turn of events, all fifty participants made it to the programme by 13 July, the first day of the programme. The rain wasn't playing a mere cameo in this programme; it lasted the entire duration, a wild and clamorous chorus in the mystical drama that was about to unfold in the lives of the participants.

The participants' day began at five every morning, and they went through a rigorous and advanced process of pranayamas, kriyas and asanas. After a two-hour break in the afternoons, they resumed their regimen at four in the evening. Their meditations concluded at midnight. It meant around fourteen to fifteen hours of sadhana or practice daily. Jaggi made it clear that these were practices that could only be pursued in the presence of a master and in a controlled atmosphere. The point of the programme, they were told, was to activate all the seven chakras and empower them to experience life at heightened levels of awareness. Some of the practices enabled them to perceive the play of the five elements in different parts of the body. Other kriyas enabled them to see the subtle distinction between the right and the left parts of the body in terms of the quality of the energy. They also discerned the presence of the central passage, or the *sushumna*.

'He said he wanted to set us on fire,' says Bharathi. 'And that's what he did. What happened in that meditation hut was fantastic. I don't think it can ever be recreated. There we were, a bunch of us, wanting nothing more than to be around this person we loved, a person who seemed always to be on fire. He was different in those days. He was a man with a mission. We could see that even though we had no idea what it was. He was a fireball, burning with a strange energy, a passion. Just being around him was enough to turn us mad as well.'

It was a rough and rugged life, Raja recalls. But there was a passionate sense of commitment that bonded the group. Their focus was Jaggi, and that made even the inconveniences seem like part of a grand adventure.

'It sounds absolutely crazy,' says Kiran who was a volunteer at the programme, 'but even an outsider like me could tell the difference between the inside of the meditation hut and the outside. Each time I entered the meditation hut the energy levels there would hit me, my eyes would close and I'd feel absolutely intoxicated. As soon as I left the place, I'd be fine again. The difference between inside and outside was unbelievable.'

Srinivas, a participant who was also responsible for recording the proceedings, concurs. 'I felt drunk most of the time. I'm not sure I even heard all that Jaggi was saying. I was just absorbing the energy of the place and the place was absolutely saturated with it. There were times when we felt we were actually living on his presence.' Bharathi confirms this. 'The energy was almost solid. I needed to come out of it sometimes, it was so overbearing. It didn't allow one a moment of peace or rest.'

Jaggi announced one evening that he had done no preparation for the programme whatsoever and that the entire proceedings were simply flowing through him naturally. 'There are many masters present here, who are filled with joy to see so many people coming forward to grow spiritually,' he said. 'They are showering their love and wisdom upon you.'

Things were certainly flowing harmoniously. The course seemed perfectly structured and planned, despite Jaggi's admission that it was all spontaneous. The participants' levels of perseverance were also high. And yet, it wasn't easy. The cheerless monotony of the diet, for one, began to slowly wear them down. One morning, one of the participants, Suman, couldn't control her tears at the sight of the ritual cup of rasam accompanied by dreary slices of beetroot.

Jaggi learnt the cause of her distress, and arranged for vegetable biryani to be served the next day. Biryani had never tasted better. It felt, recalls Suman (now Maa Gambhiri), like a party. 'The others told me to cry more often,' she remarks.

The rain wasn't helping either. The floor was slushy and patchy with fungus. Insects and snakes seemed to keep appearing. The clothes that were pegged out after a wash seemed to take forever to dry. Wild and gusty winds whistled incessantly through the hall and threatened to blow the thatched roof off altogether. Kiran remembers Jaggi sitting all night at the dais, leaning back on his seat to catch a few moments of sleep, but getting up every half hour to go out and hammer in the stay wires that kept the roof in place. 'He couldn't have slept more than an hour and a half each night.'

Sadhguru recalls the scene with relish. 'It was the fiercest storm we had ever seen. On the third or fourth day, the whole thatched hut (we called it Kaivalya Kutir) started slowly leaning to the side. It was night. The winds had picked up speed; they were doing almost a hundred and twenty kilometres an hour. I had a small room built nearby. But when I heard the howling wind, I came out at 2 a.m. to see what had happened to everybody. I saw that the wires that tied the hut down in place were slowly getting unfastened. It was a matter of minutes before the whole thing flew off. I woke up about fifteen people and we restored the roof. But the rest of them were peacefully sleeping all along! They didn't even know what was happening. That means we made them work really hard through the day!'

It wasn't just the roof that threatened to give up the ghost. 'People were meditating and sleeping in the same place. After about seven days, we found that most of their beds were eaten up from the bottom by termites. While we were sitting, the termites were busy. What to do?' laughs Sadhguru. 'We decided to move into the forest.'

A repair team moved into the hall and Jaggi led his group to the

Velliangiri Hills for four days. For the participants, it was a heady but demanding experience. At dusk, they camped on a rock beside a scenic waterfall. The rock was wet and slippery, and required them to be vigilant all night. There wasn't enough room for all forty-eight to sit, so a few spent the night standing. One found a cave and spent a relatively comfortable night, only to discover the next morning that his habitat was probably a burrow for snakes. The rain seemed interminable and many were soaked to the bone. But for all the discomfort, none was afraid. Oddly enough, Jaggi's presence put fear out of the question.

'It's difficult to believe it, but nothing was disrupted,' says Sadhguru. 'By five thirty every morning, everybody was into their sadhana. The class was not broken for a minute. The same schedule continued up there on the mountain. My daughter's clothes got wet all the time, so there was no point putting clothes on her. We just left her as she was. Nobody fell sick, and when the shed was ready, we returned and continued the sadhana. The people who went through that ninety-day programme became the real pillars of the Isha Foundation in India. They had the chance to see life in a completely different way and those ninety days changed them forever.'

Vijji arrived from Bangalore at around this time. It was a difficult time for her. Her husband seemed suddenly to have become an object of collective veneration. Coming to terms with this intrusion into their marital relationship was challenging. There were some who saw her as excessively possessive of her husband. Bharathi was one of those who couldn't understand her reluctance to be at the programme. 'It intrigued me. Why would she want to stay away? Couldn't she see the enormity of what he was and what he was doing?'

However, Jaggi's treatment of Vijji during all her emotional upheavals remained consistently gentle. His four-year-old daughter, who was yet to start school, was looked after by volunteers and spent her time running around the ashram, playing with the participants during the breaks or sitting beside Jaggi during his twelve-hour stint at the meditation hall. A participant recalls how she often fell asleep at the dais, and was carried back to the room by Jaggi after midnight.

While Jaggi was a gentle parent, he never seemed to fuss over the child unduly. Once when the girl had a severe cough, a participant remembers feeling concerned about her health. Jaggi, however, seemed quite unperturbed. But the next morning, the participant discovered that the cough had disappeared entirely. Given how intense it had been just the night before, this sudden disappearance was inexplicable. The participant wondered about it at the time, but the even more mysterious events of the next few days were to push this incident out of his mind.

For most unnerving of all was the transformation in Jaggi himself. As the programme progressed, he seemed to bear little resemblance to the warm friend and mentor the participants had known. This was a new man before them, and they weren't sure they liked the change. There were no smiles, no friendly inquiries after their wellbeing. His manner was grim, focused and forbidding, his speech was curt, and his very presence disturbing. Those who had thronged around him just a few days ago now shrank from him. Suddenly, he was a stranger. It was at this point that Jaggi—to use a phrase widely used in Isha circles—'unleashed the guru' within him. 'We suddenly saw him just the way he was. This was the core, we realized, with all the social niceties peeled off—raw, intense, molten. Being with him was unsettling, but being without him was terrifying. He was no longer a person, just an ageless presence. And that hall witnessed some scenes that no mortal can imagine,' says Kiran.

Nineteen ninety-four was the year that Nelson Mandela was elected president; it was the year of the Rwanda massacre; the year the United States sent its forces to the Persian Gulf; the year of the notorious OJ Simpson case. It is interesting to be reminded of these global events because the proceedings in that meditation hut seem to have taken place in a timeless zone. For the meditators themselves, date and time had lost all meaning. Life had assumed a curiously mythic quality. They had always known that their connection with their yoga master was much more significant and compelling than others could ever imagine. But now they began to get their first inkling of just why that was the case. The plot was larger and more outrageous than they had ever dreamt. The goldfish bowl of their lives had been lifted, and they were no longer the heroes of their own private soap operas. Suddenly they realized that they were part of a vast drama in which they had their allotted roles to play. The script—just in case they still nursed any vestigial delusions of authorship—was by no means theirs. Another hand had been writing it all along.

The realization dawned gradually. After ten days, Jaggi announced a period of silence and instructed the participants to continue with their practices. The indefinite period of silence began to wear on the participants' nerves. Suman remembers feeling bewildered and disoriented. 'I had always known the charming side of him. There was now great difficulty in accepting the other side. He could be curt and wouldn't think twice about cutting you down to size in public. It was a totally different personality. After he announced the silence, he retired to his room. He rarely came to see us. Instructions for the day would be written on a board every morning before we woke up. It was a body-breaking schedule. We never got more than four hours of sleep. But it was also psychologically and emotionally breaking. I didn't understand what was going on. I felt confused, angry and resistant.'

Snakes had been regular visitors to the programme, and were routinely caught and carried back to the woods by a few trained volunteers. But at this point the group had begun feeling directionless, and when a snake crawled in, it provoked alarm and offered a much-needed diversion. Raja saw the snake go past Jaggi's room, and knocked on the door to alert him. He had no clue at the time that his master was an ace snake catcher.

Jaggi emerged, carried the snake out and dropped it in the wild. When he returned, he looked like a thundercloud. He asked those who had broken the silence to identify themselves. Half the class warily raised their hands. This group was now instructed to turn east, and was excluded from the more advanced practices. The master seemed more unforgiving and relentless than ever. The unease grew. It was a period of deep turmoil for those who had been excluded. But Jaggi was not particularly consoling. 'If I choose among you, you will feel hurt. But nature has its own way of choosing. Those who are not entitled to something, drop out by themselves.'

Those who went on to the next phase were taught a powerful practice that lasted over three hours and concluded with a brief kriya. One of the participants recollects how his mind went entirely blank during the kriya—a phenomenon that lasted for over fifteen minutes. 'Can it really last this long?' he wondered and that was the first thought to enter his mind. He found himself becoming acutely aware of each thought that entered his mind subsequently. 'This was the first time I realized that I was part of a programme that was an opportunity in a thousand lifetimes. I also realized suddenly that I was in the presence of an extremely powerful master.' For Jaggi, as the class was beginning to discover, was not just an inspirational guide, gifted with an assortment of minor psychic powers. This man was a yogi, an adept, a man whose mastery over the meteorological fluctuations of inner weather seemed staggering and limitless. 'We'd known it all along on some deep level. But now it was out in the open. And it was scary,' says Kiran.

Many more things were coming out into the open. And they weren't designed to allay fears either. As the atmosphere in the group grew more intense and subtle, dreams began to grow more vivid and horrific. One participant found that his dreams were resumed each night from exactly where they had been interrupted the night before. Jaggi advised the participants to watch their dreams closely. He explained that the negative aspects of their unconscious mind—their karmas—were being expelled by the intense sadhanas, and these still hung, smog-like, over the hall. These were responsible for the nightmares. But he assured them that regular and sustained practice would dissolve them fully.

But there was something else more unsettling than even the nightmares. A couple of participants now began to notice an additional member in their group. He was bearded, shrouded in a rough blanket, and roamed the hall every night. But he had the ability to vanish as mysteriously as he had appeared. At around the same time, a volunteer noticed that Jaggi's bed, which was usually in a corner of his room in the triangular block, had now moved to the centre of the room. He moved it back to the corner, only to find it at the centre once more the next day.

Jaggi explained that the place was full of various disembodied beings that had been attracted by the collective intensity of their practices. 'They follow me everywhere,' he remarked. 'They're all around my bed at night. Sometimes it gets quite crammed, and I leave the cot to them and sleep on the floor. At other times, I move my bed to the centre of the room to give them more space. They are very sensitive. If someone walks noisily along the corridor, they disappear.'

But why were ghosts frequenting a place that was supposedly sanctified by spiritual practice? These, said the master, were astral beings that had just a little karma left to work out. They were naturally drawn by the presence of an enlightened being since he represented the possibility of liberation. 'They want to dissolve this karma so they don't have to be born again. So they are attracted to my presence, which has a certain significance.'

The explanation didn't offer much solace. Suddenly, the disembodied beings seemed to be everywhere. At five one morning when Suman, the first to rise, was on her way to the bathroom, she saw a figure that she assumed was a construction worker. At that moment, the figure turned and started walking towards her. It struck her then that this was neither a volunteer nor a worker, but the much-discussed 'man with a blanket'. She fled and collided headlong into another participant. Embarrassed by her alarm, she tried to feign nonchalance. But on turning around, she found the shrouded figure steadily advancing in her direction. 'The man with the blanket!' she whispered frantically, clutching her fellow-participant's hand. But he, exasperatingly, could see nothing.

Later in the programme, a woman with a beard began to make the rounds. Suman's sister, also a participant, was the first to see her and mentioned it to Jaggi. He confirmed it. 'She lived at a time when women weren't encouraged to pursue spirituality,' he explained. 'But her desire to attain enlightenment was intense. She would have attained by the sheer intensity of her desire, but somewhere within her was the idea that that she had to be a man to pursue this path. That is why she grew a beard. If she could see how many women there are in this programme, perhaps she would have felt differently. But she cannot see.'

The meditation sessions were now punctuated by sharp and persistent visions. Suman, for instance, had a vision of a tall dark young man in a jungle with a quiver of arrows. Something about the man's presence convinced her that he had an intimate connection with nature, that he belonged to the forest around him.

Another participant saw himself as a priest of a Shiva temple, also engaged in the service of a spiritual master. Yet another saw himself as part of a small group of five surrounding a man whom he recognized as his master. But this was a different-looking Jaggi. He was taller, carried a staff, and his appearance was powerful and intimidating. He saw an enraged mob attack the group. Some disciples were injured, and the group dispersed. He managed to run away and hide. In a second vision, he saw himself looking feverishly for his master. He managed to find him in a forest, surrounded again by a small group of disciples. 'How could you leave us? You've deserted us,' he reproached his master time and again.

That very evening Jaggi talked about a man who had lived three hundred and sixty years ago in Madhya Pradesh. An ardent Shiva devotee, he was part of a tribe of snake charmers that wandered from door to door, from village to village, sometimes sharing intuitive insights with the inhabitants. He happened to fall in love with a Brahmin girl, and from that moment on, his life was doomed. Hounded by her relatives, he was finally surrounded and taken captive, and one of his own snakes let loose on him. 'He still carries the mark of that snakebite on his body,' said Jaggi, and showed the class a sharply-etched imprint of snake fangs on his shoulder. There was a moment of silence. Then various participants, including Bharathi, haltingly disclosed their own visions of Bilva, the snake charmer.

Jaggi went on to speak of another lifetime. He talked of Sadhguru Sri Brahma, a sadhu and powerful yogi with a raging temper. He talked of how the yogi had done his best to gather support for a seemingly impossible life mission. Although he had the necessary technical knowledge at his fingertips, the master's purpose was sabotaged by a hostile social situation. His own singular lack of social skills made it difficult to appease this growing tide of antagonism. He then revealed how a single male disciple had accompanied Sadhguru Sri Brahma out of Coimbatore all the way to a temple in Cuddappah. That disciple, he said, was in their midst at this very moment. It was Bharathi.

For Bharathi, who sat silently listening to this, the disclosure did not come as much of a shock. She had already discovered this during her second Samyama programme when she had had a vision of herself as a male sadhu accompanying her master on a long and inhospitable journey.

Jaggi went on to divulge that before leaving his body, Sadhguru Sri Brahma had imposed a certain dimension of energy on his disciple's *ida* (the lunar or feminine side of the subtle body). As a result, Bharathi was born with two *pingalas* (the solar or masculine dimension). This ensured that her life remained uncluttered by emotional entanglements, enabling her to enter into the spiritual life with minimal impediment. He then recounted various incidents from her past and accurately described the experiences in her body during certain meditations.

Finally, he spoke of the Dhyanalinga. He had mentioned the word before to some disciples. A few of them had consulted pundits on it, and had drawn a blank. The savants had heard of Atmalingas, but no one seemed to know what a Dhyanalinga was. Indira remembers how she and some fellow-disciples had actually gone to a temple in Trichy to meet an ageing priest who was known to have powers of divination. When they had mentioned the word 'Dhyanalinga' to him, the old man reflected that he had read the word in one of the Vedas. 'He said that only a *grihastha* (householder) yogi was capable of establishing it,' she recalls.

But it was at the Wholeness Programme that Jaggi unfolded the magnitude of the enterprise. The only reason for his return in this lifetime, he said, was the Dhyanalinga. Time was short, and his only dream was to fulfil his master's mission. This was the first time his listeners had heard him mention a guru. Somehow they had assumed that their teacher was much too independent to have submitted to the discipline of a master. But a guru implied a lineage, a tradition, which, in the Indian spiritual context, also means credibility. As Swami Nisarga (who heard of this when he came to the ashram some months later) writes, 'It was like an insurance policy. I remember thinking, "For all his wild ways, this man is actually accountable."'

Jaggi now spoke of a lifetime as Shivayogi whose passage to enlightenment was paved by the compassionate intervention of Palani Swami. The very same intervention that had bestowed self-realization had also imposed a mission. The mission had been thwarted time and again. And however monumental that assignment, Jaggi was determined to fulfil it this time. He said he had resolved not merely to create the Dhyanalinga but to create an environment that would enable people to benefit from its immense transformational possibility.

The reactions to this announcement were mixed. Sadhguru was aware that many were puzzled and upset. 'Especially my wife, Vijji,' he recalls. 'She protested, saying, "No way! How can you do this?"

It took almost six to eight months to convince her of what it was all about and why it had to be done. I couldn't console her. She broke down. She said, "No way are you going to do this! You taught us that it is not about looking in buildings of stone and mud; that it's about looking within. You are the one who took away all my gods. And now I'm happy. Now you want to introduce a god into my life. I'm not going to take this!" Later we invented cleverer words for it—"multi-religious temple", "meditation shrine" . . . But at that time when I said "temple", there was this huge resistance! There were others who said, "No, let's build a school, let's build a hospital." I said, "No, all this yoga is only goodwill business. I just want to build the Dhyanalinga temple. That's all I'm here for."'

It was yet another unsettling moment, a moment of deep inner conflict, one that pointed all over again to the fact that the man they thought they knew wasn't quite what he seemed to be. Sadhguru had, in fact, warned them of the fact a year ago when he told them to prepare for changes in the imminent future. 'On the day we wanted to register the Isha Foundation, there were six people with me,' he says. 'Wonderful people, all of them. But I told them, "See, all of you are getting into this officially now; I owe it to you to tell you now that I am in disguise. When I take it off, will you still be with me?"' There were protests. One meditator exclaimed that he'd been cured of asthma, another of diabetes; how could their faith in him ever waver? Gradually, however, his meditators were to discover the challenges of living around a man with multiple masks. A mystic in mufti, they were to discover time and again in the coming years, wasn't a comfortable proposition. His restless, fluid, liminal presence was bewildering, even threatening; it was impossible to predict his next move, his next role, his next project. Even today, his quicksilver changes of persona raise the question for many who know him: who is the real Sadhguru?

Bharathi remembers feeling a surge of disappointment at the time. 'This was someone who had spoken against going to temples, and now he was proposing to build one!' But it was clear that the master was in earnest. It was also clear that he was in a hurry. 'He reminded us that he wasn't going to live beyond the age of forty-two. Time was ticking away. We had to make it happen,' she says.

She had often had several personal experiences of the way in which Jaggi's explosive meditative states pushed him perilously close to death. 'As he'd go into deeper states of meditation, his feet would sometimes grow cold and it would seem like he was about to leave the body. At such times, we'd have to vigorously rub vibhuti on his feet to bring him back.' His contact with the body at such times was so fragile that the meditators could see that their guru was unlikely to be able to sustain his body for much longer.

'I see now that he's a huge schemer,' says Bharathi. 'He's a contradiction: on the one hand, he's this tremendous ball of fire, but he's also terribly, terribly patient. He takes his time to make the kill. When he described the Dhyanalinga as a process of creating an energy form without any poojas and mantras, we began to slowly realize that this entire Wholeness Programme was not just about establishing an ashram. It was about something more, much more.'

It was also beginning to dawn on the participants that they had not gathered here by accident. There was a much larger design in this seemingly random assembly of people. And before them was a man they had trusted from the very beginning for a reason: their life purpose was inextricably linked to his own. Jaggi himself was to sum it up crisply three months later at a satsangh, 'Same place, same people, same work.'

In August, the month-long sadhana came to an end. The next two months were to be an intense training programme for those who sought to become residents and teachers. Twenty-four remained for this, while the rest returned home.

One day Jaggi went for a trek to the Velliangiri Hills. When he left, he was dressed in his usual track pants. When he returned, he was clad only in a white loincloth and turban. Those who watched him stride in and take his seat could see that he was a different person entirely. The experiences of the past month had been hair-raising enough. But nothing had quite prepared them for this sight. It was then that one of the participants spontaneously addressed him as 'Sadhguru'. Jaggi acknowledged this title. 'I am not your Jaggi any more,' he said quietly. 'I am Sadhguru.' The confirmation seemed superfluous. The remoteness of his bearing was apparent. While some of them had been disturbed and upset at the loss of a friend, they now realized they had received more than they had ever anticipated. The man before them was more than a mystic and yogi; he was a master, a guru.

Raja remembers how he and Vijji had gone up to him and curiously touched his headgear. 'Vijji tried to remove the turban. But he just turned and gave us a look. That's all it took. We backed off immediately.'

It was in the latter part of the programme that Sadhguru took the participants to the seventh Velliangiri hill. It was here, he said, that Sadhguru Sri Brahma had cast off his body. It was also here that he had made his promise: 'I will return.'

'He did keep his promise,' said Sadhguru, 'but this lifetime will be his last. Once the Dhyanalinga is established, he will never return. He will ascend the same seventh hill again and leave his body for the final time.'

A group set out in search of the exact site of the event. Sadhguru led the group. When the group halted for a break near a stream just before the seventh hill, Sadhguru went ahead on his own. When he returned, he was clearly in the grip of some powerful emotion. He sent the participants ahead with the brief comment, 'You'll find it without difficulty.'

They did. It was a wild and windy outcrop of rock dangerously located on top of a cliff. It was not difficult to find their way there. It pulsated with a fierce and explosive energy that the group had begun to recognize unmistakably as their guru's. 'We went instantly into meditative states,' says Srinivas. While some staggered, others wept, and still others were unable to open their eyes, Srinivas remembers going into an intense meditation. 'I was aware of everything that was going on around me. I could hear people chanting, "Shambho", but I couldn't open my mouth. I was there for about fifteen minutes and in my experience, I wasn't even breathing. Even when I inhaled, the exhalation came out immediately in one abrupt gasp. I felt very loose in my body, as if it was becoming separate from me. Sadhguru said that if I had been left alone, I would have left my body.'

Srinivas also remembers the time he accompanied a small group, including Sadhguru and Bharathi, to the mountain caves that Sadhguru Sri Brahma used for his meditation. The group decided to spend four days there. 'The energy there was so powerful that the air actually felt solid. You could cut through it with a knife,' he recalls. They ate, swam and meditated late into the night, and the levels of intoxication were intense. 'I was drunk all the time,' he recalls. 'Sadhguru would ask, "Shall we have a party?" He'd just blow into the air, and in a second we'd all be in another dimension altogether. Later, he'd shake me, saying, "Hey bugger, wake up!"'

In anticipation of Sadhguru's birthday on the third of September, the group planned a surprise party. The ashram was decorated with flowers and Sadhguru was regaled by a skit in which his meditators enacted how various characters from the past and the future would bless Isha and contribute generously to its upkeep. Visibly moved by the proceedings, Sadhguru embraced each one of them and offered each of them an initiation. After that, the party began. But all of a sudden, Srinivas found he couldn't stand. As the others pulled him up to dance, he kept keeling over. 'It was a condition unlike any I'd ever been in,' he says. 'It lasted for about an hour and a half. Later Sadhguru asked Bharathi to work on my ajna chakra and bring me back to normal.' Indira confirms the incident. She remembers Sadhguru being overjoyed. 'There were tears in his eyes.'

Of the incident, Sadhguru says simply, 'Things started happening at that programme. Flowers began to blossom.' But that clearly was not enough. 'If the aim is to make a few people attain, it is quite easy for me,' Sadhguru has often said. 'But we want to make the possibility available to many.'

His disciples were only just beginning to realize the fact that there was nothing particularly modest about Sadhguru's ambitions as a gardener.

‘When the Divine Descends, You Just Accommodate’

The Deepening Pilgrimage, the Darkening Night

It wasn't easy for those who had known him intimately. When Jaggi became Sadhguru, an individual seemed to have turned overnight into an abstraction. The Wholeness Programme had changed an accessible friend and guide into an impersonal figure, a forbidding persona. ‘I struggled with it for a long time,’ says one of the senior brahmacharinis. ‘The *guru–shishya* relationship in my case hasn't been a smooth one. There have been doubts, rebellions, questions and more questions. I understood that he needed to project himself in a particular way for social reasons, to gain acceptance for the Dhyanalinga and the ashram. But there were some of us who struggled with the change of image, the way in which he seemed to have become a “type”. It was everything—from his change of clothes to the ever-growing set of ashram norms and rules.’

Another resident remembers the first time he visited the ashram. Things seem to be formalizing much too rapidly. Concrete structures were appearing everywhere. His old-time friend was suddenly being addressed as ‘Sadhguru’. People around him were suddenly attired in white. Doubts assailed him. What had become of the iconoclastic Jaggi who was the first to cock a snook at organized spirituality? Had he sold out?

If these were the apprehensions at the time, one can imagine the levels of amazement when Jaggi announced that he would be initiating people into *brahmacharya*. The option to be a lay disciple remained; but brahmacharya was offered as a choice for those who were so inclined. Some were dumbfounded. And yet, to others, it didn't seem quite so preposterous. 'It seemed like a way of being with him, and there was nothing else I wanted more,' says Kiran. 'He said it was just a way of being together, of focusing one's energies as a seeker. That made sense. But I'd have done anything just to be around him.'

Those who were interested were asked to apply. Nine did. Indira was one of them. 'It wasn't terrifying at the time, because it was all so new. He said we'd jointly evolve the guidelines as we went along. He was flexible enough at the time to allow me to continue working in my computer firm, which I did for two years as a brahmacharini. When the challenges of a career started seeming pointless, I quit and joined the ashram full-time. He was supportive of both decisions.'

But what was it about? Why would such an obviously contemporary mystic set up a traditional spiritual order? It is a question many wondered at then and continue to wonder at today. I was initially baffled by it too. Here is a man with such a seemingly prodigious appetite for life, one whose approach to spirituality is life-affirming and celebratory. Why on earth would he urge others to adopt a life of austerity and self-denial? It seemed totally out of character.

Sadhguru laughed when I asked him this question some years ago. 'That's because you have a limited idea about what it means to be contemporary,' he replied. Brahmacharya, he explained, is a tried and tested path for true lovers of freedom. 'Brahman means the "ultimate", the "divine"; charya means the "path". Every human being is in search of joy, knowingly or unknowingly. Because you could not find joy, you settled for pleasure. Pleasure is just a shadow of joy—beautiful but very limited. Now, if you are a pleasure seeker, and something that gives you pleasure is taken away from you, you are broken. That means your existence is one of huge bondage, isn't it? Now, no one likes bondage; everyone has a deep desire for freedom from limitations of all kinds. You can gold-plate your pleasant limitations, but you cannot break them. Most people have gold-plated their shackles and are wearing them like ornaments; they're simply celebrating them. But brahmacharya—the path of the divine—means that you are joyful by your own nature. It means that your joy is on self-start, no longer on push-start. And anyway, if the source of happiness is within you, searching for it outside is quite stupid.'

He often quotes a line by the Buddha. 'Gautama said it is better to walk alone than in bad company. If you are alone, you could walk slow or fast, but at least you are walking in a certain direction. It's better than being dragged backwards.' Even in traditional Vedic society, he explains, about seventy per cent of the people entered family life; the option of the ascetic path was always open to the remaining thirty per cent who did not experience the same need for family situations. 'There will always be some people in the world who want more than a life dedicated to self-preservation and procreation. Brahmacharya is for them. Human beings are born alone. These are people who choose to conduct their lives in the same way. They aren't renouncing anything; it's the others in society with libido and attachment problems who are renouncing their freedom to acquire company.'

He offers the analogy of a mud pot to make his point. 'Think of yourself as a karmic pot. With the process of living, certain karmas and influences have moulded you into a certain type of person. In your childhood, this person was malleable; by the time you're a full-grown adult, it's totally rigid. So this pot is being slowly burnt by the process of life. By the time you're old, if you try to change the shape of the pot, it'll simply break. But when it was unburnt, you could very easily mould it any way you liked. That's what we're doing with brahmacharya: we're unburning people into a state where their energies become very fluid, very malleable, so we can give them any shape, any form. We can make anything out of them. That's what brahmacharya is working towards. It's a huge sadhana.'

He once asked me if I thought the *brahmacharis* looked like zombies. At the time, I replied honestly that the thought had crossed my mind. On my few visits to the ashram they seemed such shadowy presences, self-effacing to the point of invisibility. It was only later that it struck me just how much maturity it takes not to be the kind of insatiable attention-seeking entity that contemporary culture deems normal. 'They're not zombies; they're hugely intelligent people,' he assured me. 'To consciously allow yourself to become so malleable that you can turn yourself into any kind of pot—is it not good to have that freedom? I can combine ten brahmacharis and make their energies into that of one huge human being—that can be a tremendous force.' After a pause, he added, 'We've all eaten mangoes, but how many of us have planted mango trees? It's only because ten people in every generation plant mango trees that everybody else is eating mangoes. So to carry on a spiritual path in its integrity, brahmacharya is needed. It's very important that there are a few people for whom the truth is more important than their lives. When you are trying to establish a spiritual path that will live on for generations after you, it is not possible without a solid tradition of brahmacharya.'

Celibacy, he points out, is only a small part of the picture. 'Brahmacharya is a life of inclusion, not exclusion, as people suppose. The brahmachari looks away from the "you–me" relationship because he wants to establish an all-inclusiveness within himself. Brahmacharis are people who have decided that they don't want to extract joy from anything or anyone; they want to source their own inner joy. In that sense, the whole world needs to turn to brahmacharya internally. It doesn't have to be about a practice, a vow, an external lifestyle for everyone. You can be married and still be a brahmachari. It means you're ecstatic by your own nature—and that's how it should be.'

He once recounted a story about the Sufi mystic, Jalal-ud-din Rumi:

'When Rumi went to the home of his beloved and knocked on the door, his lover asked, "Who is it?"

'Rumi replied, "It is I, Rumi."

'The door did not open. Rumi was so much in love that he wept for days together. Again and again he went to the door. Each time, the voice asked, "Who is it?"

'Rumi said, "I, Rumi, and I am willing to die for you."

'The door stayed shut. One day, after all this turmoil and suffering, he arrived at a different state within himself. He went to the door once again.

'The voice asked, "Who is it?"

'Rumi replied, "It is you." And the door opened.'

Sadhguru paused like a seasoned raconteur and added, 'That is the whole process. If a spiritual practice is part of your life, it doesn't work. If it has become you, it is still not enough. It has to become more than you, more than your life. That's what brahmacharya is about.'

A *sanyasi*, who was initiated into brahmacharya in the second batch in 1996, relates an amusing incident behind his initiation. He was still wrestling with the whole business of Sadhguru-hood that had suddenly enveloped his old friend and mentor. And yet, the deep and unreasonable trust in Jaggi was still intact. One day, Sadhguru called him and casually asked him whether he watched films that starred Rajnikanth, the matinee idol of south Indian cinema. When he said he didn't, Sadhguru remarked that brahmacharya wasn't any more difficult than giving up a diet of Rajnikanth films. That settled it. The young man enrolled.

And what about the irritants of community life: the rules and regulations, the challenges of living out one's life according to the diktats of the guru, the structural pecking order, the regimentation? 'There've certainly been moments of frustration,' he concedes. 'But I see brahmacharya as a process, and not an irrevocable one. That helps. Besides, the big advantage of this life is that your spiritual process, your interiority, is entirely taken care of by Sadhguru. Why would anyone in their right mind give that up?' Is there no resentment at being subjected to a life of unquestioning obedience? 'What makes me trust Sadhguru,' he replies with quiet logic, 'is the fact that he's a man who values his freedom. That makes me confident that he'd never do anything to compromise mine.'

Somu was puzzled and alarmed by the rapidly lengthening list of ashram norms during the Wholeness Programme. 'It scared me. I followed Sadhguru one evening to his room. It was dark and I remember he was carrying a torch. We stopped at his door. He looked at me and I told him impulsively, "Jaggi, I don't want any rules." He flashed the torch in my face. He must have seen the tears in my eyes. He said gently, very gently, okay, no rules for you.'

What makes that moment memorable for Somu is the fact that Sadhguru hasn't reneged on his promise. 'Even today Sadhguru tells new initiates during meetings that he has made a promise that there will be no rules imposed on them,' says Somu (now Swami Gurubiksha), explaining that there is more of an inner party democracy at work within the monastic order than is apparent to the outsider. 'Sadhguru still says, "If there are any guidelines that you feel are unjust, just raise the matter at the proper forum and we'll change them." I trust him all the more now because I see that he never goes back on his word.'

For Kavita, a young woman who recently plunged into brahmacharya, the commitment is about unfolding adventure rather than straitjacketed conformity. 'It's about living on the edge, walking consciously. It challenges you to be conscious, alert, every moment. I've always dreamt of a situation where everyone is fired up and dedicated to dissolving the limitations of their personality. And here it is.'

A schoolteacher in Arkansas, Kavita decided to spend time at the ashram after doing some courses with Sadhguru in the US. 'I was already experiencing heightened levels of energy, clarity and vibrancy, and I thought I'd turn myself into Superwoman and go back! I was also struck by the volunteers here—their dignity, grace and gentleness. Trying to emulate Sadhguru seemed ambitious. But trying to emulate these people was an inspiring prospect.'

Before she knew it, she'd enrolled for a Teachers' Training programme and found her lofty aspirations deflated. 'It was humbling. I had thought I had to climb, conquer, and be the best. But becoming a teacher is about unlearning, melting, becoming a conduit. I found myself growing more childlike, playful, unrestricted. I liked the change and decided to stay on.' The goal hasn't changed, yet there is a subtle but significant shift of emphasis. 'Earlier, I wanted to make myself a person of worth. Now I want to unmake myself so something worthy can shine through me.'

'The more casual I seem, the more serious I am,' Sadhguru has often said. Those who have taken life-changing decisions after conversations with him, testify to that. Recently, another disciple—now a brahmachari—relates how Sadhguru called him and offhandedly inquired whether he intended to apply for brahmacharya. 'No,' replied the disciple. 'Why? Still looking for a beautiful wife?' Sadhguru asked lightly. The disciple replied, hesitantly, that he enjoyed his cup of morning tea far too much to think of renouncing it. 'Oh, we'll concoct a far more potent brew for you,' replied his master breezily. And that was that. Another one joined the ranks. The brahmachari admits that he does think about a steaming cup of masala chai every now and then, but the intensity of the craving has distinctly fallen away.

If the transition from friend to ceremonial figure was difficult for his early disciples, the impact on Vijji was obviously much greater. For a woman of simple ambitions—essentially, to be wife and mother—she now had to confront a major threat to her dearly held desires. An emotional and impulsive woman, fiercely proprietary about her husband, she suddenly found the man she loved turning into collective property. Besides, she had never regarded herself as particularly spiritual. She had seldom been particular about her sadhana. And though she worshipped her husband, she found it strange that others perceived him as a guru. 'To many of us, it appeared that he was her greatest barrier, her biggest limitation,' says an early disciple. 'It was clear to us that he was a master, but to her, he was still a husband and she was deeply possessive of him. Some of us felt she wasn't being very supportive of him in his new role.'

For the practical no-nonsense Bharathi, Vijji's temperament remained incomprehensible. She often found herself impatient with her master's wife. 'Once I asked Vijji, why are you earning a pittance doing some mundane job in a bank? Why aren't you here in Coimbatore sharing your husband's fabulous work?' When Vijji replied that she couldn't resign, given how financially uncertain her husband's life was, Bharathi was disappointed. 'It was so clear to me that what this man was holding out to us was the ultimate possibility. But it saddened me that she couldn't see it. She said that she missed the earlier life with her husband before he took up this mission. But I always wondered: surely this whole adventure is much bigger than anything any of us has known? Why doesn't she want to share in the excitement?'

Sadhguru, on the other hand, had foreseen Vijji's phase of psychological disturbance years earlier. At an early meeting, he had studied her palm and told her that she would go through an emotionally unsettling period eleven years later. He was also able to see that the new scenario wasn't easy for his wife. 'She was bewildered by the rapidity of the changes in our lives. I would keep warning her that things would change, that she shouldn't lose her mind when I changed gears. But nothing really prepared her for it. The proximity of the relationship was such that at some point she had started thinking, this is *my* man. The pace of the change, the level of travel, the months of homelessness with a child in tow, were too much for her. It wasn't easy living in other people's homes as the guru's wife; and I know I was often treated differently from the way she was. Then she also knew that my time was ticking away, that she didn't have very much time with me. It was a pressure-cooker situation. I put her through tough times. But later, the moment she sat with her eyes closed for the Dhyanalinga consecration, she did superbly.'

The change in Vijji was gradual. By early 1996, she decided to resign from her bank job in Bangalore and move to Coimbatore. Around the same time, Sadhguru refused a share in his parents' property. Both these decisions seemed impractical and unworldly to their close friends. But there were other things on their minds.

After her move to Coimbatore, Vijji's commitment to her daily practices increased. She was the first, along with Suman, to enter the meditation hall at four thirty every morning. She seemed to be quieter, less obsessed with her husband, and performed her various roles as wife, mother and disciple with greater ease and grace. The transition from child-woman to adult seemed to have happened. It was not entirely unexpected. It was also at this point that one of the most momentous events in her life had begun to unfold. She began to realize the centrality of her role in Sadhguru's mission.

For it was with Vijji and Bharathi that Sadhguru proposed to embark on his lifetime objective of establishing the Dhyanalinga. In a sense, these two were an obvious choice. Their lives had been plotted a lifetime ago in a small temple in Cuddappah. 'Their lives had been fixed,' says Sadhguru matter-of-factly. 'They didn't have lives of their own. They never had—not even in their childhood. Although they were involved in so many things, one part of them was never involved. One part of them was totally elsewhere. And when the possibility of the Dhyanalinga came in front of them, they just knew that they had to go all out.'

After three lifetimes of preparation, he was in no doubt of what needed to be done. He describes the highly sophisticated yogic process simply: 'The whole process was to make the energies of the Dhyanalinga so subtle, beyond which there could be no form. Beyond a point of subtleness, energy won't be able to retain a form. So the idea was to take the energy to that ultimate point of subtlety and encase it in a certain way that it stays there forever.

It is locked in a particular way. This consecration process doesn't involve any mantras or rituals. It is purely an energy process involving people . . . This is about making your life energies malleable. Right now, it is established as an individual. So developing the people involved in this process, putting them through years of sadhana, making them malleable and using these energies, is how we created a situation where something much higher was invited into that space. That's how the consecration happened.'

In June 1996, Sadhguru initiated Vijji and Bharathi into a process of intense practice—one that involved a blurring of boundaries between them on the energy level. 'Initially, I thought I would do it with fourteen people—seven women and seven men. That was the whole purpose of the ninety-day Wholeness Programme. People were put through very intense kriyas and other kinds of sadhana. We were in a hurry to dissolve certain karmas; we had no time to wait for these things to happen in their life, so everything was put on fast-forward for them. Trying to create those fourteen people who could be in such a state that their contact with the body would be minimal, but would still be stable enough to sit there and do what was needed, didn't happen—even though an enormous effort was made. Creating fourteen people who are one in body, mind, emotion, and who are in sufficient states of readiness, is not an easy task. I tried this for maybe a little more than a year. I identified those people, but I didn't tell anyone who they were. I tried to work with them, but I realized it was going to be difficult. Either they had the energies but didn't have the brains. Or they had the brains, but no energy. Time. It was all a question of time. So I decided to take a more drastic step—to work with three people. This was a high-risk process, but keeping two people in control was so much easier than keeping fourteen people in absolute control.'

The idea was to create a triangle of their energies: Vijji and Bharathi were to be the two points and Sadhguru the apex. In addition to the convenience of numbers, the two represented disparate and yet complementary temperaments: while Vijji was volatile and emotional, Bharathi was dispassionate and logical. Vijji was to represent the female energy, Bharathi the male and Sadhguru the ardhanari—or the androgynous principle that integrated male and female energies. Having fixed both their energies in a previous lifetime, he was in no doubt that they would deliver. Bharathi's energies had already been superimposed in a particular way so she had two pingalas, since he had anticipated that the Dhyanalinga consecration would need a woman who operated as a man.

The process was going to be a high-risk one for all the participants. 'Your energy body can just snap when you put yourself through that kind of rigour,' admits Sadhguru. 'You know, if I made them sit for meditation, it was like six hours, seven hours, eight hours. Unmoving they just sat, through the night. Every day the process started from six or seven in the evening and went on till three or four o' clock in the morning non-stop. That's not something everybody can take without the necessary sadhana. These were people who had lived in comfort. Their previous sadhana sustained them, but still there was always a tremendous risk that any one of them could just pop on my hands!'

Vijji's initial reaction to the plan was one of apprehension and deep resistance. But she gradually acquiesced. 'Perhaps,' says Bharathi, 'she had begun to see by then that if you wanted to be a part of Sadhguru's life, you had to be a part of his work.' Vijji revealed to Sadhguru at this time that she had had frequent dreams in her childhood of three people sitting in a triangular formation, engaged in some activity. The whole project, and her role in it, seemed foreordained. It seemed futile to resist.

Bharathi has no clear recollection of being formally asked to be part of the consecration process. All she does recall is being asked one full moon evening to join Sadhguru and Vijji in a meditation process. 'I sat for meditation, initially a little apprehensive about what my role would be,' she says. 'But in the presence of Sadhguru, once I close my eyes, no apprehensions or doubts remain. Some other force that doesn't seem to be mine takes over, and I settle in almost immediately into meditation. The same, and something more, happened on that full moon day. Some indomitable force and energy seemed to be surging, a force I couldn't contain. My whole body twisted and turned and I lost control over my physical senses, though I was very much aware. The process took me, over and I felt my interiority cleansed and rid of many unnecessary internal turbulences. The body became so sensitive and towards the end, an energy form, which I was not familiar with, had taken over. The deep energy contact that I experienced left me so limp in the body that I needed Vijji's help to stand and move afterwards.'

When Sadhguru suggested to Vijji and Bharathi that they spend more time with each other in order to facilitate the process, neither was particularly enthusiastic. 'For me, Vijji was always just Sadhguru's wife,' says the outspoken Bharathi. 'We had never interacted socially. I've never been very comfortable with emotional people.' Neither of the women had anything against each other. But apart from their devotion to Sadhguru, there was little in common. In the beginning, the interaction proceeded haltingly. There were times when nerves jangled and tempers flared. For what was being proposed was, in fact, outrageously simple and hugely challenging all at once: the voluntary meltdown of individual personality to facilitate the creation of a single entity. Nothing less than the hara-kiri of personal identity, in fact.

'There are so many deep layers of resistance in people,' says Sadhguru. 'I literally tore through their karma, kept it aside and put them together; otherwise, there was no way these people could have come together. They were willing to become friends; beyond that they wouldn't go. Is there anybody with whom you're willing to merge and become one? It is not so. You just believe it at certain moments, but it's not so.'

It wasn't easy. In addition to the voluntary abnegation of identity, the thinning of borders between three people meant a loss of personal privacy and a sudden acquisition of a whole heritage of thoughts and memories. 'After the two people were brought in to create a triangle of energy with me as a pivot, it was necessary that they become one in their mind, emotion and energy,' says Sadhguru. 'Now, if this person felt something on his left knee, the other two also felt something on their left knee, wherever they were. What was your life and what was their life was all mixed up in your mind. Let's say, you, me and somebody else are right now in a triangle. You didn't know what happened in my life ten years ago, but suddenly, now, you know; and what had happened in your life twenty-five years ago, I didn't know, but suddenly, now, I know. It all got so mixed up; we didn't know whose memory was whose. The mind became one; the emotions became one; the energy body also became one . . .'

As the process deepened, Bharathi suddenly knew details about Vijji's life that she had never been told before. Even more uncannily, she was aware of exactly what Vijji was thinking at certain points of time. 'Even when I was in my home in Coimbatore, I often knew exactly when she was eating, or when she was having a bath. But because we were pretty involved in certain processes by then, it didn't really amaze me.'

The process that Sadhguru had initiated them into was by his own description pretty 'drastic'. 'It was like creating a triangle of energy as an invitation to the divine. Once you create a triangle, it is like a vortex. It is a certain fierce possibility; it just sucks everything in.'

In the process of 'sucking in' the divine into their collective energy swirl, the participants also attracted more than they'd bargained for. One day, Vijji and Bharathi were bewildered by a cacophony of voices around them during their meditations. '*Pournami* (full moon) and *amavasya* (no-moon) were very significant days for practices relating to the Dhyanalinga consecration process,' says Bharathi. 'One amavasya, as I was meditating with Sadhguru and Vijji at the shrine, I heard hushed whispers and felt a certain jostling around me. I was unsure, thinking that my imagination was running riot. But the hushed voices persisted.' A few days later when the whispers seemed to have reached a crescendo, Bharathi remembers a hand on her shoulder and another body pushing against hers. She opened her eyes and was distinctly aware of a group of figures sitting huddled together beside her.

It was then that Sadhguru explained that these were simply 'disembodied beings', drawn to the spot by the possibility of personal liberation that had suddenly opened up. 'These were exalted beings released from everything, but they still had a little karmic structure. Total dissolution had not happened yet. So once you reach that dimension of energy you can hear their karmic structures just playing on, like a tape recorder. Both [Vijji and Bharathi] were clearly able to hear many people talking all at once. Any human being would have become terrified, but it seemed very natural then in that situation because the two were raised to a higher level of energy. I never expected them to take it so well. They went through these kinds of experiences in full awareness. They were not hallucinating, they were not hypnotized, and they were not under any kind of intoxication. They were in absolute awareness, more aware than anybody could normally be.'

For Bharathi, the powerful energy field around them was such a real experience that any rational argument now seemed trifling and irrelevant. 'I have always scoffed at and ridiculed anything that is beyond logic. But slowly I started keeping the mind aside and gave myself totally to the consecration process.'

For all their wariness, both Bharathi and Vijji were anxious to transcend their petty differences to assist an enterprise of obvious significance. The process started unfolding at a more rapid pace than Sadhguru had believed possible. By October, the momentum had picked up to such an extent that he was confident that the goal of three lifetimes was clearly in sight. 'I didn't know how fast or how slow the process would be, but once we put them together, everything happened beyond my expectations. They're almost like two opposite poles. One person was all reason, another person was all love. . . . When these two qualities came together, it became like one beautiful person with all the qualities; they became like a complete human being . . . But then, it became too overwhelming. Keeping these two people rooted in their bodies became difficult, so we had to stall the process for some time. . . . One thing was, these two people had their families to take care of, their day-to-day life in which they had to be totally involved. Another thing was, they had to maintain very high levels of energy and give themselves totally to the consecration process. So they needed to acquire the necessary maturity, balance and freedom within themselves to be able to handle this.'

The difficulties didn't disappear, but they were now manageable. 'These two people were complete opposites,' says Sadhguru. 'Normally, they couldn't even sit together, because they were in two totally different worlds. Now you have to merge them together. One was pure logic, the other was pure emotion. Though they did wonderfully together when we were in the consecration process, they didn't go out of their way to make it easy for me. I enjoyed it all; it was a huge challenge.'

Bharathi remembers the distinct change in Vijji once she began to realize her role in the bigger picture. 'The amazing thing about Vijji,' she says, 'was that once she decided to cooperate, she gave herself totally to the processes, despite her struggles. Maybe she was left as choiceless as I was. I don't know. Maybe she still carried her insecurities afterwards. But when we sat together, we were both totally involved. In some ways, she was more giving than I was. I'm sure there were times she feared and loathed me, but she was also fond of me. Perhaps the advantage of being emotional, like Vijji,' she reflects, 'is that you can bring love into your heart, and then maybe things begin to happen.'

At the same time, the rational Bharathi was also aware that a shift was taking place within her. She acknowledges that until then, a certain part of her had always been somewhat scornful and dismissive of Vijji. 'It felt like by being married, my master had allowed himself to be subjugated to someone who was irrelevant.'

But the process initiated a subtle change of perspective, a softening on her part as well. 'Both of us were possessive of Sadhguru in different ways. When we sat for this process, our personalities were no more a hurdle. Through Sadhguru a deep level of connection began to grow between us. The warmth increased. Besides, the processes were so powerful, that I began to see Vijji less as a human being and more as a certain kind of energy. I always saw myself as an instrument for Sadhguru. There was no personal choice about it. Despite my ego and my eccentricities, at the time of the process, I could just empty myself and sit there and allow him to do what was necessary. And so could Vijji. I had a certain respect for her because of that.'

And yet, it all seemed much too smooth and harmonious to be true. 'I knew something had to go wrong,' says Sadhguru. 'I knew a project as mammoth as the Dhyanalinga could never be established without something going wrong somewhere.' The anticipated hurdle was social. That was where things had gone wrong in an earlier lifetime. Sadhguru instructed his disciples to be particularly careful in their interactions with the outside world. Social goodwill was essential to this undertaking. Little did he know that the seeds of the problem lay much closer home.

More than two decades ago, when Jaggi was still a happy-go-lucky collegian, he happened to be ranging the hills of Karnataka on his motorcycle. He had run out of food, but that was nothing new to him. He had been in situations like this before. But after five days of near starvation, he was determined to get himself a meal. At this point, he happened to glimpse what looked like an ashram on a hill. He turned his bike in that direction right away. When he reached the building, instead of dismounting, he rode right up the fifteen steps to the cottage. It was an unceremonious entry. Scruffy and unwashed, his clothes crumpled and soiled after days in the wilderness, Jaggi was not a particularly prepossessing sight.

The guru of the ashram, Swami Nirmalananda (revered as a saint in those parts), stood at the head of the steps. In his present condition, Jaggi was unsure of the reception he would get. But to his surprise, the Swami smiled, walked up to him and—to his utter stupefaction—touched his feet. The gesture rendered Jaggi speechless. He had no clue how to respond. At that moment, some constriction within him seemed to crumble. He wasn't sure what was happening. But he knew that for some inexplicable reason he had been honoured by this saint, and he was moved.

'I never got off my motorcycle unless it was a must,' he recalls. 'So I rode up all the steps right up to his residence. I was covered with mud and slush from head to toe. This man was over sixty years of age, I was just about twenty. He was known to be a great sage and saint. I never was interested in sages or saints. I was just hungry and I wanted food. There was no other place to go; there were no restaurants around. I said, "I'm very hungry, I need to eat something." And I had a few rupees in my pocket; I could pay. He just looked at me and burst into laughter and tears, and fell at my feet. This shook me. I had never bowed down in my life to anybody. Now I can bow down to anything, even to an ant. But at that time I wouldn't bow down to anything, and this man coming and touching my muddy boots disturbed me a little. Then I just shook it off and said, "Okay, I'm hungry; you got some food?" He said, "Come" and he made me sit down. He wanted to unlace my boots; I said, "Don't do that". They were filthy. So he baked bread for me; not very good bread, but he didn't have anything else. And he had honey. He gave me honey and bread, and I ate it all up. He just sat there, tending to me like I was a little baby. I ignored all that. I ate and left.'

Swami Nirmalananda was a silent saint. He had spent several years in silence and communicated only through notes and letters. After that meeting, Jaggi visited him several times, often carrying an offering of fruits with him. Since he had never seen himself as a spiritual seeker, he never sought any guidance from the Swami.

But their relationship grew and the two spent many companionable moments together. 'I remember sometimes he would speak to me. But most of the time he would converse with me through notes. He was always warm. And I warmed to him too. I didn't bother about whether he was enlightened or not. That didn't mean anything to me. I didn't want to concede that I was going to a spiritual person, because spirituality and I just didn't go together, but I started liking the guy. It became like a silent kind of love affair. He was a wonderful human being. And he lived gently. If he wanted to offer flowers for his daily worship, he would wait for the flowers to fall. He would never pluck from the tree. And he ate only fallen fruit; he'd never pluck them off the tree. He was that kind of man.'

After Sadhguru's spiritual life unfolded, he grew far too busy to maintain contact with the Swami. But soon after his marriage, he took Vijji with him to the Swami's B.R. Hills ashram. The Swami welcomed them silently. Initially, he seemed unable to place Sadhguru whose appearance had changed considerably in the past decade. 'I had a full beard now. Vijji was with me. I was gentler. From the wild strapping youth I had once been, I had now grown a little tamer,' says Sadhguru wryly.

But when Sadhguru introduced himself as Jaggi, the Swami's eyes suddenly brightened. 'The motorcycle man!' he gestured. Sadhguru nodded. The Swami then wrote something on a piece of paper and handed it over. It read, 'I recognised your smile.' (The Swami had always considered the smile to be an important index of a person's personality and spiritual development.) 'He welcomed us and he made us sit down,' says Sadhguru. 'Every time I went after that, you know, even before, whenever I went he gave me a can of honey. That's one thing he always had as a gift for me. He always gave me two or three litres of honey to carry home. We would have a long conversation he would write his questions and I would speak. Every day he wrote a minimum of eighty to a hundred letters. This is the way he kept in contact with people around the world. After that meeting, he started writing letters to me. I was travelling most of the time so I didn't reply very often. I didn't have a desk of my own—no home, no hearth, nothing. I was travelling so much at that time. Once in a way I wrote back. He never travelled. He hadn't travelled for probably twenty years. He didn't step out beyond those two acres of the ashram. He just lived within those confines. The ashram was located on a cliff. He would sometimes go to the edge and look out at the mountains and valleys and come back; that's all.'

That encounter was significant in many ways. It was Vijji's first meeting with a man who would change her life goals in a way she never imagined. She took an instant liking to him and was eager to visit him each time they were in Mysore. It was also memorable because of a dangerous incident the couple encountered on their return journey. As they hurtled homeward through the jungle on Sadhguru's motorbike, they suddenly found themselves disturbingly close to a wild elephant. Jaggi turned off his engine. Vijji clung to him, terrified. There was less than three feet between them and the beast. The elephant stood, facing some trees, and evidently hadn't seen them yet. Just behind was a small sloping path. The elephant sensed human presence and turned. It was now or never. Sadhguru plunged his bike downhill, whizzing right by the elephant. The beast trumpeted loudly and seemed to lurch in their direction. Vijji, who hadn't been expecting them to move, was alarmed by her husband's daredevilry. 'She was angry and crying, and beating me up, saying, "Have you gone mad? Why did you do that?" She was so terrified she peed in her pants!' laughs Sadhguru who had laughed away the incident even on that occasion.

In June 1996, Sadhguru and Vijji, along with their daughter, visited Swami Nirmalananda once again. He was older now, and looked somewhat worn and listless. He had emerged from his phase of silence. He told Sadhguru that he had lived as a yogi and wanted to die as one. Reluctant to linger on as an invalid, he said he was keen on shedding his ageing body before the next summer solstice.

He had already built a small samadhi for himself. In the course of the meeting, he had many questions for Sadhguru about the *mahasamadhi* state. His chief concern was how to leave the body without pain or discomfort. 'He said he was seventy-three and wanted to die as a yogi, not a rogi, an invalid,' says Sadhguru. 'He wanted to know if it would work, what exactly would happen, all sorts of details. That's the first time I opened up about this subject and spoke to him about a completely different dimension—what it is that stops a person from leaving, how to overcome these hurdles. I went into certain details.'

As Sadhguru clarified the Swami's doubts, Vijji listened intently to the conversation. She had become an inadvertent witness to a highly advanced esoteric discussion—one that would customarily have never been conducted in the presence of a neophyte. 'As she was listening to all this, she burst into tears,' recalls Sadhguru. 'She just cried and cried. I ignored her and continued to speak because Vijji was capable of crying for any reason—for joy, for anything. She was so overwhelmed by what I was saying that she couldn't stop. Nirmalananda also started weeping every now and then. And he continued asking me questions. We went into great detail about matters I have never spoken of anywhere.'

Vijji was unusually quiet on their return journey. In an effort to cheer her up, Sadhguru stopped the car and reminded her of their close shave with the wild elephant on the previous visit. But she didn't smile. 'I was trying to make light of the whole thing but she was in some kind of mood. I was just standing on the road. In front of me was this incredible view. My daughter was playing around nearby. And Vijji suddenly fell at my feet. She said, "I want to go like him."

'I said, "You want to go? Just jump off the hill; what's your problem?" I was just trying to joke and dismiss the whole thing.

'She said, "No, I want to leave like he is—consciously. I want to leave like that."

'I said, "Okay, when are you going to leave? Tell me the good news." I was still joking with her.

'But she was overflowing with emotion and tears. She said, "No, I am really serious. You must help me."'

It was then that the alarm bells began to ring. Vijji's role in the consecration of the Dhyanalinga was pivotal. This desire for mahasamadhi couldn't have been more inopportune. Sadhguru knew it could not be allowed to get out of hand. But that was just the beginning. Subsequently, Vijji often raised the subject of mahasamadhi with her husband. He saw she was in dead earnest and refused to be distracted. It was disturbing, but Sadhguru was aware that she was still a spiritual novice. She had neither the maturity nor the intensity required to attain her goal. It was a process that demanded sadhana and Vijji had never shown any inclination for sustained practice. Thankfully, she was still unripe, unready.

What he hadn't bargained for, however, was her determination. Because after that day, Vijji was a changed person. Her face had a new lustre, her life was infused with a new sense of purpose. 'From that day she was another person altogether. People who knew her were aware of how frivolous she was, most of the time acting like a six-year-old girl. But suddenly in the last eight or nine months she became all focused. It all started from that day. I said, "Okay, are you willing to do some sadhana? Let's see how seriously you do it." I never thought she would have the perseverance to stick to it like forever. It takes twenty-four hours of attention, of commitment. I never thought she'd have the determination for that. At the same time, I didn't want to deny the possibility to anybody.'

Sadhguru was already far too preoccupied with architectural plans for the Dhyanalinga shrine to pay much heed to any warning signs. As Vijji's sense of resolution increased, he was only peripherally aware of the change. In any case, he was confident that she would never be able to accomplish such a feat on her own. 'If there was anyone who could do it, I thought it would be Bharathi because she had a certain dispassion about her. But Vijji was always clinging to me; I never thought she was capable of it.' He mentioned it to some people around him, but they laughed it off. If anyone seemed singularly incapable of mahasamadhi, it was Vijji. It seemed a distant and unattainable aim for the most single-minded spiritual seeker. Even with her newfound maturity, Vijji seemed far too whimsical and erratic to qualify as a candidate.

'I gave her some very simple sadhana but she went very intensely into it,' he says. 'In a few months, I saw she was going really far. She even started talking confidently about leaving in another six months or eight months. Then I tried to discourage her, slow her down a little. I reminded her that after all these twelve years of being on the road, we finally had a place to live. For the first time, she had a place where she could call her own. She could cook and keep house. I knew these things meant a lot to her. Our daughter was going to be seven. And Vijji herself was just blossoming. After a certain phase of immaturity, problems, struggles within herself, things were working out well for her. So I said, "Why now? What's the hurry?"

'She said, "Right now, I am feeling absolutely beautiful inside, and outside everybody is wonderful to me. I don't know how long I will be able to maintain this. All my life, I have been confused; I've been in turmoil, had emotional upheavals. Right now I am in a place where I want to be. Tomorrow if something happens to my child, or to you, I may again allow that to affect me. But right now nothing matters to me. I am in that state. This is the time for me to leave."

'I had no argument with that because I know it's true. I said, "Wait a few years; enjoy this and go."

'But she said, "Right now, you don't want me to go. But after a few years, maybe you will."'

Sadhguru laughs at the recollection. 'Against such wisdom I had no argument! So I made some attempts to discourage her as a husband. But as a guru, I couldn't stop her.'

The consecration practices played their role in giving an additional fillip to Vijji's resolve, bringing her dream within her reach. 'I wanted the people involved in the Dhyanalinga to be in certain states of samadhi,' says Sadhguru. 'One aspect of samadhi is your contact with the body becomes minimal. It can be brought down to a one-pointed contact. We call that *nirvikalpa samadhi*. It means that your contact with your body is minimal, like a thread. If you break that thread, then it is mahasamadhi. But it's nice to hold a single thread and continue to live because then you are almost free from it [the body] and still alive. There are a few things you have to do: you still have to eat a little, go to the toilet. But in every other way you are free from the bodily process. It's a good way to live. Normally, when people are like this, we keep them in certain levels of inactivity and safety. We keep them in protected atmospheres. We don't expose them to outside situations, because with the smallest disturbance, they may leave the body. Just a pin prick and they may leave the body for good. But when we were consecrating the Dhyanalinga, I wanted people who were in samadhi states but still physically active. This was risky. But the process required it. So I was teaching them how to be active. This gave Vijji a tremendous opportunity to develop a certain capability. She started going all out.'

In October 1996, Sadhguru happened to be planning his programme schedule for January. At that point, he had a sudden intuition that the proposed classes wouldn't be possible. He decided to cancel them. 'I told Raja, "I feel the programmes in the last week of January will not happen. I don't like this. Push it to first week of February." Raja asked me if I had any personal engagements. I said, "No, I just feel programmes fixed for that time may have to be postponed."' Others around him asked why, but he could offer no explanation.

By the end of November, the edifice of the lingam had arrived in the ashram. Sadhguru now undertook a journey to Sambalpur in Orissa to initiate the renovation of the Mukteshwar temple there. He took Vijji with him. It proved to be a strange trip. A senior disciple recalls that after visiting the temple, Sadhguru started walking through the surrounding forest at a great pace. It was night, and a few people followed him. When he reached a small pool of water (fed by the river Mahanadi), he suddenly stopped short. He signalled to the others to halt, and continued on his own. He walked around the pool and abruptly stopped before an old tree. He gazed at it for a long time, tears streaming down his face. Then in one swift gesture, he removed his garland and placed it on the tree. This act evoked equally baffling responses from the bystanders. Some wept; others fell to the ground and rolled, as if possessed. The atmosphere seemed charged with an intense energy.

When he returned to Coimbatore, Sadhguru revealed that he had, in fact, visited a temple that he had known intimately in another lifetime. 'Bilva was trying to shift a large group of people from his tribe to Sambalpur and had often camped beneath this tree with his family. It was amazing how the tree had stood all these centuries. No one had brought it down. The old tree had died and just the bark remained. Inside that, its offspring grew within the shell of the old tree, so it was the same tree, in a sense.'

In December 1996, Sadhguru took Vijji and several inmates of the ashram to visit Swami Nirmalananda. He seemed physically weak, and it was clear that the day of his mahasamadhi was not far. He was a man at peace with himself, and his presence struck his visitors as sacred. Some were moved to tears. The Swami consoled them. 'I may not be here the next time you visit,' he said quietly, 'but you will be able to feel my presence everywhere.' His advice to them was to remain fearless. He assured them that they had a guru who was capable of leading them to the highest spiritual attainments. 'Trust him and be true to your sadhana. He will do the rest,' he said.

The last few months had been difficult for the Swami. His announcement of his mahasamadhi had provoked a controversy. Rationalist groups in Karnataka labelled this an attempt at suicide and led a vociferous protest against what they saw as an obscurantist practice. There was even a police inquiry at the ashram. 'When we went there, there were two police constables in the ashram,' says

Sadhguru. 'He held me and wept. He said, "See, I have not even plucked a flower from a single tree in this ashram all my life, but they've actually posted policemen in my ashram."

'I said "Why are you bothered? Two men sitting here, what are they going to do to you?" He said, "But they think I'm going to commit suicide."

'I said, "You don't bother; you know you just have to do this, this and this," and I went through details of what needed to be done. But he was distressed, because the police were monitoring him all the time, to make sure he didn't take his life.'

The Swami eventually released a statement in which he explained that for someone who had lived a long and spiritually fruitful life, the decision to leave the body was as natural a process as an old leaf falling off a tree. For a man who has attained self-realization, he said, the body becomes an unbearable burden; others could have no idea of just how painful it was for such a person to retain his hold on the body. This non-violent and conscious relinquishing of the body, he said, had many honourable precedents in the country's spiritual heritage. He requested the protesters not to create any unnecessary confusion in the minds of people, and asked to be allowed to make his final exit in peace. The seventy-three-year-old Swami eventually left his body on the 10 January 1997. 'On a fine January afternoon,' says Sadhguru, 'he came and sat in his samadhi. With about fifty-five people there to witness this, he just left. The police couldn't catch him! The rationalists argued, "He must have taken some poison; he must be post-mortemed!" But how could a man who had consumed poison walk to a samadhi, sit cross-legged and smiling, and leave like this?'

The last meeting with the Swami made a deep impression on the Isha meditators. 'Watching the Swami and Sadhguru together,' says one meditator, 'was special. It was the day of the Arudra darshan [the Tamil festival celebrating the cosmic dance of Shiva, considered to be the longest night in the year]. Seeing them together on that occasion gave the moment an added significance; it was like seeing the sun and the moon together.'

In the third week of December, Sadhguru telephoned Bharathi. He asked her if she would join Vijji, his daughter and him on a fortnight's car trip. Although reluctant to accompany them on what she assumed was a family holiday, she agreed. It meant making arrangements for her family again. 'But by then, I'd learnt to scheme,' she smiles. 'Since it was the Christmas–Pongal time, my kids had school holidays and I sent them off to my brother's place in Hyderabad.' She left with Sadhguru and his family on 26 December. No one had any clue to the purpose of this trip, and none of them—not even the participants—guessed how path-breaking it would prove to be.

Although the Dhyanalinga work was proceeding apace, Sadhguru was aware that certain 'karmic barriers' remained and impeded the complete integration of the two participants in the process. While Vijji and Bharathi were quite willing to cooperate, there were unconscious areas of constraint that still needed to be addressed. The ideal way to disentangle these deeply buried knots was to jointly visit places that were of importance to their previous lives.

Bharathi, who was as clueless as Vijji about the purpose of the trip, recalls times during the journey when she felt it would have been easier if she hadn't accompanied them. 'It was becoming clear to me that Vijji was possessive about her husband and insecure about the way in which young people were increasingly regarding him as a godlike figure and going crazy about him. She also made what I thought was a foolish comment to Sadhguru about wanting to attain mahasamadhi. I felt it was like a child talking about a Barbie doll, and I asked her, "Why mahasamadhi? Why die? Why not live and assist him?" She would just retreat into her shell when I said such things. I felt a certain anger towards her at the time—anger that my guru was married to someone who couldn't understand the magnitude of his life mission. Now I think I could perhaps have been easier on her. I never understood her pain as a woman and was often condescending. But that was because I couldn't understand why she wanted to reduce him to just a husband when he was so obviously so much more than that.'

The first halt on the journey was Sambalpur on the western border of Orissa. A town with a considerable tribal population, it is located sixteen kilometres south of the Hirakud Dam. An ancient centre of the diamond trade and currently famous for its textiles, it is also a well-known centre of Vajrayana Buddhism. The group headed for the small Mukteshwar temple about an hour's drive from Sambalpur.

As they approached the ancient temple, Bharathi was distinctly aware that the place was not new to her. It evoked a mix of longing and grief that grew increasingly unbearable in intensity. The powerful feelings made her turn silent and withdrawn. 'In the course of the journey, Sadhguru explained several things to Vijji—the reason we were making certain visits, their significance, and so on. For me there were not many questions. I had already had certain glimpses during my Samyama programmes that made many scenes instantly familiar.' The three meditated at the temple for three days. Bharathi slipped into her meditation practices easily. She found the place electrifying in its energy, and was often unable to stand after her meditations.

A senior disciple who had made arrangements for both their visits to Sambalpur now noticed that Vijji seemed decidedly different from the way she had been on her visit just a fortnight ago. Her approach to Sadhguru was less casual, more reverential, and there was something indefinable about her own presence that induced respect.

Now Sadhguru decided to pursue the trajectory of Bilva's life. He knew that the snake charmer's hometown was likely to be somewhere in the vicinity. But he had no idea of the name of the town or in which direction it lay. Undeterred, the foursome plunged into what might have seemed to any onlooker to be a wild-goose chase—an uncertain search for an unknown destination. They had no map, no clues, no leads. It was a journey that could have taken them months to accomplish. And yet, they encountered no blind alleys. They were travelling by jeep, and Sadhguru directed the driver, guided entirely by his intuition. He navigated the vehicle to the town of Raigad in Madhya Pradesh, on the other side of the Orissa border.

As the jeep drove in, Bharathi was assailed again by an overwhelming sense of déjà vu. The place seemed achingly familiar; she had no doubt that someone very dear to her had lived here. They headed directly to a small Shiva temple. As soon as she set foot in the shrine, Bharathi knew it was the temple she had seen in a vision during her second Samyama programme. The sound of temple bells had often haunted her dreams as a young girl. The sound of this particular temple bell was exactly the clangour to which she was so accustomed. 'Ever since I was a child, there has been a small faraway temple in my vision. As soon as I saw this Shiva temple, I knew that I used to come here as a young girl to worship in an earlier lifetime,' she recalls.

For Sadhguru, the experience was just as alive. 'That Raigad street was just the way it had been. Everything was as I remembered it—the same Brahmin colony, the temple, everything. Soon after, this temple was renovated. But at that time, it was as if everything stood still in time, just waiting for us to revisit it and recognize it.'

After meditating in the temple, Sadhguru led the party to a tree outside the temple. It stood before a stream, and although it stood among several other trees, there was no doubt that this was different. It still pulsated with a raw energy, instantly recognizable to the visitors. Four hundred years later, it could still transport the travellers into another dimension of space and time. It was here that a young man had breathed the last few minutes of his life. 'When Bilva fell,' Sadhguru says, 'it was face down. The energy of that body was just intact when we approached the tree. Nothing had changed.' And those last minutes in Bilva's life, as Sadhguru points out, were spent, by some intervention of grace, in full awareness. 'That's why breath-watching at Isha is always tinged with venom,' Sadhguru has often said. 'Elsewhere breath-watching is a very cool process. At Isha it is very hot. Here, if you sit and watch your breath, it drives you into a maddening frenzy. It's like you are on the edge of life and death. That's because this man watched his life breath when it was ebbing away. The awareness did not come easy. It happened when his breath was almost gone.'

On their return journey, the group passed through Vishakapatnam in the state of Andhra Pradesh. Here, too, Sadhguru decided it was time for exploration. Luck was on their side again; every detour seemed intimately linked to the main course, every digression proved to be just another lane home. Sadhguru had often asked Bharathi about a place that was likely to be in the Rayalseema area of Andhra Pradesh. He did not know its name. Since she belonged to the coastal part of the state, she was unable to help him. Now the group decided to deviate from their plan again. Instead of returning to Coimbatore via Bangalore, they decided to drive to Hyderabad. After spending a night there, they hit the road again. Four hours later, they approached the small town of Cuddappah. Guided yet again by Sadhguru's unerring inner radar, they drove directly to a Shiva temple.

A silence descended upon Sadhguru as they neared the shrine. Bharathi experienced a familiar upsurge of energy as she entered it. She knew immediately that this was the place in which she had spent time with her master in an earlier lifetime. It was here that Sadhguru Sri Brahma and his faithful disciple had created a blueprint for the Dhyanalinga, plotting the lives of future disciples, right down to the wombs in which they were to be born. They travellers meditated here for a while. The place, they learnt, had lain derelict for several years and had only recently been renovated.

For some reason, Vijji found that she was unable to look Bharathi in the eye during their time at the temple. Although Bharathi was puzzled by this, a part of her knew why. There was a marked change in her attitude and body language in the temple. 'I knew that a great deal had happened here between me and Sadhguru, and felt suddenly protective of him. I knew I had seen my master in a state of pain and defeat earlier, and I didn't want to see him fail again. I felt a fierce determination, and whoever came in our way seemed insignificant. There was also a certain indignation: why has my master, my guru, this king of kings, chosen to get *married* in this lifetime?'

It was later that she realized that the time she had spent with Sadhguru Sri Brahma in the temple in her previous lifetime had been a period of great hardship for both of them. It was a time when her attitude towards her master was protective to the point of being belligerent. The powerful energy of the temple had stirred that deep-seated ferocity yet again. This inexplicable mood change, not surprisingly, intimidated Vijji. As they drove away from the temple, however, the surge of aggression abated as swiftly as it had arisen.

The immediate fallout of the trip, Bharathi recalls, was that it released her from 'a few small fairy-tale attachments' she carried towards certain relationships and events. This reduced the tension between her and Vijji considerably. The cleansing hadn't taken place on a purely psychological level either. Something deeper had happened. And Sadhguru's daughter inadvertently confirmed this. When they emerged from one of their long meditations in one of the temples, she ran spontaneously up to Bharathi, calling her 'Amma'. She realized her mistake a second later. The incident was subtle but an important testimony to the fact now they both exuded energies that were far more harmonious than before.

It had been a whirlwind tour: they had covered six states and five thousand-odd kilometres in twelve days, and six of those days had been spent driving, with many of the nights spent in the car itself. But for the travellers, it had been much more than a hectic trip. They had actually zigzagged through several lifetimes, their journey opening their eyes to the many independent strands that wove together the tapestry of their lives. No wonder Sadhguru termed it a 'karma yatra'. It was nothing less than a pilgrimage, a chance to dissolve deeply embedded blocks and unconscious identifications by revisiting their past histories.

On their way back, the Dhyanalinga suddenly seemed less remote and dreamlike. It looked like an imminent possibility. 'As we were driving back, I made Vijji and Bharathi take a vow that by the next pournami in February we would finish the consecration,' recalls Sadhguru. 'I said, no matter what family compulsions, no matter what it takes, we will finish it. They agreed. I said, "That's not enough; you have to really take a vow." So I actually made them shout it out aloud three times. And they did.'

Although he was exhausted, Sadhguru immediately called for a satsangh, eager to share with his disciples the fruits of their journey as well as news of the breakthrough that it represented. 'I've nothing to show you, but definitely we have brought a tremendous gift for you,' he announced. He described the karma yatra as a journey so free of hitches that it seemed as if 'the whole of existence was waiting for us to do it'. He instructed Vijji and Bharathi to sit at either end of the hall, creating a triangular formation. He then led a group meditation, which his meditators remembered for a long time afterwards as extraordinarily powerful.

'It was such a powerful experience,' he was to say later. 'These two people went through a fast-forward of life, a quick progression; so many events of their past life just happened . . . I would describe the place exactly before we would enter the town, so that doubts didn't arise in the minds of even these two people. They shouldn't think that they're only imagining those things. I would tell them how the vibrations would be, which chakra would get activated when you walk into the place . . . and it would be exactly the same in their experience; it couldn't be any different . . . Whether it is Cuddappah or Sambalpur, we know exactly where to go, because once we start approaching that place the vibrations are such that the past connection just pulls you there. We could have chosen so many other places where both their pasts were involved or where their pasts were separately involved, but we wanted to go to those places which were of spiritual significance. When we went there, the spiritual dimension became a living experience for both of them. So when they went through these kinds of processes, all the structures which were holding them were shaken loose. After that the consecration became very easy. Even before that, the urge to break the karmic bondage was there; the sadhana was there towards that, but this acted like an extra boost.'

And so, the goal seemed nearer than ever before. But intimations of trouble were already in the air. It was soon after the karma yatra that Bharathi left for her family home in Vishakapatnam to celebrate Pongal. On their way back from a trip to her father's ancestral home in her native village, one of her sisters-in-law suggested that they stop and visit a local saint named Venkanna Babu who lived by the Godavari riverside.

With her long-standing mistrust of godmen and temples, Bharathi was reluctant to join them. But since the saint's home was on the way, it seemed churlish to refuse. Venkanna Babu was venerated as a holy man in the area, and was believed to be gifted with powers of prescience. He entertained a small assembly of visitors every Saturday evening. It was his practice to emerge after long hours of prayer and meet his gathering. He would stand before them with his eyes closed and a silver flute in hand, listen to their questions and offer his advice.

Bharathi and her sisters-in-law trooped into his simple home. The visitors sat before him in a row on the floor. Each person was given their chance to ask a question. When her turn came, Bharathi was silent. But the saint continued to wait. When her sister-in-law nudged her, she felt obliged to ask a question. 'My guru wants to establish something,' she said awkwardly. 'What do you think about it? Will it happen?'

There was a pause. Venkanna Babu's eyes remained closed for a length of time. Then he spoke. 'There is something that Sadhguru seeks to establish,' he said. 'But it will not happen as soon as he desires. There will be difficulties; there will be delays.' There was a pause. Then he added, 'Your guru is no ordinary being. He is vaster than the ocean, but the present circumstances are adverse and they will take their toll upon his health.' His final words were of reassurance. 'You are walking a certain path,' he told Bharathi. 'And it is the right one.'

When Bharathi reached Vishakapatnam that night, she called Vijji and Sadhguru immediately. Anxious not to dishearten them, she mentioned the barest details of her encounter with Venkanna Babu. 'I told Sadhguru that he had said there would be some hiccups in the process. I also told him that he should take care of his health. Vijji told me that Sadhguru already seemed to be anticipating some delays. When she had asked him whether the consecration would be over soon, he had fallen silent. She said he seemed to know something would be amiss. It worried her.' Bharathi herself was not unduly worried by Venkanna Babu's prediction. Sadhguru seemed to be in control of the situation; the consecration seemed nearly complete, and she couldn't anticipate what could possibly go wrong at this stage. She was struck, however, by the reverence with which Venkanna Babu had spoken of Sadhguru, despite never having met him.

In the meantime, Sadhguru had taken Vijji to Bangalore for a cousin's wedding. 'In the twelve years that we had been married, we both had been so busy that none of my relatives—other than my immediate family—had ever met my wife. I never went to any of the family functions. I never visited anyone because I was always travelling and teaching, building a whole new family, in a sense. So I decided to go because I wanted everybody in my family to meet Vijji. By now, after the karma yatra, she was glowing like the full moon. People who saw her in those last few weeks could clearly see that she was different. Everyone met her and they all said, "Wow, what a wife you have. No wonder you never came to see us earlier!" All that stuff.'

But the grand family conclave was also something of a leave-taking, although no one but Sadhguru and Vijji had an inkling of it. 'I knew that she was preparing for her mahasamadhi and that after the consecration was over, by February–March, she wanted to leave.' He did hint at it, but no one took it seriously. 'They wouldn't believe it. They said, "What nonsense! She is so beautiful and joyful; why would she suddenly go?"'

The couple visited Vijji's parents as well as Sadhguru's family in Mysore (his mother's death ceremony was on the eighteenth of the month). 'I gently mentioned to both sides of the family that Vijji had been saying she wanted to go, that she may not be around for too long,' says Sadhguru. 'My father dismissed it as rubbish. Others were a little taken aback.'

Twenty-second January, 1997, is a day that Bharathi remembers vividly. She was back from Vishakapatnam by then. The doorbell rang that night. It was Vijji at the door. She said she had come to Coimbatore to conduct a satsangh and had decided to pay Bharathi an impromptu visit. Bharathi invited her in and served her dinner. Vijji gave her some pongal *prasadam* from Bangalore. 'I remember she was looking very nice that evening, and I told her so,' says Bharathi. 'There was something mellow about her. She seemed particularly at ease with herself.'

Twenty-third January was a full moon day. Sadhguru had told them that he wanted to complete the Dhyanalinga consecration either that day or by the next full moon. But Bharathi had her daughter's school play to attend that day. Although she hadn't mentioned it to Sadhguru or Vijji, she doubted that she would be able to make it to the ashram that day. 'Vijji didn't ask me if I was coming for pournami, and I didn't tell her about my plans to go for my daughter's school programme, either. Later, I regretted it. If I'd gone to the ashram that day, it's possible things would have been quite different.'

At that time, however, none of them knew just what was about to happen on the twenty-third. Probably not even the person who set that dramatic turn of events in motion. For her, it was still a plan—a fierce all-consuming plan perhaps. But plans, she knew as well as anyone else, were notoriously unreliable.

The events of the day unfolded unremarkably. Maa Gambhiri remembers that Vijji handed over a diary to her early that morning and told her to mark Sadhguru's engagements in it. It puzzled her a little because Vijji had always been in charge of his appointments and there had never been the need for such a diary in the past. But she put the event out of her mind as she busied herself with her duties in the kitchen.

Sadhguru did notice that Vijji had risen early that morning and done her sadhana. After a few hours, she had a bath and did her sadhana again. She repeated this procedure several times. At ten o'clock, he had lunch with her. There was a monthly teachers' meet that day, and participants recall Vijji championing the cause of a few teachers who were singled out for criticism. There was nothing significant about this. Vijji was often vocal in her support of ashram volunteers and teachers. 'I remember I was supporting Sadhguru on some point, and Vijji strongly opposed it,' says Raja.

She left for her home at four thirty that afternoon. The special full moon meditations began at dusk. 'It had been part of Vijji's sadhana for a few months to cook and serve the brahmacharis and brahmacharinis by hand on full moon days,' says Swami Devasatwa. 'We'd assemble in the shrine in Sadhguru's home, and the two of them would feed us handfuls of bisi-bele-bhat, followed by curd and rice. But first, there were the meditations.'

Sadhguru remembers that Vijji suddenly rose in the middle of the meditation and left. He was puzzled since it was unusual for anyone to interrupt the meditation.

'I had my eyes closed but I knew when she got up and walked away,' he recalls. 'I was a little irritated. Nobody dares to just get up and walk away from a meditation. Once they sit, that's it. Within about eight or ten minutes she got up and walked away and within five minutes she came back and sat down. She had gone into the bathroom, and left all her jewels there, from the toe ring to the nose stud. These are things that a woman in India doesn't remove normally. These are things that are never spoken or written about, but if there is metal in certain strategic parts of your body, you cannot leave your body by accident. So whenever anybody comes to the ashram, if we put them through any kind of intense sadhana, the first thing we do is give them a simple copper ring to wear. It was only much later after everything was over, when I went into the bathroom that I saw that all Vijji's jewellery was placed next to the washbasin. She had removed it, come back and sat down. When she sat down she must have realized that this metal had been the only thing holding her back. There was a sudden explosion of energy. Within seven minutes of her return she was gone. '

Swami Devasatwa remembers the scene clearly. 'She was sitting on Sadhguru's chair. She was chanting with the rest of us. The next moment, she just sort of fell to one side. I remember there was a smile on her face.'

There was a flurry of consternation. Someone informed Sadhguru that Vijji was 'not waking up'. In a moment, he was by her side. He worked ceaselessly on her chakras, while the others looked on, uncomprehending. It was not entirely unusual. People had slipped out of their bodies during meditations before, but they usually returned. An hour later, Sadhguru looked up. His eyes were wet. 'She's gone,' he said. 'She left through her anahata.'

The news reached Bharathi when she was in the middle of the school programme. 'As soon as I heard, my first thought was, oh my God, this woman did it! I felt a grudging admiration for her. Then came anger: why did she have to do it now? How will we complete the process?'

Sadhguru's daughter, seven years old at the time, reports her version of the events with an impressionistic clarity. The message that her mother was unwell reached her in boarding school. By the time she reached the ashram, she knew something was wrong. 'When I came in, people were bawling. I saw my dad crying, my mother lying on a bed full of flowers. It was three in the morning. I was tired. I hugged my dad. I remember I said I was sleepy.'

She had realized what had happened, she says, but no, she had no questions. 'Weird stuff was always happening around my parents, anyway,' she says simply. 'I was used to it.' Having sat with her father on the dais during the Wholeness Programme and several Bhava Spandana programmes, she was accustomed to the sight of people weeping, staggering and experiencing a whole gamut of states of altered consciousness. 'The next day, I saw people pulling out the ashes from the pyre,' she says. 'I remember wondering then: how do they know the difference between bones and logs?'

On some level, her mother had prepared her for this day. Just a few days before the event, when they were driving her back to her boarding school in Ooty, Vijji had told her that she wouldn't be with her for her birthday that March. The girl had listened silently. She recalls Sadhguru remonstrating with Vijji for needlessly worrying her. Vijji had replied that she knew she wouldn't be able to retain her body for more than two pournamis. Sadhguru, too, recalls the conversation. 'She was telling the girl that she would be gone before March so I would come and meet her instead. The two of them were just talking in a very matter-of-fact manner. I said, "Why are you doing this to the girl? Just leave her alone. You don't know whether you will go or not." But she said, "No, no, I have to tell her. I will definitely go." She had announced that she would leave on a full moon evening some eight months ago and had started working towards it. She was very clear about it. We came back on the twenty-first evening from Ooty. The twenty-third evening is when she left. This sounds like a fairy tale. But it is true.'

Sadhguru's daughter remembers Vijji as little more than an archetypal mother figure. She remembers her as the woman who decorated her hair with hibiscus leaves and white flowers, who did her holiday homework with her left hand ('so no one would know she'd done it for me'), and who would bring her home-cooked food to school on parent visits. 'I didn't really know who she was, but I still feel I kind of do know her,' she says. 'I intuitively know what she'd have liked and disliked.'

Recently, on Vijji's tenth anniversary celebrations, another facet of her mother's identity was revealed to her. 'Listening to people's responses, I thought, oh my God, maybe she wasn't just my mother and my dad's wife. I realized suddenly that there had been much more to her.'

Not many had realized just how much more to Vijji there was. It was her mahasamadhi that brought it into sharp focus. 'Behind her emotions, there lay an intensity that none of us had guessed,' says one of the sanyasis. 'I'd always seen her as a thoughtful person, a considerate one. I remember how she gave me one of Sadhguru's warm woollen shirts because I'd joined the ashram without bringing any winter wear. I remember the packets of Little Heart's biscuits she'd always send for me with Sadhguru every time he returned from Bangalore. But she was also very volatile. Many of us thought that her love for her husband was the biggest barrier to her spiritual growth. But there was a change in her after the consecration work started. And in the end she got what she wanted—before any of us did.'

Others remember her warmth and great capacity for affection. 'Whenever Sadhguru rebuked me—and that was pretty often—Vijji would immediately leap to my defence,' remembers Srinivas. 'She had talked to me about mahasamadhi just a week earlier,' says Raja. 'We often discussed it. I had visited Swami Nirmalananda as well and I had been moved by that meeting. I used to tell her that I longed to attain it too.' While he had never anticipated that she would leave as soon as she did, he wasn't entirely surprised either. 'The atmosphere was different in those days. Sadhguru seemed far fiercer, more intense. We were younger; the unexpected didn't surprise us. We were all full of confidence and hope. Everything seemed possible.'

One thousand people attended Vijji's funeral. Sadhguru remained in his home for ten days after the ceremony. Ashram residents remember him pacing furiously up and down his veranda, his face a study in grief. On the eleventh day, he conducted a special aradhana or memorial function. Three thousand attended it.

'It has always been hard for me to explain to people what Vijji is,' he announced to the gathering in a short but moving address. 'When I say "Vijji", I am not referring to her either as my wife or as a woman, just as a being. As a being, she has always been truly wonderful in my experience. But as many of you know, she was a person of very intense emotions. In her childlikeness, she never knew what should be expressed or what should be held back in a group of people. Whatever emotions were within her always found expression, irrespective of the situation.'

A husband's loss struggled with a guru's pride. 'This is not child's play,' he reminded the assembly. 'Even accomplished yogis would struggle to attain this. As some of you know now, Swami Nirmalananda, who spent his life in spiritual sadhana, in the last few days before his mahasamadhi, was in doubt about whether it would be possible for him or not, and that's what he expressed to me when we visited him for the last time. With divine grace, he attained mahasamadhi. Even a gnani, who had spent his lifetime in spiritual sadhana, struggled to attain this. To throw this life out of this body without injuring the body takes something else. One has to generate a tremendous amount of energy, which requires intense sadhana. Vijji knew the methods to achieve this. But at this stage, we never imagined that without my assistance, she would be able to generate the necessary energy. The swiftness with which she has achieved this was just made possible with her love, probably the only thing she knew. When I look at the whole series of events, it is very clear that there was a direct intervention of the divine. It seems like Shambho that her heart was crying for, has taken her by the hand. Out of sheer love, she made it possible.'

His pain was palpable. But he did not miss the opportunity to point out that Vijji's mahasamadhi was not a mere individual's triumph, but an inspiration to many. 'For all spiritual seekers, mahasamadhi is the ultimate goal, the very culmination of their sadhana, a chance to dissolve into divinity. Whenever you get an opportunity, let people know that even this kind of opportunity is available to man, that it is possible to take hold of the very process of birth and death into one's hands. Generally, people believe that all these things are over with the sages and rishis of ancient times. But spirituality in its highest possibility is still very much alive. The public at large has come to the conclusion that the age of genuine saints is over. Now, the present situation here is clear proof that it is not. And it never will be. I did not wish that at this stage anybody here should leave the body and go. But she aspired for it and she has dissolved into the maha-mantra, "Shambho." It is not for me or anyone to ask whether this is right or wrong.' He added quietly, 'I am not big enough to question him.'

He has often described devotion as the quickest and most intelligent path for a seeker. 'Devotees often look like a bunch of idiots to the rest of the world, but the wisest ones are always devotees. This is a different kind of wisdom which logical minds can never understand.'

It was clear that while Sadhguru was aware that Vijji was going to leave her body, he had no idea it would be so soon. 'She was determined to go,' he says. 'I often told her that after twelve years, we finally had our own home, a growing child, some stability in our lives. But she was adamant. And I knew I couldn't stop it. In the last few months, her very breath had become "Shambho". But I thought she would leave a month later. I believed the consecration would be done by then.'

He remembers that on their drive back from Ooty a couple of days before her mahasamadhi, Vijji, who had been chanting 'Shambho', as she usually did, suddenly began weeping. She clutched his hand and asked him to stop the car. When he complied, she had declared that he was the only Shambho she had known in her life, and begged him to help her realize her dream. Sadhguru lightly replied that even if she didn't know Shambho, Shambho certainly knew her. 'If you remain sincere about what you're doing, you will definitely experience him and know him beyond my form.' No one, he added, could deny her her dream. She seemed comforted by this. After their return, she pursued her practices with increased fervour.

But perhaps there was another subliminal motive that underlay Vijji's resolve to attain mahasamadhi: the fear of outliving her husband. 'It scared her, the fact that he was going to die at forty-two,' says Bharathi. 'I do remember her saying she didn't want to live after him.'

One still can't help wondering how a yogi of Sadhguru's attainments could have been unaware of the imminence of Vijji's departure. 'I was anticipating an impediment, but I thought it would be social,' he says, pointing out that for centuries social norms had been the traditional obstruction in the path of the Dhyanalinga. 'So I instructed all the people around me to be extremely careful not to get into any kind of trouble anywhere; not to create any kind of resistance with anybody, because I knew something was coming. I thought I'd fixed the situations around me sufficiently . . . Though on one level, I knew this was coming, the situation around me and what was demanded out of me at the moment blocked my conscious cognition.'

Besides, he adds, Vijji was not an accomplished yogi and her departure was not as premeditated as it might have seemed. 'Though her leaving was very much of her conscious will, she had no moment-to-moment control over the life forces. But the last few minutes before she left, she was aware and accommodated the dissolution of herself by removing all the metal on her body in the form of ornaments. When the divine descends, you just accommodate.'

Even if her husband had had no clue to the course of events, the heavens seemed to have colluded with Vijji in her single-minded aspiration. 'It was a very special day in terms of the way energies were moving for this planet,' Sadhguru explains. 'There was an exceedingly rare and archetypically appropriate planetary alignment, a moment in time expressed in the heavens as a perfect six-pointed star. This pattern comes on the exact day where three outer planets, Jupiter, Uranus and Neptune are conjoined together for the first time in almost two hundred years. On 23 January, this cluster of planets centred on the first degree of Aquarius, joined by the sun with the full moon opposite them all. This pattern may also be seen as a symbolic representation of the long-heralded dawning of the Age of Aquarius. It is also the *thaipoosam*, a day that many sages of the past have chosen for their own mahasamadhi.'

Sadhguru's voice holds a definite note of exultation at his most unlikely disciple's attainment. 'As a husband, I was in shock and grief. She had lived like my shadow for twelve years. There was not one moment when she was not there. But as a guru, I was proud. She had accomplished her ambition through the intensity of her emotions. She just dissolved into her love. And she left without doing any harm to her own body; she simply discarded it like an old garment. When a person leaves in full awareness, shedding the body without causing any injury or damage to it, that person is truly no more. She doesn't exist as a being any longer. It means she has just melted away. The game is up—completely.' Particularly significant was the fact that Vijji had not undertaken any fast or penance before her departure. 'Even if I were to leave my body, I would prepare for it. I would not eat for at least twenty-four hours before the event,' Sadhguru admits. 'But she did it effortlessly, without any obvious preparation. Such a simple process of sadhana I gave her, but she just took it to such heights. It's very rare.'

The effortless exit of a thirty-three-year-old woman in perfect health was a source of wonder to many. But there was also a very real grief. A concise tribute to her memory comes from Srinivas, a man of few words: 'Vijji,' he says, 'was an ordinary woman capable of an extraordinary amount of love.' He is among the many who miss her. 'She was one of the most natural and spontaneous people I've known,' says Maa Karpoori. 'Initially I felt anger at her departure. I wondered why Sadhguru hadn't prevented it somehow. Now I realize that perhaps her mahasamadhi happened at the best possible time. She would have faced tough times ahead, as the scale and significance of Sadhguru's sphere of activity increased. But for all of us, her going meant a vacuum.' Says Raja quietly, 'Now, I feel like I'm part of a great organization, but she had made me feel like I was part of a family.'

Vijji's ashes were buried in the shrine adjoining her home. Several meditators still choose to spend silent hours at this small and unostentatious spot. 'There is a quality there that's special,' says Hoda, an ashram resident. 'I never knew her. But when I sit there, I feel I do. There's a gentleness there, something soft, a great sense of peace.'

Sadhguru himself has testified to this. Although the concept of mahasamadhi does indeed mean that there is no residual personhood, a person's fragrance, he says, cannot be exorcized. 'For this being, there is no more bondage of a physical body. Her name is Vijaya Kumari which means "victory's daughter"—the highest possible victory for any being became hers. But even if the flower is no more, still the fragrance can remain. And the fragrance of this flower is forever. It's never lost . . . The physical fragrance may die, but the energy fragrance that we're talking about can't be killed. That corner of the ashram nurtures a very different type of energy altogether. It is very mild, very subtle, very pleasant and beautiful. If you sit there for a while it can you give you a bodiless kind of feeling. That space is fundamentally anahata. It's like a solvent. It can slowly melt you down.'

On another occasion, as we were walking in the garden around his home, he remarked, 'That woman knew nothing about the spiritual life. She had no great accomplishments. She was as ordinary as ordinary can be. She had been through bursts of devotion and confusion, devotion and confusion all her life. When she managed to hold on to a devotional spell for long enough, she made it—just like that.'

He carelessly tossed a petal in the direction of her shrine. 'She left my home empty but our hearts full.'

'If You Drop Your Fruit Willingly, Stones Can Be Minimized'

Countdown, Crisis, Denouement

Vijji's mahasamadhi represented a strange irony—a tragedy for her husband and a triumph for her guru. And by a twist of fate, of course, both master and mate were the same man. Even for the guru, however, this wasn't an unalloyed triumph. For while Vijji had left like an exemplary disciple, the timing of this event couldn't have been more inconvenient. The realization of her personal dream had become the obstacle to a larger one. The Dhyanalinga had been thwarted, not by a lack of zeal or commitment, but by too much of it; not by social immaturity, but by an excess of spiritual maturity. A fruit had ripened sooner than expected, and had no option but to fall.

For Sadhguru, it meant putting aside the deep sense of personal loss and addressing the mission of lifetimes all over again. 'Once Vijji attained mahasamadhi, we were back to square one,' he said. 'Ninety-five per cent of the work was done. Just a little more time, in one more week, we would have completed the consecration, but now we got stuck.' There was another factor that made this setback all the more aggravating. Time was running out. At thirty-nine, Sadhguru knew he didn't have much longer to live.

He had already tried to prepare his daughter for this possibility, and remembers being astounded by her quiet acceptance and exceptional level of understanding. 'Her mother had just passed away. I brought her back home and kept her with me for some days. When I was taking her back to school after three or four days, I saw she was just fine. I thought maybe she didn't understand what had happened, maybe she hadn't even grasped it. I asked her, "Is it okay that Vijji is gone?"

'She said, "I know she's gone. She told me that she would go."

'I said, "Do you know that you will never see her again?"

'She said, "Jaggi, do dead people come back? I know she won't come back."

'Then I asked, "Is it okay with you?"

'"She had talked to me about it. It's okay with me."

'Then I said, "Is it okay if I leave?"

'She said, "Wait till I grow up and then leave."

'That's when I thought, okay, I have somebody really beautiful on my hands.'

In the next year and a half, Bharathi saw her master go through an excruciating time. 'I won't forget the struggles he went through,' she says. The urgent need was to find a replacement for Vijji. Sadhguru experimented with several meditators, but to no avail. 'He tried many people,' recalls Bharathi, 'but it wasn't the same. I knew it too. I could feel it.'

That was when Sadhguru had to take a tough decision. There was clearly no time to put a third person through the preparations that Vijji had been through. He had no option but to play the role himself. 'Time was short,' he says. 'There were many people around me in high states of energy, but that energy wasn't supported by adequate mental maturity. For the consecration, we needed fluid energies; this loosens the fixed boundaries of who you are. If you make a person's energies fluid, he's a nuclear bomb. But the moment you do this, people start doing immature things. They start getting protective of their privacy; they want to preserve aspects of their personality. You need a certain distance between yourself and your thought processes if this is to work. I had many good people around me, energy-wise, but their minds still weren't sufficiently mature. This is still the case.'

Playing Vijji's role meant the recreating of her energy body with his own. This reconstruction was so detailed and complete that that many felt Vijji's presence tangibly around the ashram in the months that followed. 'Many times it appeared to me as if Vijji was there back with us,' confirms Bharathi. 'We could smell the familiar smell of her body and her energies. But this required a tremendous amount of energy and was not done unless absolutely necessary. Sitting at Sadhguru's feet, nothing seemed impossible anymore.'

But the process took its toll. After five hours of the consecration process, Sadhguru would emerge drained and exhausted. Managing two bodies with a single person's energy severely depleted his resources. 'In eleven months' time, I aged about twenty-five to thirty years,' he says. 'I became old and sick. All kinds of bizarre diseases were there in my body. When they took my blood test in the United States, they couldn't believe it . . . The results were as if I had some devastating diseases in my body.'

As her master pulled out the stops to complete the process, Bharathi was put through a strenuous personal regimen. 'I did lots of sadhana. We didn't want the energy we'd built up to dissipate. At the same time, I could see his health failing. I could see the decline. He'd be weak and fragile. His kidneys were failing, his liver was damaged. There were lumps on his body. His blood was a mess.'

The photographs of Sadhguru at the time reveal a man who seemed suddenly to have aged drastically. 'In those eighteen months, I lost almost twenty to twenty-five years of my life. You wouldn't believe it. This moment I would be perfectly okay, but if you saw me after one hour, I'd be absolutely, medically sick. Not just tired. Medically ill. You could take my blood samples and see everything is wrong. They'd tell me I had cancer. After fifteen days, they'd check and everything would be okay with me. If I sat here for one process, huge lumps would appear in my body. After another three hours, you'd see they had gone. It was unbelievable. I don't expect you to believe it.'

What sustained him through the physical storms and ravages was the knowledge that he would shed the body as soon as the consecration was complete. For his disciples, this was a tense and difficult time. They knew that something momentous was being attempted, but they also knew their time with their master was short-lived. They watched, silent and ineffectual, as his physical condition deteriorated rapidly before their eyes. 'The deterioration showed in his day-to-day work, his reflexes and body as a whole,' says Bharathi. 'Many times, I stood by helplessly, not knowing what to do when I found him in physically broken condition after certain sessions. At times, in very difficult situations, it appeared to me that Sadhguru might just have to leave to make the Dhyanalinga happen. But these thoughts never stayed very long. Something within me told me we'd have both Sadhguru and the Dhyanalinga with us.'

But something darker and more disquieting was to consume the attention of the residents of the ashram and the citizens of Coimbatore for the next eighteen months—something that shook the fledgling Isha movement to its very foundations. For Vijji's departure was followed by another crisis, but this time of a magnitude that none had expected. It was the long-awaited social backlash, but far more savage and vindictive than they had ever imagined. Venkanna Babu had warned of this eventuality months ago. Sadhguru had envisaged it too. 'I instinctively knew it was coming, but I didn't know how and from where it would come.'

And yet, at the time of Vijji's mahasamadhi, he had already put his finger on the likely source of the problem. 'Here we live in a different atmosphere,' he had told his meditators. 'For us this situation is very natural. But in the society outside, many doubts and suspicions will be cast upon the whole event.'

He was right. It started when the uncle of a meditator swooped down on the ashram with a bunch of hired goons and took the young man home by force. The story was a familiar one: the meditator wanted to live in the ashram; his family was opposed to it. This was in itself not an entirely a new occurrence. Families of new meditators and initiates were often hostile. There was one strand of Coimbatore society that remained suspicious of Sadhguru's rapidly-mushrooming flock of disciples. Sadhguru had urged the family to discuss things with the meditator (a 32-year-old, and not an impressionable minor by any means) and take him home with his consent. But when neither pleas nor threats seemed to work, the family had decided to resort to force.

The meditator revealed later that he was kept drugged for several months and had no clue of what was happening around him. When the meditator's resolve to relocate to the ashram showed no sign of wavering, the family decided to go on the offensive. The uncle proceeded to instigate a smear campaign by provoking a family that was at the time at its most vulnerable. Vijji's parents, still shell-shocked and bewildered by their daughter's sudden death, were swayed by the man's outrage. Events followed in rapid succession. A police complaint was filed against Sadhguru for the murder of his wife. (Ironically, it was eight months after her death.) Allegations of dowry harassment were flung around freely. The campaign was swift and precisely aimed. The media joined the fray, a Tamil magazine spearheading the movement.

Sadhguru was abroad at the time of the fracas. But he was surely in no doubt that the darkest hour in Isha's history had arrived. The carefully cultivated goodwill of the past decade seemed to have been gutted in a matter of weeks. He says the slander mattered little to him personally. And yet, the accusation of a dowry-related murder could not have left undisturbed a fiercely independent man who had just lost his wife. But the focus of his attention had to be one-pointed. And he knew that for the Dhyanalinga, there could not have been a more ill-timed setback. 'We were expecting trouble, but it came in every way, from every direction. We spent a year or eighteen months in daily crisis management. When I say crisis, I mean that these people had created a situation that was threatening our very existence.'

The time to act had arrived. Sadhguru says he returned to the ashram and set about doing what he is usually reluctant to do. 'I settled them,' he says cryptically. Coming from a yogi whose sphere of operations includes the invisible and esoteric, one is not quite sure what that means. But it does suggest that he intervened in the plot in a way he wouldn't ever have allowed himself under normal circumstances. In a short span of time, the vested interests that had been instrumental in whipping up rage and revenge found themselves dealing with unexpected havoc in their own lives. The complaint was withdrawn and the campaign died a natural death. 'And today, less than ten years later', says Sadhguru with a gleam of quiet amusement in his eyes, 'we are a phenomenon in Tamil Nadu. Our work is concentrated in this state, and the vested interests have fallen silent.'

While his knowledge of the human psyche is profound, Sadhguru still marvels at certain acts of compulsion of which the human species is capable. Jealousy, he says, is an emotion he has never understood. It is an emotion that he has attracted a great deal over several lifetimes. His air of self-possession and his refusal to care for the opinions of others have no doubt been responsible for people's fear and resentment. But despite having confronted the emotion at close quarters, he says it makes little sense to him. 'It's unfamiliar to me. I've never understood how people can allow jealousy to become so big in their lives that they're willing to actually destroy someone because of it.'

At the same time, there is nothing tame about the Isha spiritual process and he knows that it can be deeply threatening to those who prefer a cosier weekend spirituality. 'I am not into the solace-peddling business which will always find appreciation in the world,' he admits. 'When you talk about a fundamental transformation in life, you will find enormous resistance in the world. If you want to do hardcore spirituality, it is very difficult because it demands a drastic transformation in a human being. This spirituality is not for people who just want to feel good; it is for people who are truly seeking to move from one dimension of life to another. So usually, this never grows popular. Why many great masters never started large movements is because when you start a large movement, you have to compromise. When Shiva was around, or when Agastya was around, this kind of spiritual transformation happened in a big way. But in the last few thousand years, such a hardcore spiritual process hasn't really gathered momentum. Somehow with dedication, cunning and an enormous amount of grace, we have achieved even this much. But it is very rare.'

For the Isha volunteers, this was a particularly testing time. Many of them had flouted parental wishes and renounced familial obligations to commit themselves full-time to the movement. But now their life choices were being held up to scathing public scrutiny. Allegations of cultism, dissolute lifestyles and chemically-induced 'trips' (fostered by the hallucinogenic magic gruel!) hung thickly in the air. 'That's when we decided to turn aggressive,' remembers Raja. 'We had focused so far on sadhana and individual growth. Now we decided to make a concerted effort to reach out and share what we had. We wanted to touch people, to let them know what we were, what we had to offer, what we were capable of. The alternative was to be wiped out.'

For Raja and his Isha teachers, the regimen that unfolded was more gruelling than it had ever been. Three classes of three hours each were held each day by a single teacher. A class was held within every sixty kilometres, covering the entire state of Tamil Nadu. Each programme was for thirteen days. 'There were nights we got only two to three hours of sleep. And sometimes when there were four programmes in immediate succession, I wouldn't come home for two months at a time.'

Facing the suspicion of the participants wasn't easy. There would always be two in a class of fifty who had questions, recalls Raja. They were all the predictable questions about the credentials of the guru and about the rumours of drugs and sex. It was tricky. 'Two disruptive participants could mean that you could lose the rest of the forty-eight,' he says. But the teachers remained determinedly calm, answering the questions with an unstudied sincerity.

The commitment of the teachers commanded respect. They lived with the families of local meditators, and their integrity was increasingly apparent to all those who interacted closely with them. Word gradually spread that the Isha volunteers—whether you agreed with them or not—actually walked the talk. 'It took us three to four years,' says Raja, 'but the tide of opinion did change.'

He recounts how in a dramatic volte-face, one of the Tamil journalists involved in the Isha sting operation actually did the programme many years later. 'It was in 2001 in Chennai. I was told that he was among the participants. I was conscious of his presence, but I paid no particular attention to him. At the end of the thirteen-day programme when I was about to board the train from Chennai, he came up to me, apologized profusely and wept. There were tears in my eyes too. Today, years later, we're actually good friends.'

It was at this time that Sadhguru and two hundred meditators undertook a trip to the Someshwar temple in Cuddappah. The group was aware that the temple had special associations for their guru. Sri Palani Swami had been there. Sadhguru Sri Brahma had spent the last months of his life there. This visit obviously had a deep significance. It was also intended, many of them guessed, to help dissolve some of the blocks that had plagued them on their journey. 'Sadhguru took a golden snake as an offering for the linga at the temple,' says Maa Karpoori. There was a particularly warm and generous local reception in Cuddappah, she recalls, and Sadhguru was treated with much reverence.

But now another challenge presented itself. As Sadhguru approached the sanctum, the temple priests turned suddenly hostile. A slew of objections poured forth. 'They said I wasn't a Brahmin, they started talking about caste, gotram, kulam, all kinds of things, and said the linga would be finished if I entered,' says Sadhguru. 'The temple trustee tried to reason with them. He said, look, this man's brought an offering, he has a past association with this temple, let him in. He even said my gotram was 'Shiva'! But the Brahmins were adamant. So there was this huge argument going on. I was just watching this, a smile on my lips. On the one hand, here was this temple and all that it meant to me, and on the other hand, there were these guys who work for a salary, telling me I didn't have the right to be there. I was just standing there, watching this whole farce, but I wasn't relenting either. And that's when Bharathi suddenly got mad. She just tore into those guys like a bull terrier.'

Maa Karpoori remembers the scene with clarity. 'I've never seen Bharathi like that before. She told the priests that if they didn't allow it, they would have to face the consequences. She was actually saying, you'd better let him in now, or else.' Whether it was in sheer shock or terror, no one knew, but the priests took to their heels. The temple was available to Sadhguru and the meditators for three energy-saturated days. 'We did our own pooja to Shiva,' says Sadhguru. 'And the situation was just explosive. Those were different days. I won't set fire to a situation like that ever again.'

Eventually, the outraged priests were mollified and coaxed back into the temple by assurances from the trustee and the Collector that they would be compensated for the many elaborate purification rituals they had had to undergo to restore the 'defiled' linga. While the group remembers that Bharathi's outburst had turned the tide of events that day, Sadhguru recalls the moment for other reasons as well. 'It was one big joke,' he says, 'because that's exactly what happened a lifetime ago when Sadhguru Sri Brahma and Vibhuthi walked into that temple. The Brahmins had objections then as well. But when these two men—who were just burning with intensity at that time—turned and looked at them, they simply scooted. And here was Bharathi doing the same thing all over again. I had a big laugh. It was the same situation replaying itself!'

Whether it was the visit to the Someshwar temple that did it, no one was quite sure. But Maa Karpoori recalls that the obstacles on the path to the Dhyanalinga seemed considerably reduced. 'On a personal level, our spiritual journeys seemed easier as well. Things began to return to normal.'

Looking back on the first fraught decade of the Isha movement, Sadhguru says, 'In the first ten years of our existence, people threw stones at us. But people only throw stones because they unconsciously know your fruit is valuable. Bearing fruit,' he adds, 'is more significant than being stoned. Because fruit attracts birds, animals and people, not just stones. Also, those who throw stones don't cut you down. They only do what they know best—throw stones.' After a pause, he remarks, 'And if you drop your fruit willingly, stones can be minimized.'

Perhaps that made the difference. A dream that aimed to make the fruit of self-transformation available to all could be deferred, but not destroyed. Having waited centuries to reach its fruition, it could now no longer be denied. The stones were part of the journey. But they meant little to a tree that sought to share its fruit, not withhold it. None was to be discriminated against; everyone was called, everyone chosen. The Dhyanalinga's hour seemed to have come.

Those who witnessed the process knew they would never be the same again. 'It was exhilarating,' says a brahmacharini, her eyes still radiant at the memory. 'The energy levels were unimaginable. We didn't know what was going on, but we knew we were participating in something enormous.'

Perhaps the enormity of the accomplishment is only evident when one hears Sadhguru speak of earlier attempts that had ended in disaster and futility. In addition to his own concerted efforts for three lifetimes, an even more dramatic and poignant story is that of the Dhyanalinga-that-almost-was over a thousand years ago. It happened in Bhojpur, near the city of Bhopal in Madhya Pradesh. Fourteen people—seven men and seven women—were prepared for several years for the ambitious project. However, in the final stages of the consecration, just the evening before its completion, in an incident eerily reminiscent of Vijji's mahasamadhi centuries later, one of the women left her body. 'The temptation to leave the body is so much,' said Sadhguru, 'because here, you have an opportunity where your contact with the body is so minimal, that with little effort, you can leave it. It's absolute dissolution.' There was also probably the euphoria of seeing the end in sight. Her efforts slackened, her focus wavered at the last moment, and the goal was missed.

The yogi in charge of the process was disheartened, but did not give up. 'He decided to play the roles of the man and the woman, using his ida and pingala, which is an enormous stress on the system. He played this role and would have completed the process because what was left was very little,' says Sadhguru. Here again, the scenario was uncannily similar to the Isha counterpart. The end seemed almost in sight, when a local invasion occurred. In the ensuing combat, the yogi's left foot was severed. Now his ida was rendered useless, and the entire process came to a grinding halt once again.

The situation was desperate. Another woman was trained rapidly for the task. It was now decided that there was no alternative but for yogi and the woman to shed their bodies and merge with the linga, thereby completing the consecration. Another disciple was put in charge of locking the chakras once they were energized. This was a vital function; without the locking of the chakras, the energies would dissipate.

The scene was set. The participants were fully prepared. And then came the fall. The disciple in charge of locking the chakras was overwhelmed by the situation. To remain unperturbed and vigilant while his beloved guru left his body wasn't easy. 'The situation was too overwhelming,' says Sadhguru. 'Your guru, your master, your life and breath, dropped his body. You were sitting there watching. It was too much. He couldn't do it.'

And so the disciple hesitated, the chakras weren't locked in time and the linga remained tragically misshapen. 'Immediately,' says Sadhguru, 'the linga cracked vertically through . . . The whole project was abandoned. It was ninety-five per cent done, but it is a painful form. Two people gave their lives. They had done so much work on it, but it had not been fulfilled . . . The linga remains just like that, very powerful, but slightly distorted. The energy is not receding. If it had been consecrated with mantras, it would have receded by now. A thousand years is a lot of time, but it hasn't receded. The linga stayed there, incomplete, broken.'

When Sadhguru visited Bhojpur with Bharathi at the time of the Dhyanalinga consecration, he said he felt an excruciating pain in his spine when he was about eight kilometres away from the shrine. When they reached the temple, there was a sudden numbness in his left foot, making it difficult for him to get out of the car. For Bharathi, the linga became such a powerful experience that she almost left her body. She thought she had been sitting in meditation for a few minutes, but three quarters of an hour passed, and Sadhguru had to work intensively on her ajna chakra to bring her back. Both had experienced the tragic history of the crippled, incomplete linga in their own ways.

To rectify the Bhojpur linga, said Sadhguru, would have been more demanding than creating a new one. Besides, the shrine was in the hands of the Archaeological Society, and objections to any kind of intervention were likely to be considerable. Sadhguru and Bharathi left the place, uneasily aware that the story of the distorted Bhojpur linga could repeat itself yet again. It almost had.

Sadhguru's description of the Dhyanalinga consecration has to be the most lucid account in recorded history of an incredibly arcane yogic process.

The aim, he says, was to create an energy form with seven chakras operating at their optimal condition. In the human being, the chakras are held in place by karmic substance. For the Dhyanalinga, however, he was clear that no karmic substance was to be used. And yet, without it, the chakras could not be locked, which would mean the entire form would dissipate. The challenge, therefore, was to lock the chakras with pranic substance from all three participants, although this lacked the tenacity of its karmic counterpart.

'If the other two involved in the consecration were with me, I would have locked it with so much more ease,' he said later. 'Since one person was missing, creating three threads of prana without karmic substance from three different bodies, taking and weaving it and tying it up in a certain way, was difficult. . . . The three threads were actual nadis or channels, one from Bharathi, one of mine, and another also from me created in Vijji's flavour. Taking nadis out of one's system could be damaging. It had to be done with care, and elaborate precautions were taken to limit the damage.'

Since his own role was 'multifunctional' it was not easy to avoid damage altogether. The result was that his body was besieged by a host of major and minor physiological difficulties. 'I didn't want to play the music,' he says lightly. 'Initially, I thought there would be fourteen people and I would do the conducting. But here, I ended up playing the music anyway. And after Vijji left, I had to play double music. Two instruments at the same time.'

Other than the actual act of binding the energies which entailed some amount of karma, there was no individual karma invested in the Dhyanalinga. Each chakra was established and locked, moving systematically from top to bottom. Although the process of locking the higher chakras was more subtle, the more physically demanding were the lower chakras. 'The main challenge,' said Sadhguru, 'was the lower chakras, the swadhishtana and the muladhara. Since one person was missing, the process took an enormous toll on my body, weakening my *swadhishtana* and muladhara. It was like I could leave at any moment.'

Raja accompanied him to Chennai where he chose a specific kind of stone for the linga. Much of the actual consecration work, however, was done with a copper rod that Sadhguru kept in his home. 'We bystanders didn't know what was happening,' says Raja. 'We would be sitting around, watching him as he sat and supervised the establishment of the stone linga. But when the process started—which was usually late in the night—we would know right away. The energies would be so high.' He describes his own role as that of a 'soldier' at the time, a trusted lieutenant, not quite sure of what was going on, but ready to guard his guru's mission with his life against a hostile world.

Even Bharathi who was actively involved in the process had no clue to the technicalities involved. All she could see was that she was in the charge of a bravura conductor. 'I remember the *lingarandhram*—the copper tube containing mercury, energized with qualities of the seven chakras—which was to be inserted into the lingam and sealed before the completion of the consecration. This was a major step. Each chakra was energized with intense sadhanas lasting many days at a time. We were oblivious of day and night, as these indescribable energy situations occurred. The energies leaped and danced in my chakras and nadis, tearing my body apart. After energizing each chakra, Sadhguru would share the process with the brahmacharis and inmates in the ashram. These satsanghs were pure ecstasy. Many days of sadhana was shared with them in a short time.'

For those who witnessed the process, perhaps the most intriguing was the locking of the throat chakra or *vishuddhi* (known as the seat of power). Vishuddhi meditation, Sadhguru explained, is rarely encouraged, since it can create needlessly powerful people who lack the responsibility and balance to handle that power. Since time was short and the vishuddhi needed to be energized, Sadhguru eventually decided to use a one-time yogi for the process. 'He was a disembodied being, looking for dissolution,' he said later. 'It was late night on an amavasya and over five hundred or six hundred people were witness to this process . . . We used a coconut in a certain way to trap this being and do what we had to do. He was being willingly trapped, not unwillingly. Once he realized how he was going to be used, he was more than willing . . . So we actually trapped this yogi, made him into pure energy and put him in the vishuddhi chakra. He became a part of the Dhyanalinga.'

A brahmachari recalls that once the coconut was set in a certain place, a little snake crawled up to it right away. Sadhguru explained later that snakes are invariably attracted to a certain kind of energy. It wasn't surprising. The energy that night, recalls the brahmachari, was tremendously powerful.

When questioned about the dubious ethics of trapping a disembodied being, Sadhguru's reply was crisp: 'As long as something is serving the purpose of liberating people, everything is okay with me. Just about anything is okay with me. I'm not somebody who is coming from some value structure, or ethics or morals. What I'm saying may sound dangerous to you, but anybody who is on the path, this is how they are.'

He did add, however, that the whole process of sadhana for any spiritual aspirant is about moving away from a limited set of identifications, physical, mental and cultural. In this process of individual dissolution, the aim is to terminate entirely the notion of a separate. 'There was a "he" when we caught him, but when we put him there, when the vishuddhi was consecrated, there was no "he" any more. It's like somebody was making a pot, a mud pot. The pot was done, but not burnt yet. I took it and again made it into mud, and then again made a linga out of it. That's how it is. You're thinking in terms of, "Oh! That person, is he trapped there? What will happen to him? What about his evolution?" There is no "him" anymore. I just made him into the Dhyanalinga. It's just that we used this energy which was going around like a fool, as an individual. I destroyed his individuality and merged him into the Dhyanalinga. So there is no "him" really, but that's how far language can go.' And what happened to the karma of the disembodied being? How did he dispense with that? Did he take it upon himself? Sadhguru's reply was brief: 'Where else to take it?'

The most distinctive feature of the entire consecration process was the fact that it entailed no rituals or mantras. This, Sadhguru has often pointed out, is a characteristic of the south Indian tradition of yoga, associated with the sage, Agastya. 'Everything here is done with pure energy. We don't care to use mantras. We simply use energy. Simply direct force, as it is. This is a completely different path and attitude. It's a different dimension altogether.'

Perhaps what awed those who witnessed the entire Dhyanalinga process most of all was Sadhguru's unwavering clarity. Despite the constantly changing variables, he never seemed flustered or agitated. And he showed no doubt or hesitation during what was clearly a highly sophisticated and elaborate process. It was a knowledge evidently born of the simple act of his guru's, touching his forehead with his staff two lifetimes ago. 'Whenever the need to know any dimension of life presented itself, at that moment, the answers were always there within me,' he says. 'Life has always been like that for me.' As he said recently at a satsangh, 'The only thing I'm really good at is making the air around me crackle with energy. I'm not a great teacher, you know. I do that only because without blabbering all the time it doesn't work in the world.' Those around at the time confirm that what they witnessed was indeed someone with a masterly understanding of atmospherics. The crackle was very much in evidence.

Another dramatic moment was when Sadhguru created a hairline crack in the stone structure of the linga with a simple clap of his hands. Those who watched were stupefied. They were well aware that the linga was made of the highest-density granite in Asia ('of over four-thousand-two-hundred-plus units'). But by this stage, such casual miracles seemed almost common around their guru. He explained it to them later. 'During the process of consecration, just in case I shed the body, we knew locking the energies would be a huge problem. We didn't want such a problem to happen . . . I have always kept it as a possibility that in case the consecration didn't happen as planned, the only way for me would be to merge into it and somebody else would have to lock the energies; it would have been very much possible that the linga, unable to contain the energies, would have opened up. As a safeguard against this, I effected a minute vertical crack in the linga.'

There are those who remember how he fell after the mammoth challenge of locking the swadhishtana. It seemed like the end had actually arrived. 'As each chakra was locked, I felt it distinctly in my energy body,' says Bharathi. 'When it came to the swadhishtana—the most difficult part of the process—as his physical body was very unstable, Sadhguru was in utmost physical pain.'

Sadhguru was not unaware of the risks involved. 'There was every possibility that I could lose my body at that moment. I kept everything ready, to a point where I had arranged legal adoption for my daughter, the ashram—how it should be maintained, everything was written down. I had the samadhi ready and I just asked them to park a vehicle outside. If I totally lost the body, that was fine; they knew how to handle it. But suppose I became incapacitated and I needed to be brought in, then the vehicle—an old Tata Sierra—would be there.'

Raja recalls that the brahmacharis were asked to sit facing the linga, while the householder disciples were instructed to sit facing away from it. After a few meditation processes, Sadhguru climbed on to the base of the linga. He told the assembly to close their eyes. They complied with bated breath. A little while later, they heard a thud. When they opened their eyes, they found that he had fallen. The consecration was complete. But Sadhguru, it seemed, had paid the price.

The residents watched as a team of brahmacharis carried his inert body out to the car. He seemed alive, but only just. They knew it was touch-and-go. For three days, he couldn't stand. He had lost his speech and communicated only through notes. 'My body was broken beyond repair,' he says. 'Medically, I was definitely beyond repair. To start again was almost like trying to create a new life.'

Bharathi did her best to restore his broken system, but there seemed little hope. He remained silent, frail, unresponsive. At one point, at her wits' end, she asked him, 'Shall we hit the road?' It was a shot in the dark. If there was anything that could rekindle his zest for life, it was possibly his wanderlust. 'That's when a gleam returned to his eyes,' she recalls with a smile.

Why did a man, who had been prepared for the last seventeen years to leave at the age of forty-two, consider staying back? 'Not because I was desperate to live,' he quips. 'The more deadly serious a situation is, the more of a joke it is for me. When Bharathi asked me this question, I thought, okay, let's see, just for fun, if I can put my body together again. Later, it became a challenge.'

Despite his playful take on it, the decision to put the body mechanism together was no doubt motivated by the fact that he now had a group of disciples for whom 'Sadhguru' meant their very life breath. He was also probably aware that his continued presence would make the social acceptance of the Dhyanalinga that much easier. 'There was the social consideration,' he acknowledges. 'But above all, there were too many people around me who were at the point where I needed to push them and see them through. These people have stood by me in more ways than others understand. They stood like solid rocks. There have been many who have been willing to stand by me, emotionally. I'm not belittling that. But you don't interfere with death for emotion. These people were different. They were willing to live or die for me. They became so involved on an energy level that they didn't know the difference between me and them. They have mingled and merged with my very life process. My staying behind was for them, to see them through to the end.'

While his health is considerably better now, he says he is still on 'life support'. 'I used my energy so excessively in the consecration process it caused serious damage to my system. My energy system was badly mutilated. Since then I have had to be dependent on certain people for my survival. I am still not hundred per cent recovered. Right now I can seem to be in perfect health and in the next moment I can be seriously ill—medically ill. But I have largely come out of that phase.'

He is often asked about the prominent snake-shaped copper ring he wears around his right ankle. 'It's a shackle,' he has explained. 'It keeps me anchored to the body. Restructuring this body has been a huge challenge. Many people literally gave me their lives so I could I use their energies to slowly restructure this body. I'm almost eighty per cent all right now, and I could fix the rest if I had just a one month break. But I haven't had the time. Since my health keeps fluctuating, people around me have been very afraid that I will leave. So they've put this shackle on me. It stabilizes the system; it doesn't allow me to accidentally slip off.'

And what does it feel like to live your life on constant 'life support', I once asked him. 'It means tremendous freedom,' he chuckled. 'But it also means enslavement.' He added, 'The day I remove it you know I have very little time left. Within forty days, I'll be gone.'

The Dhyanalinga consecration was completed on 23 June 1999. The shrine was opened to the public in November that year. The last year of the millennium marked the end of what must surely have been the darkest chapter in Sadhguru's life, and in the youthful history of Isha. While the mood at Isha was exultant, the world was as yet unaware—and much of it continues to be—of the historic significance of the achievement. Sadhguru has often said it will take a couple of generations for the world to fully appreciate just what the Dhyanalinga signifies for humanity at large.

And what exactly is the Dhyanalinga anyway? It remains an enigma even to those whose lives have been profoundly touched and changed by it. What every viewer sees is the imposing black stone ellipsoid. But Sadhguru has often said that the form can be dispensed with altogether; the only reason for its existence is that most people need a visual focus for their meditation. The actual linga is essentially a fully functional subtle body, entirely invisible, with all the seven chakras operating optimally. Its function is essentially meditative. While the well-known Jyotirlingas in various parts of the country address specific issues of health and material wellbeing, the Dhyanalinga is the only linga that addresses all the seven chakras simultaneously. Sitting in its precincts is equivalent to sitting in the presence of a live master—one who showers his grace unceasingly, freely, impartially, silently. 'It is the highest manifestation of the Divine,' says Sadhguru. 'It is like a living person, with all the seven chakras manifesting themselves at their peak. It is alive.'

There have been certain recurrent questions about the linga that Sadhguru answers patiently each time, as if he were negotiating them for the very first time. Why the Shivalinga form, is a frequently asked question. He replies that sitting in the intensely charged space of the Dhyanalinga requires no specific belief system. 'You don't need any belief. You just need to be open, that's all. Let's say a non-believer drives a car. Will it go? This is what you're asking. Or if a non-believer sits here, will this light still make him see? The question is of that nature. It doesn't matter if you're a believer or a non-believer. The moment you turn on the light, it is there for everybody. Believers don't get any extra light.'

He explains that the first primordial energy form is in the shape of an ellipsoid, and the final energy form before dissolution assumes the same shape. Hence, the linga. Indian culture came up with the figure of Shiva to represent this deep understanding of the existential dimension. Shiva, as Sadhguru reiterates, means 'that which is not'—an unsettling concept, and an even more threatening reality, if one allows it into one's life. 'We use Shiva because it's very difficult to get attached to him. In Tamil Nadu, you have been told that you shouldn't keep Shiva's form in your house . . . If he's there, his very form is such that all your attachments will get destroyed, and you don't want that. You have made big investments in your attachments, and even though they have brought you very painful dividends, you still can't throw them away. These investments may melt away without you knowing what's happening. That's why they told you to banish Shiva from your house.'

The Dhyanalinga, then, is a project that virtually ensnares the most radical, the most terrifying and luminous divinity in the Indian spiritual pantheon. It is a project that turns 'that which is not' into 'that which is'—to the extent that such a paradox is possible. 'The Dhyanalinga,' says Sadhguru, 'is almost like trapping Shiva and keeping him fixed there. He doesn't come down easily. He demands his own price, in his own way. It is a very deep science.'

Is the linga a phallic symbol? This is another routine query. Sadhguru explains that the linga is a combination of the feminine and the masculine—one of the most unique and audacious ideas conceived by Eastern spiritual culture. 'When the masculine and the feminine meet at the lowest level, it is known as sex. When the same masculine and feminine meet at the highest level, it signifies the union of Shiva and Shakti. In this conjunction, Shiva is *rupa* or form; Shakti is *shoonya*, or nothingness. Shiva is Purusha; Shakti is Prakriti, the undifferentiated force of nature. The linga–yoni as the manifestation of the Shiva–Shakti principle demonstrates the persistence of all pairs of opposites. Nothing can exist in this universe without its opposite or contrast.'

At the recent consecration of the Linga Bhairavi, he explained this further. 'The Dhyanalinga temple is like a womb; it's the yoni of the Devi. When we say yoni, we mean the womb, which was seen as a sacred space that all of us have to inhabit in the most crucial part of our making. . . . Always, wherever Shakti and Shiva, the linga and yoni, are presented, it is the inside of the womb that you're seeing, not the outside. So when you enter the Dhyanalinga space, you are actually inside the womb.'

And why are there no rituals in the Dhyanalinga? Is it to cater to the sensitivities of those who visit it as a multi-religious shrine? Sadhguru explains that rituals are traditionally a means to renew the energy of a sacred space. But the Dhyanalinga has been consecrated through pure energy work and requires no maintenance or revival. 'Performing any ritual would be absolutely meaningless because Dhyanalinga has gone through *prana pratishtha*. It is in the highest level of intensity that any form can be. If you intensify the energy beyond this, it's bound to become formless. . . . It is a complete system of energy. . . . In a space like this, rituals would be of no significance and out of place.'

The south Indian tradition of yoga, associated with the sage Agastya, is evidently known to specialize in this kind of *pranic* mastery. 'Among the *saptarishis*—the seven sages, all direct disciples of Shiva, who started the process of yoga—Agastya is the ultimate in Kriya yoga,' Sadhguru has said. 'If you say "kriya", it means Agastya; that's how it is. Anything and everything that can be done on the level of human energy has been talked about and done by this man in a miraculous way. So everybody who comes from the tradition of Kriya naturally claims their lineage to Agastya—not to claim a pedigree, but just to express gratitude to a man who was so much larger than life. He is supposed to have lived for four thousand years. We don't know about that. But he definitely must have lived for an extraordinary length of time to have made the spiritual process a reality for every human habitation on the Deccan plateau. He brought yoga into people's lives without a label, without a format, just as a simple everyday life process. The southern part of India is still enjoying the benefits of his work.'

Sadhguru terms the shrine with quiet authorial pride as an 'engineering marvel'. 'The elliptical dome that we built to house the Dhyanalinga is seventy-six feet in diameter and thirty-thee feet high. No steel, no cement and no concrete have been used; just brick and mud mortar, stabilized with lime, sand, alum and herbal additives. It's the only structure like this on the planet right now. The simple technology used in this is that all the bricks are trying to fall down at the same time, but the way the dome is made, they can never fall. The nature of the design ensures a life of at least five thousand years for the dome. And it is built upon a sand foundation which ensures that it's unaffected by seismological movement.'

What is not immediately apparent to the visitor is the extent to which the average anonymous Isha volunteer has contributed to the actual making of the temple. 'Even the building of the temple was undertaken by volunteers,' says Maa Karpoori. 'There were two hundred and fifty labourers and one thousand of us, and we worked on that structure brick by brick.' They knew that each of those bricks had been hard earned for they had been equally involved in the preceding months of spirited fund-raising. Sadhguru's cause had become their cause and all his disciples were determined to do their bit, right down to the little schoolgirl who decided to hoard and contribute her bus fare by walking home from school for a month. Maa Karpoori remembers trudging with her fellow-volunteers Bharathi and Lalitha day after day, from one shop in Coimbatore to another, attempting to convince a spectrum of puzzled, suspicious and indifferent tradesman—from grocers to teashop owners—of the importance of the cause, and feeling a surge of triumph with every five rupees that came their way.

As an energy form, the Dhyanalinga is what Sadhguru has famously called 'a concoction of pure awareness and madness'. 'In the future, if one day, some realized beings who are very sensitive come to that place and access the Dhyanalinga the way it really is, they will go crazy with laughter . . . It is so dead serious on one level, and done so playfully on another level . . . It was built like that, slowly. It is life-sustaining in one way. It is life-taking in another way.'

For those who have experienced Sadhguru as a master, there seems little difference between him and the Dhyanalinga. One is made of flesh and blood and the other of stone, but the quality of the presence—the 'subtle body', in yogic terms—feels essentially the same. What is the difference, is another question that Sadhguru is often asked. None whatsoever, replies Sadhguru candidly. 'It's just that I still have the problems of eating and sleeping. He doesn't. . . . Another difference is that I took three lifetimes to become like this. He managed it in three years. . . . Above all, once you have a physical body, people's ability to experience what is beyond that will decrease. Because once you see a person, you start judging—seeing what's right and wrong about him, what appeals to you or doesn't. All these judgements will take away your ability to experience that being . . . When you sit in front of a living guru, you have many problems, judgements, likes and dislikes, because invariably you end up looking at his personality. . . . With the Dhyanalinga, you don't have these problems, because he doesn't carry a physical or mental body. If you experience him once, every time you sit, you will look up to him reverentially. If he had a physical body, one moment you would be looking up to him reverentially, the next moment you would be judging him and condemning him for something . . . So he has come with extra advantages!'

And that remains an ironic but accurate summation of the distinction. For those who have known and been touched by him, however, the master with the physical body—however overbearing, however challenging—remains a distinct improvement on the master endowed with only a subtle one. The Dhyanalinga is a transformational experience. But Isha meditators would probably consider their generation the lucky one: they have had the privilege of knowing two gurus in the same lifetime.

'Time to Graze the Valleys of Life'
The Master, the Man and his Message

Perhaps the most fascinating aspect of my interaction with Sadhguru has been the chance to watch him segue on a moment-to-moment basis between the individual and the archetype, man and guru. In our arguments, I've often believed he is contradictory. But on another level, it's those very contradictions that I find baffling and intriguing all at once.

There's his ability in the middle of an intense discussion to suddenly stop and draw my attention to the limpid quality of sunlight, or the trajectory of a feather falling through the clear afternoon air. We were talking about his past lives once when he suddenly paused, mid-sentence, to point out the presence of an owl, half-concealed, on the tree in his garden. I was on a long walk with him when he talked about nirvikalpa samadhi, cracked a risqué joke, drew my attention to the changing colours of the clouds, and had an animated exchange with a tribal woman about the nature of her work—all in the course of a few minutes. On another occasion, we were in his car, having an argument, when he informed me—casually, mid-sentence—that there were two snakes in the rear of the car. My capacity for argument turned suddenly feeble.

Time with him has a curiously elastic quality. Many find that even a five-minute meeting with him can be packed with intensely rewarding insights, and an extraordinary amount of material for future reflection. As he once remarked, 'I utter every word consciously, not habitually. That gives the words power. Spirituality is about not allowing anything to happen to you unconsciously.' It is this heightened level of aliveness that he brings to each moment which makes every meeting with him such an unpredictable business. You could go in, prepared to discuss a book—as I once did—and find yourself doing a meditation practice instead.

In an Isha yoga course, particularly the higher-level Samyama programme, he is very much the master—remote, majestic, formidable. At a public lecture or at a satsangh, he is a charismatic speaker, fluent, witty, gentle and yet unsparing in his replies to the many questions that come his way. In an informal one-on-one exchange, he can be mischievous, teasing, irrepressibly boyish. This capacity to swing from a moment of gravitas to a lively involvement with the minutiae of life is one of his most endearing traits. I've found myself wondering if the man avidly discussing caller tunes on his cell phone with a brahmachari could be the same man who called me out of the blue when I was going through a particularly difficult time in Mumbai and told me to 'stop doing this' to myself. Or who rang me up one afternoon after I had spent a sleepless night worrying about something and asked me why I had 'pulled' him out of his game of golf. I've wondered if the speed demon who whizzes by in his car like some adolescent on a velocity trip can be the same man who called up to gently condole with me after the death of my cat (a gesture that silenced my doubts once and for all about whether I had found my guru).

He can be so emphatic, so dead-certain about things that he often runs the risk of sounding arrogant. He has acknowledged his dictatorial streak. 'Yes, I am authoritarian because I don't listen to anybody. About the simple things of life, if even a child speaks I will listen with great respect. But when it comes to certain aspects of life it doesn't matter if even God comes, I will not listen to him because I know better. This sounds absolutely egoistic and stupid. . . . But what can I do? It's true. You quote the scripture to me; I will dismiss it. You bring your pundit to me; I will dismiss him. You wake Buddha up from his grave and bring him here; I'll still dismiss him unless he agrees with me. So I am a total authoritarian when it comes to the fundamentals of life.'

And just when the autocratic manner begins to rile you, he can disarm you with moments of extraordinary humility. At a recent satsangh, he remarked, 'I hesitate to say this because the word will spread and spoil my reputation! But I am a devotee. You'll say, "Oh come on, Sadhguru, you a devotee? You're arrogant!" I can tell you, it takes a lot to look arrogant. Then you'll ask, "What kind of devotee are you? Oh, you must be Shiva's devotee." No. Shiva is my partner. I'm not his devotee. This will be very hard for you to digest, but I am devoted to you . . . Devotion does not mean that I have to bow down to you or touch your feet or sing your praises. In every way I live for you; that's devotion. I took this very birth to make this happen for you and that's devotion.'

He has often been known to declare, 'To all those who are willing, I am available to you in ways that are beyond your logical understanding.' Almost every disciple has experienced this compassionate availability in one way or the other.

Manju's father, who had never seen Sadhguru, insisted (when he was shown a photograph) that it was 'this very man with a turban' who had sat by his bedside for much of the night when he was critically ill in a Mumbai hospital. Manju's father recovered rapidly after that night.

Shahnaz remembers the time she found a lump in her breast. Deeply distressed, she mentioned it to Sadhguru at the first possible opportunity. His reply was predictably flippant: 'What do you need a breast for?' But the next day when he called her, he seemed to know the exact whereabouts of the lump. He advised her to switch to a raw food diet while he located a reliable specialist for her in Coimbatore. The days passed. He was travelling and Shahnaz didn't hear from him. And yet, she found the lump growing smaller by the day until it disappeared altogether. A fortnight later, after his return, he summoned her to him. 'There's no need for a doctor now,' he said simply.

An American doctor with a heart problem was keen on joining the meditators on their annual trip to the Himalayas, but knew that it was impossible. In addition to her cardiac condition, she needed tracheal support and was unable to function without a ventilator. When she told Sadhguru of her desire, he told her to go on the trip. A couple of days after she reached the ashram, she was taken off the ventilator. After a week at the ashram, she joined the rest of the group on the Himalayan sojourn. She was not only able to walk the entire distance of eighty kilometres but even braved an altitude of over 14,000 feet.

Another meditator who was advised immediate knee surgery by specialists in the US because of a torn cartilage was told by Sadhguru to 'leave your leg and come'. He was in excruciating pain and demurred. But eventually he decided to throw caution to the winds. He joined the Himalayan trekkers, walking all eighty kilometres of the distance over twelve days, and was even able to keep pace with Sadhguru. 'So I went about telling everybody, this man tried to con me for ten thousand dollars,' Sadhguru joked later. 'Now you can call it a miracle if you want. I just call it another kind of science, that's all. . . . This life energy in you created your whole body. These bones, this flesh, this heart, this kidney and everything, can't it create a piece of cartilage? If your energies are kept in full flow and proper balance, they are definitely capable of recreating the physical.'

A dramatic case in point was the time Sadhguru healed himself in 2007, confounding a spectrum of doctors across continents and flouting the dire predictions of his medical reports. It started when he found himself running a temperature during a programme in Los Angeles in April. The fever persisted during a programme in London (despite multiple doses of Paracetamol). It continued unabated even after his return to India, on his subsequent trip to Australia and well after his return to a hectic television-shooting schedule in the ashram. Never having cancelled an engagement in the past two and a half decades, Sadhguru had no intention of doing it now. 'My temperature was constantly 104 and 105 degrees. I was sweating so profusely that I had to change my clothes every two hours. One day in the ashram, I thought my brain was going to burst; I just checked my temperature and found it was 107. I just went and stood under a cold shower, as I was, clothes, turban and all,' he laughs. 'Later a US doctor told me it was the smartest thing I could have done at the time. With that kind of fever, I could have gone at any moment.'

His ailment baffled the medics everywhere. He found himself treated for two kinds of malaria, dengue and typhoid. He travelled back to the US and in the middle of a talk in California, a concerned member of the audience—a doctor who noticed his acute perspiration and obviously weakened condition—raised his hand and informed him that he ought to be in 'the Emergency Room right now'. Sadhguru agreed. He was rushed to hospital immediately, and spent the next couple of weeks connected to a mobile intravenous port with which he continued with his frantic spate of engagements in California, Atlanta, Tennessee and North Carolina. 'With this kind of travel schedule, not being able to eat and with seven weeks of constant temperature, I almost collapsed by the time I got to North Carolina. I could feel my system breaking down, and I was hyperventilating. The doctor there termed my blood report "esoteric",' he chuckles, 'and I was sent to Atlanta and then to a New York hospital. By then I had gone through sixteen blood tests and four MRIs, and I had built a thick file of all kinds of weird blood reports.'

By the time he reached New York, he discovered a swelling in his neck and was in excruciating pain. 'Must be all the people around me,' he joked about his mysterious 'pain in the neck,' refusing to allow the gravity of the situation to dampen his ability to pick out a joke where there was one. 'The doctors said that most probably my lymph nodes had become malignant. All my systems were slowly receding and collapsing, and they didn't know why. They said, "You may have two weeks," and it was better to inform my family. I had to be operated for my lymph nodes and was on my way to an anaesthesia test. I was sitting in the waiting room when I just looked at my system. I knew that something was wrong that they couldn't handle even with surgery. The problem was elsewhere. And I thought, "I don't want this guy to be cutting me open and looking into me." I said, "Enough. I want to go home." That's the good thing about the US: if you tell the doctors you want to go home, they cannot force you to stay. They took all kinds of signatures from me to indemnify themselves and said, it's up to you.'

He stayed in a New York apartment for a few days, 'worked' on himself and had soon employed his own brand of esoteric wisdom to defy the collective wisdom of all the esoteric medical reports! 'In two weeks' time, I recovered,' he says. 'In less than twenty-five days, I was in Kailash. I drove all the way from Kathmandu to Kailash and then trekked up.' Despite the dramatic turnaround, he was still visibly weak at the time. But he was, after all, in the vicinity of what he has often termed 'the greatest mystical library in the planet'. 'I looked at Kailash and there was so much information waiting to be accessed. I just got in touch with one aspect of that information and used it on myself in a certain way. After that, I just bounced back. I looked younger, and even my voice had changed—just in about an hour's time. The results were visible. There were almost two hundred people who witnessed this.'

As a listener, it is only possible to listen to such a story in silence. Aware of the demands it makes on your credulity, Sadhguru is quick to treat it lightly. 'It's the kind of story that even your great grandmother would be embarrassed to narrate because it's too far-fetched.' But why did you allow yourself to be subjected to this medical rigmarole before intervening and setting yourself right, I ask. 'Because my schedule didn't allow it; I was travelling all the time and this needed time. And in any case, once I place myself in a doctor's hands, I don't tell him what to do. But once the doctors termed it a fever of unknown origin and said it was untreatable, I knew I had to look inward and fix this.'

And before you can begin to train the spotlight on his capacity to access and decode the mystical archives of the world, he has adroitly turned the focus of the conversation to the wonders of Kailash. 'There are really no words to describe it. If there is any absolutely "unreasonable" place on the planet, it's this mountain, this outcrop of black granite. It's beyond reason. It's beyond anything in your wildest imagination. Right from my childhood I have made trips to many places, wild and wonderful places. But I have to say that in terms of possibility and the sheer immensity of what it has to offer, I have never seen any thing like Kailash until now. If there is some physical form in this existence that could be seen as nearest to what we refer to as Shiva, this is it.'

While he has evidently reached out to many in situations of medical distress, Sadhguru has always been careful to avoid the vulgar appellation of 'miracle-monger'. Ever the rationalist, he demystifies the process of healing by describing it simply as 'knowing how to work with the energy body'. 'I don't want this termed a miracle, because that means you are dismissing a whole science, a whole wisdom, a whole understanding of life. Let us make a distinction between an infectious disease and a chronic disease. Infections you have to be careful and protect yourself against. But when it comes to a chronic ailment, whatever it may be, the root cause is always in the energy body. Once it is disturbed, the mental body and the physical body are bound to be disturbed. If people are willing to do a certain amount of sadhana to balance and activate their pranamayakosha, or energy body, they can definitely be free of all chronic ailments.'

Compassion he has in abundance, but insiders know that this is not unmixed with ruthlessness. There is a well-known dictum in Isha circles: when you get close to Sadhguru, beware! 'He started as a friend, later turned guru, and that's when I realized what a tough taskmaster he is,' says Maa Karpoori. 'When he put me through a period of silence (which eventually lasted three years), I felt his presence enter me like a cyclone. It felt like I wasn't in control any more. It was like being flooded, choked, wrung inside out. It felt like death. But after months passed, I felt so completely cleansed that I realized that he had actually brought me to the other shore. My brahmacharya has been a battlefield, full of conflict. But when I finally took sanyas after my three years of silence, I was at ease. Today I feel I am near home finally. My house is lit. I can see it and I am content.' She believes the master's brutal compassion—which compelled her to drop her friendship with him only to discover a far deeper connection—had a vital role to play in her spiritual journey.

Shopping for a guru is obviously a vulgar business and Sadhguru has often talked of its dangers. But how is a seeker to know he has stumbled upon the real thing? What are the signs? 'You don't look for your guru,' says Sadhguru firmly. 'You just deepen the longing in you. When you know the true pain of ignorance, a guru will happen. You don't have to look. If you sit with him, everything in you should feel threatened. You want to run away, but there is something in you which keeps on pulling you towards him—you can assume then that he is your guru. If you feel very comfortable around him, he is not. Maybe he's your friend; maybe he's a good man; maybe you should seek his blessings. But good intentions and a pleasant nature do not make a guru. A guru's intention is to awaken you, not to put you to sleep. He is somebody who disturbs all kinds of conclusions that you have drawn. He is not a solace-peddler. He is there to assist you towards your liberation.'

He concedes, however, that it is possible for even the serious seeker to be sidetracked by the neon blaze and the seductive packaging at the display window. 'Yes, it can be a hard job because sometimes the counterfeit looks better than the real thing. First, you must see, what is it doing to you? Maybe you saw God. So what the hell? What has it done to you? What is the transformation it has produced? That is the question. Has it in some way transformed you into a more joyful, more intense human being? Have you become a better life? Better, not in terms of morality, but just as life, have you taken a step within you? If it is so, even if the guru is fake, what's the problem? Use him. What is he demanding out of you? If he's demanding your money or your property, it is not worth it. You must go only to that place where they are demanding your life.'

That sounds alarming, of course, but then Sadhguru's style isn't known to be reassuringly avuncular. 'Someone who is demanding your life, what can he do with it anyway?' he asks. 'But I demand life, nothing less than that. If you give it, *I* don't get it. But the fact that you are willing to give away your life—that changes you. It transforms your life. If these gurus are demanding anything less than your life, you can conclude they are a fake. But first see if it is bringing about some transformation. Even the conman initially gives you a free sample. Later on maybe he tries to con you. But initially when you go to a mall, they give you a free sample of something. Eat it and come. What's your problem? They won't poison you—poisoning is not good for future sales anyway.'

What has always fascinated me about Sadhguru is his breathtaking sweep of knowledge about varied aspects of life and the effortless manner in which he seems to garner it. Whether it is his impromptu discourses on the mysteries of Mount Kailash and Lake Manasarovar, his ability to talk at length about the consecration processes in various sacred spaces, or the intimate details he seems to have about each person's inner life, the limits of his knowledge seem truly astounding. How does he know? And how much does he really know? I have often tried to find out. 'When you simply look without the dimension of your logical thinking, there is no time and space,' he once said. 'If you simply know how to look, everything is right here all the time. This moment is eternity; here is everywhere.'

He is always at pains to sound casual about it, but for all his attempts at demystification, he clearly cannot explain the process beyond a point. 'As there is an Internet, there is also an "inner-net",' he told me once. 'All the work that has ever been done in the realm of consciousness, lives. And it can be accessed.'

While there is no conventional logic here, there is clearly an intrinsic logic at work. 'All mystical knowledge comes from that dimension of existence that people are unable to access with their sense organs,' he says. 'This is a completely different dimension of perception. What you can see, hear, smell, taste and touch is limited. There are types of information that cannot be perceived by your eyes, ears, nose, tongue and skin. Think of a camera or a periscope which offer you other ways of seeing. Think of ultrasonic or subsonic sound; your ears cannot hear it, but it exists. Likewise, the X-ray is able to see what your eyes cannot see. Similarly with mystical knowledge; it is just about accessing a type of information that cannot be perceived by the sense organs. It's another dimension of perception. Metaphorically, it is termed the third eye.'

I once happened to ask him how he replenished his vast and ever-expanding repertoire of jokes. He always seems to have a new one for each satsangh. Nothing prepared me for his reply. 'Oh, I just pick them out of the heads of fellow-passengers on those endless flights,' he said breezily. He looked at me for a moment as if assessing my potential, and then shook his head regretfully. 'No jokes in there!'

Apparently, it's on transcontinental flights that he also 'picks out' ideas from the brains of unwary passengers that come in handy at global seminars! 'At some medical conferences, people were quite amazed at my grasp of modern medicine,' he chuckles, happily unapologetic about these acts of intellectual burglary.

Once during a car ride, I asked him if there was anything he immediately 'knew' about his surroundings. 'If I am passing a place that is consecrated in a certain way, I would know right away,' he answered. 'And if someone is recently dead around here, I would know that as well.'

It apparently happened in the case of his mother's death in 1989. Susheela was diagnosed with lupus and was rapidly heading towards renal failure. It was clear that the end was near. 'I'd fixed a class in Hyderabad. My dad was mad at me because I didn't cancel it. The whole family was totally freaked out,' says Sadhguru. He spoke to his mother before he left, however, and she urged him to continue with his work. 'I knew she would go soon, but I had fixed the schedule. In these last twenty-six years, I have never cancelled a single programme. So though I knew she was dying, I told her, "See, I have to go." She said, yes, go ahead.'

Sadhguru remembers conducting the introductory class on a Friday. 'There were many enrolments for that programme. In the middle of the enrolments, I suddenly knew. I announced that I wouldn't be able to conduct the programme, and rescheduled it fifteen days later. I took my bike and started riding back. I stopped at a telephone booth in Penukonda at one in the morning and called home. I said I knew what had happened, and that I was on my way back. I reached at six thirty in the morning well in time for the funeral in the afternoon.'

His ability to judge people's personalities and read their thoughts is well known, as many have discovered (often to their discomfiture). There are also other trivial, but useful, details he is able to gauge. A notoriously fast driver, many of the risks he takes on the roads are evidently due to his ability to assess which roads to take, which to avoid, the possible hurdles or impasses along the way. A German meditator remembers a breakneck drive from Germany to France in which Sadhguru intuitively sensed where all the traffic jams were likely to occur. 'He avoided them all effortlessly, and reached his destination in record time,' he says, still awed.

While his knowledge of the phenomenal world is startling, he often offers sudden glimpses into the work he does on other realms. He once recounted a strange anecdote about the time he was walking in the Appalachian Mountains. The year was 2000. 'I was alone and walking through the woods. I suddenly saw a man standing still, frozen in a position of despair and shame. He was in the regalia of someone from a Native American tribe. He was just there, immobile, and I saw he had been standing like that for close to three hundred years.'

Although he had no physical body any more, the man's energies remained frozen and unchanged. Intrigued, Sadhguru retrieved the man's biography. 'If anyone is in extreme movement or extreme stillness, I immediately involve myself. The in-between level of movement doesn't mean anything. But people in extreme movement or stillness—I can't stay away from them, because that's my playground. I found that this man had the responsibility of protecting his elder brother, who was a kind of leader in the community. He held his elder brother in great esteem, and considered it a great privilege to walk by his side and protect him. Then a situation happened by which they were both deceived and the elder brother was killed. So now this man just stood there, in absolute failure and distress. These were such extreme emotions that he had stood that way for over three hundred years! Obviously, the body fell back to earth, but the rest of him just stood there as he was at that moment. It was time he moved on, I thought. Too much time in shame and defeat is not good. So I just helped him to move on from that situation.' As always, his own intervention is presented with a casual air. Sadhguru is one of those storytellers who knows how to throw away a line, how not to press a point. It frequently leaves his listeners in agonies of suspense. But that is clearly the idea.

His schedule grows more frantic by the year. His speaking engagements and programmes take him out of the country for several months in a year. When he is at the ashram, he seldom sleeps more than three to four hours every night. When asked about his personal regimen, he replies that his daily 'maintenance practice' is one surya namaskar (over which, he says, he takes forty minutes) and 'twenty seconds of yoga'. 'That's what it takes to unleash the Creator within,' he says enigmatically.

I ask whether gurus are exempt from rigorous sadhana. He laughs. 'Kriya is neither about the body nor the breath. You don't know

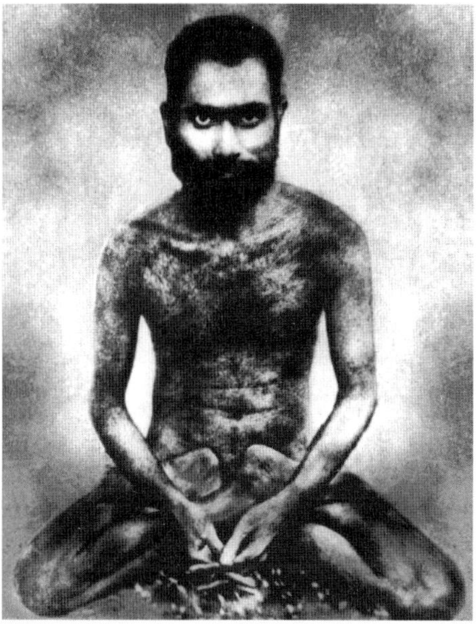

'I will be back.' Another time, same mission.
Sadhguru Sri Brahma

With his siblings. Jaggi is seated.

The legendary 90-day Wholeness Programme at which Sadhguru 'unleashed the guru' within him.

'We suddenly saw him just the way he was . . . no longer a person, just an ageless presence.'

In the mountain cave frequented by Sadhguru Sri Brahma.

The two who acted as one. Vijji and Bharathi.

The art of turning a piece of rock into the divine:
the alchemist at work

'Her name was Vijaya Kumari which means "victory's daughter".
The highest possible victory for any being became hers.'

The dream of lifetimes: the Dhyanalinga was consecrated on 23 June 1999.

The compassionate embrace:
Sadhguru with a prisoner on death row.

'The only thing I'm really good at is making the air around me crackle with energy.' The high-voltage touch.

As much at home in rural Tamil Nadu as at a high-powered world conference: Sadhguru with the villagers of Dhanikandi.

'Have lived the peaks too long/ Time to graze the valleys of life...' The guru at a game of golf.

The seasoned trekker contemplates Kanti Sarovar, where 'the world's first-ever yoga programme' (supposedly conducted by none other than Shiva, the Adi Yogi) took place.

'This one will graze human beings' predicted an astrologer at his birth. Sadhguru at a maha-satsangh.

Hell on wheels: The 'fast-forward guru'.

Sadhguru with Bugsy and Leela.

On an off-road adventure.

Plotting the divine: Sadhguru scheming the birth
of the goddess Linga Bhairavi.

A primal bond.

Birthing the Devi: a goddess comes to life.

how to activate the energy body, so you use your breath and body as a means. But if you don't have that limitation, you can activate it in a very short time.'

There has never been anything of the puritan about him and that extends to his dietary habits as well. He eats twice a day: at around eleven thirty in the morning and seven thirty in the evening. He is vegetarian, his meal invariably comprising more vegetables than cereals. When vegetarian options are not easily available, particularly when travelling, he is known to relish seafood. This omnivorous diet once perturbed a group of vegan Americans to such an extent that they cancelled their proposed visit to the ashram. The sanyasi with whom they were in touch urged them to come and experience the place at first hand before drawing any conclusions, but they were apparently too shaken by the disclosure.

His love of life extends to other areas as well. He enjoys cooking when he finds the time, and claims to make the meanest *masala dosa* on the planet. His daughter vouches for this (and adds with cheerful extravagance that he is 'the best cook in the whole world'). His passion for sport is legendary. When he is in the ashram, he is often to be seen joining the inmates for a fierce evening game of volleyball. Golf is a sport to which he is now staunchly committed. Whenever he is able to steal a couple of days off from his gruelling schedule, he escapes for a golfing weekend. Then there is his fondness for music (he learns classical music whenever he finds the time, and his teacher describes him as an eager, if somewhat distracted, pupil), as well as an affinity for poetry (he has often talked wistfully of his years in poultry farming when he had hours to devote to his own writing).

His love of fast cars endures and remains his most well-documented passion. 'I can be with people at a satsangh, get intoxicated with them, cry with them. The next moment, I could get into my car and become the most aggressive driver ever,' he once told me with pride when discussing how a yogi manages the ida and the pingala—the lunar and the solar elements—within himself.

'On the Kailash trip this time, I was the most aggressive driver in China. The Tibetan drivers believe only they can do the drive. But what most people do in three days, I did in one day flat. When I reached and got out of my car, those Tibetan drivers stubbed out their cigarettes and stood in front of me with folded hands. Not because I'm a guru or anything. Just because of my driving! When you know how to manage both aspects within yourself, you can be meditative or outgoing—as the situation demands.'

He laughed and added, 'Shiva drew two lines for everyone and only one line for me.' Why such partisanship, I demanded. 'Oh, because he's my partner, he's biased,' he chuckled and then explained: 'For an enlightened being, the sun and moon don't exist. The duality is no more. The two lines merge into one.'

Apparently, one who can conduct the solar and the lunar elements in balance has the freedom to respond to situations as he desires. 'Once in a way when I have the time, I cry,' he says. 'I'm capable of that. I can move from laughter to tears in just one moment. This is because what is happening within is conscious. There is enough in this world to cry for; and there is enough in this world to laugh for, isn't there? If I want, I can look at a flower and cry. I can look at a bird or cloud and cry. I 'm not emotionally crippled; I'm capable of emotion but I can choose not to be compelled by situations.'

Despite his capacity for dry understatement and caustic wit, no one who knows Sadhguru can be in any doubt of the existence of that emotional side. As an ashram resident observes, 'I guess we've all been touched in some way by that tenderness and vulnerability which is what Sadhguru is all about. He is quite simply the kindest person we've known. That's what keeps us going through the difficult moments.'

At the close of almost each of his *mahasatsanghs*, he is invariably in tears. Are those tears of love or compassion, I once asked him. His reply was simple and unhesitating: 'Of intensity and inclusiveness.'

At the recent consecration of the Linga Bhairavi temple, Sadhguru's tears flowed freely. He admitted that it was the energy of the goddess as well as the tremendous devotion of the five thousand meditators present that overwhelmed him. 'I am jammed from two sides,' he said wryly. 'The power of the Devi is just blasting me out. So if I look this way I cry; and if I look the other way, I cry.'

He admitted that no one who saw him on the street would consider him a sentimental man. 'But to know life in its full range, one needs to be not just a man and not just a woman. To be a total man if need be, to be a total woman if need be, to be a child if need be, to be a demon if need be, and to be divine if need be—this is the possibility that human consciousness has come with. This is the possibility that every human being should know.'

His openness to people and situations often evokes a protective impulse in those who know him well. There are some who express a sotto voce concern that Sadhguru's spirit of inclusiveness is at times indiscriminate, verging sometimes on naïveté. 'Shiva is called Bholenath, isn't he?' a meditator once asked me. Her implication was clear: Sadhguru was perhaps just a bit too trusting for his own good.

Sadhguru himself seems to treat his good-intentioned protectors with an amused and affectionate indulgence. Recently, he offered an interesting perspective on the disarming insouciance with which he seems to live his life. 'I live a life which is completely unguarded,' he said. 'Just about anybody can deceive me. It's very easy. Not because I lack the intelligence to guard myself, but simply because what I have cannot be stolen. If anyone could take it, I would be very glad! It is just that you cannot deceive me and ever think of living well. That's not going to happen. This is not a threat or a curse. It is just the way of life. You cannot spit at the sky and hope you will not receive the shower of your own spittle.'

When a sprightly journalist once asked him what he would do if he ever met a terrorist, he replied, 'First of all, I don't identify someone as a terrorist; I see everybody as a possible terrorist. If you provoke them sufficiently, everybody is a possible terrorist. But if someone who has been involved in terrorist activity comes to me, I'll probably embrace him. That never fails to work—if he feels some pleasantness within himself, if his anger and hatred recede for some time, he's no more a terror for anybody.' So far the reply was within the acceptable limits of 'guruspeak'. But then Sadhguru being Sadhguru couldn't resist adding, 'But if I happen to meet the man when he's in action, I'll kill him!' The journalist looked shocked. 'You would actually kill?' Sadhguru retorted, 'What would you have me do if the guy is spraying bullets around the place? Say "Asataoma sadgamaya"?'

And that is, of course, a typically Sadhguru response. Nothing—not even non-violence—is a creed. He can be compassion itself with a person in need; the next moment, he can be as brutal as the situation, in his estimation, demands. 'You just have to be aware and do what's needed. That's intelligence, that's awareness, that's life. You don't need a moral structure when you have consciousness. That has always been the strength of this culture: whenever there were dips in consciousness, the right kind of people came, worked on it and raised it. Now unfortunately we're reaching a dangerous point where there is neither morality nor consciousness. If we don't do something urgent to raise human consciousness we will fall into the horrible trap of morality. And if we don't do either we'll fall into total chaos.'

He has evidently changed a great deal over the years. Bharathi says Sadhguru is no longer the man she once knew. 'He was like a fireball when I first met him. Now he's much mellower. That almost-physical fierceness about his presence has gone.' Maa Karpoori agrees. 'He sometimes seems so smart, polished and clever now that I find it difficult to connect him to the raw, intense man I once knew. But I'm not socially connected to him anymore—only the inner connection remains—so the behavioural change affects me less.'

Sadhguru confirms that he has indeed allowed a certain transition to occur. 'After the consecration, I wrote a poem in which I said:

"Have lived the peaks too long/ Time to graze the valleys of life . . ." That's what I'm doing now—grazing the valleys. Earlier I was like a suicide bomber. There was only one thing I wanted to do, and I didn't give a damn if the body broke up after that. My energies were wired towards one purpose and nothing else. That was to get all these people to go in one direction—people at different levels of resistance, misunderstanding and entanglement in life. It needed a certain forcefulness. But after the Dhyanalinga happened, I allowed myself to change my whole personality.'

While many have been disconcerted over the years by his mercurial changes of role and demeanour, Sadhguru has remained consistent about one pragmatic aim: the importance of doing what needs to be done. As his disciples have watched him oscillate between the dispassionate sage who created the Dhyanalinga and the ecstatic devotee who consecrated the Linga Bhairavi, there have been periodic plaintive voices that demand to know what exactly Sadhguru and 'Brand Isha' are about. Sadhguru laughs it off. 'I'm not really concerned about any brand. My only concern is about where you stand. Are you standing facing the possibility or are you standing facing something else? My effort is just to see that you stand facing the doorway. Even in unawareness if you're facing the right direction, it's okay. Even if you sleepwalk, it's okay; you still cross. I think the essential brand has always been no nonsense—just doing what works. That's my brand. It doesn't matter whether it's written in the scriptures or not. It works—that was my brand, and that's still the brand. Maybe,' he admits with a chuckle, 'it's getting a little more complex nowadays . . .'

The urgency is there certainly, but is probably more muted. There is no doubt that he is more accessible now, socially more savvy. His playing field is global, and he is not unaware of how to play the game in diverse and often tricky situations. Heading a yoga centre with multiple social outreach projects obviously takes large quantities of tact, guile and ruthlessness, an ability to woo corporate honchos, appease government officials and steer his organization clear of troubled political waters. And he is evidently equal to the task.

It is a facet of him that I still grapple with internally. I see the need for some measure of political awareness for a man running a spiritual community of this magnitude. I am also aware that if he had not engaged in some measure of outreach, many—including me—would be unaware of his existence. But I remain more comfortable with the idea of the low-profile unassuming spiritual master—the kind who shuns the limelight, who leads a quiet life of meditation, is available to a small band of committed meditators, offers advice on spiritual matters and refrains from commenting on other issues. And instead, here is the irrepressible, exuberant man who has become my guru, playing chief guest at the Indian Premier League matches in South Africa, gallivanting to high-end economic conferences, wearing exquisite silk shawls, making public comments on questions ranging from feminism to homosexuality.

'Making your peace with the establishment?' I once asked him, perhaps a little saucily, on the eve of his departure for the World Economic Forum. 'It's not about making peace,' he replied patiently. 'It's about putting your resources and energies where it produces maximum results. You don't plant your seed in a stone; you plant it in fertile soil. The point is, till now, the spiritual people have always been copping out. Copping out is not a contribution. If people are your business, society is your business, corruption is also your business, and the World Economic Forum is also your business. In this country, gurus always went to the kings, not because they were looking for money, but because if you give some advice to that guy, people will live well. If you went and worked in isolation in a village, the king could raze your work in a day. To do just spiritual work, I don't need any publicity and advertising. For the first fifteen years, I never held any press meet, never appeared on television; there were no banners or posters. But my hands were always full. I don't need publicity for spiritual work, but for the social part of my work, I need lots of publicity.'

So, are the days of the reclusive loincloth-clad sage over, I persisted. Today's gurus seem to be a highflying and jet-setting bunch, clued in to market demands; isn't something lost in this transition? He laughed. 'Yogis were always highflying!' he retorted. 'They were always flamboyant people. Mystics were colourful people too. Only people who are striving to become that way are loincloth-clad! Because of sadhana they're like that. I've also been a loincloth person. It takes a while to realize that a loincloth will not make you spiritual. But everybody has to go through the loincloth stage to know that. Only if you go through this loincloth phase of your life, you are able to wear this [he pointed to his own attire] with a different air. This never sticks to you because the loincloth oils you so well.'

On another occasion, he said, 'Let's say I could get George Bush to meditate. Now the decisions he makes will be qualitatively different. If he'd meditated before Iraq, he'd have acted differently. I'm not putting Bush above a tribal woman in any way. There's no difference between the two. But instead of creating suffering and then trying to relieve it, we can try to avoid active suffering by reaching out to those in positions of social responsibility.'

Whether it is a politician or a pop star, he claims to have no compunctions about imparting yoga to either. But isn't there a fine line between being inclusive and indiscriminate, I once asked. What about the dangers of this turning into a Page Three spiritual jamboree? 'I'll never compromise on what I'm doing,' he replied. 'But I would definitely do a programme for a Michael Jackson if he were willing to make it happen to everybody. The logic is simple. I want to teach meditation to everybody. Now just the fact that someone like Michael Jackson is meditating will make millions of fans close their eyes and emulate him. That's not a bad thing. He'd be more effective than me. I have no issue with that. Looks commercial to you? I just think it's sensible.'

A long-standing volunteer points out that, while he has faced his share of 'to stay or to leave' dilemmas during his journey with Isha, what has kept him on course is the fact that it is fundamentally a fair organization. Brahminism, feudalism and nepotism in all their varied avatars have been consciously kept at bay. 'Unlike other spiritual organizations in this country, caste, creed and family are not the controlling factors,' he says. 'If there are family members who want to play a part, they have to grow with the organization like anyone else. They aren't given any preferential treatment. In so many other spiritual outfits in India, the spiritual process is taught by dedicated volunteers, but when it comes to money and property, it is closely monopolized by the guru's family. What does that say about these set-ups?'

Although Sadhguru relishes the public role, he prefers to remain, as he says, 'consciously uncivilized'. So while his manner is seldom socially inappropriate, he isn't the world's smartest diplomat either. The first year that he attended the World Economic Forum, he apparently floored several participants with his incisive speech and clear thinking. But then, by his own admission, he 'blew it' in the evening by joining in the dancing—and doing it with much gusto. Such behaviour clearly wasn't an acceptable part of the 'holy man' package deal and it left some industrialists and their wives quite shaken! 'They were all getting drunk and hesitating to dance. Because I am always drunk anyway, I just went and started dancing! Some fell in love with the yogi who dances and others couldn't handle it at all!'

'A guru's job is to transmit. Transmission is much more important than teaching. Teaching is only a way of knocking on the door,' Sadhguru once said.

From a man who regards belief as an encumbrance on the path to self-discovery, it is not surprising that there is no doctrinal system that can be described as a 'Sadhguru teaching'. His aim, he says often, is to demolish all accumulated beliefs, not add to the already tottering pyramid of sacred supposition. While the Isha yoga programmes entail a fair amount of discursive input, it soon becomes apparent that the point of the course lies elsewhere.

'I appeal to your logic because that's the only way I can get you to sit with me,' he often says. 'The moment I stop being logical, you will get up and leave. So I'm logical, but only up to a point. If I talk enlightenment, it will only be a tall story as far as you're concerned. And if I unleash myself, you won't come back tomorrow. In any case, the logical mind, by definition, divides everything into at least two. But enlightenment means just one. So you can't talk enlightenment; you can only talk around it.' And he's pretty good at talking around it, judging, if nothing else, by the fact that many of his listeners keep coming back for more. I discovered some time ago that if you're determined to find holes in Sadhguru's logic, it isn't difficult. But finding holes is only for those who look for a bulletproof consistency. Like many mystics before him, Sadhguru can be perverse and paradoxical, but no less compelling for that reason.

What does it mean—really mean—to be a mystic, I once asked him. He replied, 'There were two cows grazing on an English meadow. One said, "What's your opinion on the Mad Cow disease?" The other said, "I don't care a hoot about it. Anyway, I'm a helicopter."

'If a cow realizes that it is a cow, it becomes a celebrity—a holy cow. It's that simple. It's just a question of realization. In India, we've always called mystics "realized" beings. It is not about inventing or discovering something; it's just about realizing who you are. If there is something you do not understand it's mysterious to you. Someone who seems to know what others do not is called a mystic. But the mystic is just someone who has realized what is there. Others don't because they're too self-engrossed to pay any attention to life.'

Then what's so special about that knowledge? What's the big deal about being a cow that realizes its 'bovinity'? 'If you know life, if you know the truth, you know how everything works,' he says. 'If you want love or ecstasy or bliss, it's yours. The deepest human desire is freedom. And that's available too. After the experience I had on Chamundi Hill, time and space started flipping in me. Suddenly what was there was here; what was then was now. I could see everyone's past, present and future at the same time. It was all one grand confusion. But it was also utterly beautiful. I realized then that all human experience is self-created. Though most human beings believe that their experience is created by events around them, I realized that it is hundred per cent self-created. You can make your experience whichever way you want. Just to feel a moment of pleasantness within oneself, how much indignity each human being is going through. Just to experience one moment of completeness, what a circus people are making of their lives. And it will never be enough. There will always be a longing in human beings for something more. This compulsion to go beyond compulsion is a fundamental human need.'

One of Sadhguru's jokes suggests that he holds an opinion of human beings that isn't particularly flattering. 'Two crocodiles met. One was looking nice and fat; another was looking like a year-long Samyama programme [alluding to a 7-day advanced Isha programme where to call the diet frugal would be an understatement]. Now, this lake where they lived was next to the court house.

'The skinny one said, "Oh my friend, how do you manage this? Both of us are eating the same diet, but you look good. Look at me. I am mostly skin and a little bone."

'So the fat one asked, "How do you get your prey?"

'The skinny one said, "I go wait at the parking lot where the lawyers park their cars. And when they are just opening their car doors, I go from beneath the car, grab them, pull them under the car, shake all the shit out of them and eat them."

'The other one said, "That's the mistake. If you shake all the shit out of them, all that's left is a briefcase."

'So if we shake all the karma out of you,' says Sadhguru with a laugh, 'what is left? Nothing much.'

But then this is the central paradox. If the human being is no more than a heap of shit—and a briefcase—what makes the guru spend his entire lifetime spent addressing the human condition? What is the rationale? What is the motivation? 'It's a totally wrong notion that you have to be fired up to do something,' Sadhguru once told me. Total involvement without concern for the result, I asked. 'Do I look uninvolved to you?' he asked, instantly alert to the possibility of perpetuating any pat clichés about *nishkama karma* or dispassionate action. 'I'm very involved. But if it doesn't happen, I won't be broken. With thousands of people, I am very deeply, passionately involved. If you are free from the fear of suffering, would you hesitate to involve yourself in life? Right now you are hesitating simply because of the fear of suffering. If the fear of suffering is taken away, wouldn't you give yourself absolutely to everything around you? Wouldn't you throw yourself into life? Wouldn't you love more rather than less? This ashram, these buildings, whatever we are doing—personally, it doesn't mean a damn thing to me. The moment I say this, people get shocked. Or they ask, "If it doesn't mean anything to you, why are you doing all this?" That is what you need to understand. Though, personally, it doesn't mean a damn thing to me, I am willing to waste my life just doing it. I am not doing anything because it means a lot to me. I do it because it is needed. That's all.'

What appealed to me about Sadhguru's approach from the very start was his refusal to divide faith and reason, spirituality and science, the sacred and the material, into easy binaries. 'You are a spiritual being dabbling with the material, although you think it's the reverse,' he often reiterates. 'Liberation is not my idea; it is the fundamental longing in every form of life. There is a simultaneous need in every human being for containment and expansion, for self-preservation and boundlessness. As the longings of the body, the longings of the being are constantly in play. Physical nature is trying to protect itself, while spiritual nature is trying to expand. But only the body needs protection. Beyond that, the impulse to protect and preserve is imprisonment. Spiritual lust is inborn, but because of excessive teaching, people think it's coming from outside. You cannot stop the longing to be all-inclusive. There is something within a human being that dislikes boundaries. This thirst to be boundless is not created by you; it is just life longing for itself. You can go in instalments, if you like. But the basic longing is to grasp something boundless; until then, this longing won't be settled. It's just sensible to be consciously spiritual, rather than unconsciously spiritual.'

He uses the age-old metaphors of the butterfly emerging from its chrysalis, or of a plant from a seed, to make his point. For all their seeming discontinuities and ruptures, these are natural processes. 'If a seed is not broken, a new sprout will never happen. If you try to save the shield that protects the seed, no new possibility will ever come. The seed goes through the tremendous struggle of losing itself—losing its safety and integrity and becoming vulnerable to every outside force that's around. But without that vulnerability, without the breaking of the shell, life won't sprout.'

What does it take for that life to sprout? Evidently, aligning oneself with the way things are, rather than fighting the inevitability of this process. 'Growth happens anyway. Your only choice is to grow willingly or unwillingly. If you are willing, it's love. If you're not, it's rape.'

Another aspect of Sadhguru's approach that appeals is his refusal to reinforce a deterministic definition of karma. 'If you are willing to make your life process conscious, there is no destiny for you,' he often says. 'Destiny is hundred per cent your creation. Even now that is so. It is just that you are creating it unconsciously. But you can also create it consciously. Yoga is about becoming a master of your destiny to the point that the very process of life, death and birth is in your hands. The very womb you choose to be born in is by choice. As your understanding and perception of life deepens, you will see that everything is in your hands.' He often jokes that most people are willing to take credit for their success but attribute their failures to karma or divine will!

Any deep identification—with scripture, ideology, opinion, philosophy, prejudice or belief—becomes the hurdle on this journey. 'The moment you believe in something,' says Sadhguru, 'a fight with the opposing view is inevitable. You only postpone it with moderate talk. But if you don't mess with the human mind, it's very natural for human beings to seek. Unlike a believer who thinks he knows, a seeker starts from the position, "I don't know". As soon as you become an "I don't know", life begins to happen to you in a huge way.'

Any brand of self-righteousness, in this scheme of things, can be a dangerous snare. 'Because even goodness,' says Sadhguru, 'is a certain level of prejudice. Schoolteachers, followed by parents, have, with all their good intentions, probably perpetrated more collective evil on humanity than Hitler. He simply organized the suffering. If you are seeking liberation, you are not trying to create better karma. You're trying to drop the load of karma altogether. There are teachers who teach good and evil. And there are those, like me, who try to destroy both.'

If he is sceptical of trite belief, he is equally dismissive of glib cynicism. 'Faith,' he said once with epigrammatic precision, 'is mature reason. Atheism is immature reason.' Faith, in this view, has nothing to do with belief. It is merely the fuel that keeps the seeker going on the road that so often seems like a cul-de-sac; the octane that motivates her to take the terrifying plunge into the unknown. Doubt, he acknowledges, can be an important and inevitable step in the journey of faith, but suspicion he terms just 'a disease.' He often tells an apocryphal story from the Buddhist tradition: when a devout believer questioned the Buddha about the existence of God, the great master denied it; when a committed sceptic asked the Buddha the same question, the master affirmed it. The story is obviously meant to remind questioners time and again that truth is necessarily beyond belief and unbelief; that the spiritual journey needs seekers, not believers.

And what exactly is that truth? Like the Buddha before him, Sadhguru remains silent on that one. It is not a destination, a conclusion, or a matter of metaphysical speculation, but a 'living experience' is all he says. It cannot be articulated, only perceived. But there is nothing exclusive about that experience, he reiterates. The possibility of that experience is available to all. It is only the levels of readiness that vary. And these can be worked on. 'This body can be just a bundle of flesh and blood and bones. Or this body can be made into a powerful instrument. When it's come as a pure biological entity, the only forces which work through it are self-preservation and procreation. But if you do a little bit of work with this, you can transform this piece of earth into the divine itself. You can make it into a deity that's worthy of worship. The significance of human nature is that you have the discretion to decide how God should function within you.'

That 'little bit of work' is yoga—the path of inner alchemy by which a biological being transforms itself into a spiritual one. It is the ancient inner science of aligning one's body, mind, emotion and energy, in order to realize one's deepest potential as a human being. 'Where there is just teaching, there will be adoration, there will be worship,' says Sadhguru. 'Only where there is a method, there will be transformation.'

In one conversation, he described the method in a striking image. 'In yoga we don't believe in sudden enlightenment. We make enlightenment into a process. In Zen, they wait for enlightenment to happen like a blossoming flower: a sudden enlightenment. But in yoga, we let it happen gradually, because, if it happens suddenly, you could leave the body. We don't want that to happen. We want you to grow stage by stage. When you come to a certain level of understanding, you move into the next level of realization. There is no suddenness. There is no shock.'

But does that make for less magic? Less romance? Less flamboyance? Less drama? He concedes that it might. 'Perhaps, to some extent, there is less beauty. When a flower blooms suddenly, it is beautiful. But this is a slow process. Flowers will bloom, but in yoga we are not bothered about flowers. Here we are like gardeners. The work seems to be dull. We plant the seed. Our job is only with the soil. We don't bother about the plant. We don't bother about the flowers or fruits. Our hands are always in the soil. We make a system out of gardening. You can't make a science out of blossoming flowers, but you can make a science out of gardening. If you do a good job of your gardening, flowers will come anyway. That is the science of yoga. This is the deepest understanding anywhere. As you go along, there is an endless peeling. You peel one layer after another of understanding. Suppose I plant a hundred thousand trees and only one tree bloomed. Could I call myself a gardener? That one tree would have come even if I were not there, wouldn't it? But if at least fifty thousand bloom, then I could call myself a gardener. This is the difference. And the system works even if I am gone.'

And yet, for all his unromantic muddy-fingered agrarian metaphors, the spirituality that Sadhguru offers is far from cheerless. While it does take dedication, it is less about grit-toothed penance than about celebration. There is nothing life-denying about it. In fact, there are times when his descriptions are positively bacchanalian. 'I am one hundred percent for intoxication. I never drink nor do I take any drug from the outside. I've just learnt a different way of getting drunk; all the time at no cost—no hangover, and at the same time remaining fully balanced. And it is good for your health. Isn't it a better way to drink? Such a shift—from wine to the divine!'

Or yet again: 'You can make the body so pleasurable that just sitting here and breathing is a million times more than anything that you have known. And breathing is on twenty-four hours a day. If breath can become such a pleasure, why should you go for anything else?'

Sadhguru's approach has always stressed involvement rather than detachment, engagement rather than navel-gazing withdrawal. If you are not involved with life, he often says, you are dead. The challenge is to remain involved without getting entangled. 'Our lives become beautiful not because we are perfect. Our lives become beautiful because we put our hearts into what we do. You will never know the beauty of life unless you are deeply involved. At the same time, you cannot enjoy the beauty of involvement if you get attached. If you don't get this subtle distinction, you will suffer.'

The conventional taboos of the spiritual life—lust and lucre—aren't treated with puritanical horror either. 'Sex and money aren't problems. Sex in the body is fine; money in the pocket is fine. It's only a problem when they enter your mind.' It is true that he has initiated a group of brahmacharis and sanyasis at Isha, but he proposes no moral rationale for this. 'Brahmacharya,' he says simply, 'is just a way of organising your energies in such a way that your peace and your joy are all your own. It is a way of giving up your personal agendas and moving from compulsion to choice. If you do it unwillingly it can be absolute torture. But if you do it willingly, it is wonderful. Celibacy, on the other hand, is an ugly word that suggests only the physical aspect of refraining from a natural urge that is in the body and much more in the mind.'

In this whole journey of self-recovery, peace is not the aim, just incidental by-product. 'Peace is not the ultimate attainment of life, but the very foundation of life, the birthright of all human beings.' The logic is simple. The process of becoming inclusive—of seeing the world as part of oneself rather than 'out there'—dissolves the very seed of separateness. 'Anything that you experience as a part of yourself, with that you [can] have no conflict.' Joy is part of it too. And in the process of deepening involvement, one's life becomes an expression of joy, rather than a pursuit of it. 'Happiness has always been an internal phenomenon. The source of your happiness is inside of you. But right now, though it is inside, the switch is in somebody else's hands. The starter button is somewhere else. It is in the stock market, or in your wife's hands, or your children's hands, or the neighbour's hands. You've given it to everybody, except to yourself. The reason why somebody is happy or unhappy is not because of what is happening in their life. Either you know how to manage your inner climate or you don't. That's all.'

If peace and happiness are just a part of the process, is there a larger point to the whole human pilgrimage from unawareness to awareness? What lies at the end? Is there a wider scheme, a cosmic plan, some grand universal design?

None whatsoever, it would seem. The 'point' or 'purpose' or 'denouement' is the last illusion to which the utilitarian mind cussedly cleaves. But even this has to be dropped at the end. 'Divinity does everything purposelessly,' says Sadhguru. 'Purposefulness is an illusion of the mind. The universe is an empty shell where your mind frolics infinitely. And you know this only if you can play. If you're dead serious, you miss what is here, and you miss what is beyond. If you're playful and intense, you'll be receptive to life. If you're too serious, you'll miss it.'

Self-realization, then, Sadhguru reminds us, like so many mystics before him, is less about getting somewhere than about realizing there is nowhere to go. It entails not an acquisition of knowledge, but an unlearning of received wisdom. 'What was limited knowing has become a boundless unknowing. That's wonderful enough for me,' he once remarked. 'Most people are in a condition of part knowledge and part ignorance. But enlightenment is a condition of borderless ignorance. When you really don't know, you're not bound by the limitations of creation. You're blessed with the freedom of the Creator.'

And what's left after that moment of self-knowledge, or after that acknowledgement of 'borderless ignorance'? Judging by the man before us, the answer, it would seem, is aliveness—exuberant, unfettered, roaring aliveness. 'And that aliveness,' says the master, 'is not a small thing. It is the greatest phenomenon on the planet.'

As he once asked a group of listeners with exasperated incredulity, 'The very Creator is within you; what are you thinking about? The very source of creation is throbbing within you. What are you thinking about that is more important than this?'

'The Ball Game' and Beyond

The Master Plan

His life has been led increasingly in the public eye. In the past ten years since the Dhyanalinga, Sadhguru's programmes and speaking engagements have grown at a stupendous rate and the stamped pages on his passport are many and varied. Even while he rubs shoulders with the rich and powerful in the drawing rooms of Delhi and conference rooms in Europe, his grassroots projects—from Action for Rural Rejuvenation to community health services for the regional population—remain close to his heart. His pioneering tree-planting project in Tamil Nadu has turned him into an iconic figure in the state. It won him a national award—the Indira Gandhi Paryavaran Puraskar—recently. And at satsanghs, judging by the response his entry elicits, he is nothing short of a rock star.

He makes light of the effect he has on crowds. 'It's not about feeling a high,' he said when driving away from an amazingly high-voltage satsangh in Kotagiri. 'It's more of a coming home—the sense that one is among people who recognize you for who you really are. It's like a plant finding itself in fertile soil.'

Although his schedule is punishing, the more esoteric dimension of his inner life is still apparently active. He has often said he has initiated into the spiritual path more people he has not met than those he has, suggesting a parallel level of rigorous spiritual activity. Since the Dhyanalinga, there have been other consecrations as well, including the Mahima Hall at the Isha centre in Tennessee, and the Linga Bhairavi in Coimbatore.

Plans and projects seem to mushroom on a daily basis. The Isha Centre in Coimbatore is constantly abuzz with construction activity. The pace of operations bewilders residents and visitors. 'Who can believe we started out here with a small shed and a thatched-roofed meditation hall just fifteen years ago?' asks a sanyasi, looking around in wonder at the enormous Spanda Hall, the Home School and the fast-burgeoning residential quarters around him.

What are Sadhguru's plans for Isha exactly? He seldom addresses that in any detail. But no one doubts that there is an undisclosed master plan. 'Every master plans,' he says enigmatically. 'Gautama Buddha did. I do. Gautama is a guru who knew the consequence of his teaching perfectly well. And I know the consequence of my teaching perfectly well. I am not teaching something impulsively. If I tell you the various aspects of my life, the impossible complications, and with what deadly accuracy I am going at it, you will probably feel I am ruthless—or maybe you will think I am playing God! But there is a consequence to everything, including the teaching, because the teaching is a karma. Especially when you perform spiritual activity, the consequence is there in a very huge way. So what is the consequence that you will create in the next hundred to five hundred years? This is something that every guru has to look at.'

How then does he map the future of Isha? 'In the case of Isha, the process will last in a very active way for six hundred to seven hundred years. After that, it will continue in a lowered way. But the energy part of it is indestructible. Though, right now, the teaching looks like the major part, it is actually just a small part in my life. The real work that I do is not in what I am saying or doing around the world. The real work is in the "eggs" that I lay which can't be destroyed, which will be there forever.' The 'eggs' are apparently certain energy possibilities—the essence of his inner realization—which he says every guru leaves behind for future generations of seekers. This invisible but vibrantly alive bequest is the real legacy of every master.

He once said that he does not plan to leave any single spiritual successor. The Dhyanalinga will be the primary guru, and there will be other 'spiritual possibilities' offered presumably by various people. It is clear that there will be more rules, and that life in the ashram will become more orderly after his time. 'Right now it is a carefully crafted situation of chaos and exuberance, maintained to keep everyone sufficiently confused. There is enough confusion to make you keep seeking, to make you keep wondering, "Is this worthwhile?" But there is never enough confusion to make it totally chaotic. Maintaining this balance is a huge feat. It takes lot of effort. If people become too settled, if it becomes too organized, there will be no spiritual quest and the ashram will become a corporation. But at the same time, how much anarchy can you take?' He sees the change as inevitable. A certain fluidity is possible when there is a live guru, he explains, but after his time, a greater measure of organization will be imperative.

On the one hand, Sadhguru can seem full of childlike excitement about Isha's expansion projects. And yet, as he often reiterates, it matters little to him on another level. 'I do want things to improve. If the necessary opportunity and resources are there, my mission would be to consecrate the planet itself. That's what I would like to do. No man, woman, child, animal or insect should exist in a space that is non-consecrated. Nobody deserves to live or die in barren places. And if we can generate the money, the resources, the technology, there is a great deal that can be done to reduce poverty, hunger, ill health in the world as well. As a human being, I am in the business of making things better and I am willing to strive and stake my life for it. But as a guru, it doesn't really matter to me. If you want to end the game tomorrow, I'm ready to end it. If it works, it's fine. If not, that's fine too. Maybe I'll have tears in my eyes and laughter on my lips. That's how I am most of the time anyway.'

While he has not revealed the time of his own departure, Sadhguru has often said he intends to make sure he chooses the time and date. 'I'll hang on as long as I see thirsty eyes around me. The moment I don't see those any more, I will leave. And I will walk to my grave. Nobody will have to carry me there, I promise you that. If you have sufficient mastery, if you're able to leave your body consciously, you should leave when everything is well. I'm not in a hurry. But I will leave when I'm well. I live quite a spectacular life within myself even if it's not visible to most people. And the way I die will be visibly spectacular—like a signature.'

He refuses to say more. He simply laughs and adds, 'But that's if all the calculations go right. Something else could happen—I may crash my car or something. But that is also going to be spectacular because if I do, I'm going to crash it at very high speed!'

He has declared that he will retain his subtle body for eighty years after his death, for the sake of those disciples who live on after him. When I ask him to explain, he replies quietly, 'When a person leaves his body consciously, it means dissolution. The very fundamentals of an individual are dissolved. But you can delay that, if necessary. When you leave the body, you can ensure a certain kind of discretion is left in you. There is no individual presence that can be seen physically, but you're still around. You can even hold a satsangh, if you like! The transmission will continue; only the speaking will stop.'

In any case, he points out with a twinkle in his eye, there is little proof that he is around even now. An old woman saint named Bengali Maa in Tapovan in the Himalayas once scrutinized his photograph and announced emphatically that he was dead. When dazed meditators reported this to Sadhguru, he merely laughed and said, 'I'm off the record as far as existence is concerned. I may have fooled all of you, but here is a woman who could not be fooled.' On another occasion, when he allowed himself to be subjected to certain tests, scientists measured the gamma waves in his brain and were stupefied. 'They told me, either you're dead or your brain is dead. I said, the latter is too insulting, so I'll settle for the first.'

And what does he intend to achieve by staying back in his subtle body for eighty years after his death? 'Mop-up operations,' he replies briefly. 'To take care of all those people, associated with Isha in one way or the other, who live beyond me. All those people who made the mistake of sitting with me even for a moment.'

And what happens to them, I ask. Do you assure them of liberation? 'Liberation for those who are willing,' he replies. 'At the time of death, most people are willing. And for the rest, a better life next time round, one that hastens their spiritual growth.'

I wonder whether he would ever consider returning to the physical body. There's no room for negotiation on that one. 'Not again. I've done it three times. Once you are realized, you can't imagine how stupid it is to go through the process of embodiment and birth all over again. Being in the body means you have to play with the world. The ball game is inevitable. And once you're realized, that game is like playing with a child. You either do it with disinterest or with love. But there's no challenge. You can't confine certain things in a contained space beyond a point. As it is, I spill over too easily. Never again.'

Postscript

That conversation took place during an early morning walk around the ashram. It is a morning I remember clearly.

Around us the forest explodes in a dozen dialects of green: from dew-stippled watercolours, suffused with light, to the more voluptuous textures of oil painting, from the flamboyant green of parrot-wing to the darker mysteries of jade. The morning air is sharp with expectancy. The mountains stand shadowed, watchful, still swathed in cloud and memories of a chill night wind, not quite awake yet to this festival of sun.

There is nothing remotely somnolent about my walking companion, however. He seems as awake as it is possible to be, his conversation incisive, his mind snapping at ideas, his entire being as alert to movements in the undergrowth and the shade of sunlight as it is to the antics of his dog and the smallest shifts in my psychological weather.

I enjoy these morning walks. It fits the image I've always had of an ideal learning situation. I've often imagined myself walking beside a friend and teacher across fields and along winding wooded lanes, listening, questioning, reflecting. It makes deep sense to me, this meandering mobile tutorial. I like words, laughter, the crackle of argument, but above all, I know I learn best when I am relaxed, when I can absorb an atmosphere, soak in a presence.

We re-enter the ashram gates. Our rounds are punctuated by frequent halts, as he stops to greet individuals and bless groups of meditators. They throng around him, watching him with an intentness and fervour that humbles me even as it scares me. I marvel at the intensity of that trust. And yet, it is not new to me. I have probably looked at him with an equally blazing intensity on occasion. I wonder at how he handles it, how he lives with the responsibility of all those lives invested to his care. He is, as always, completely present with each person he talks to, and yet, the next moment, he strides along, resuming our conversation with ease.

Our interaction does not conclude without an argument. I am uncomfortable with something he has said in the press. He says he was misquoted. But he then spends the next half hour justifying the misquote. Perverse, I think, and yet typical of the man.

I leave the ashram that evening, strangely energized, as always, by the interaction. At the same time, I mutter under my breath about his views with which I cannot bring myself to agree. On the flight, I think about it again. 'Why is this man my guru? For all his seeming liberalism, he can be downright reactionary. I disagree with him on several issues. He's abrasive, impatient, not to mention inconsistent. And it's infuriating not to have time enough to complete an argument.'

A recurrent cycle of thoughts returns. I wonder whether spiritual guides should plunge to this extent into worldly affairs. I wonder whether he isn't getting too big, whether Isha's plans aren't getting too ambitious. I wonder whether he runs the risk, like so many others, of getting corrupted by power. I wonder at his sudden imperiousness and obstinacy. I wonder if I will ever be able to come to terms with his personality or make my peace with his impersonality, his ability to belong to everyone and no one, all at once.

I think about friends back home. I wonder how I can ever explain this anomaly of a guru to them. I visualize their polite inquiring faces when I talk about his clarity, his transmissions of energy, his past lifetimes of spiritual mastery. I imagine their incomprehension at my periodic disappearances to the ashram, their murmured anxieties about my immersion in a new cult, my need to substitute the 'real' world and its 'real' issues with some pathetic midlife recourse to organised spiritual feel-goodism. Will they ever understand what makes this person and this journey so significant in my life? Can I say, in all honesty, that I understand it myself?

I remember what I wrote in my first article on him five years ago: 'Let's say we disbelieve the whole story about his yogic mastery and enlightenment. We're still left with an interesting deal. There's a bracing wit, a refreshing lack of piety . . . a razor-sharp intelligence, . . . a contemporary vocabulary, the teaching of a meditation process that requires no faith, only committed practice. Sadhguru Jaggi Vasudev wears the air of a man who's figured out how to lead a life of sanity. Perhaps that is enough?'

Is it enough? If everything else were to be taken away, and I was left with the practice, would that really be enough? As I watch the reputations of established gurus collapse, leaving behind legions of disciples in states of anguish, conflict or ostrich-like denial, I ask myself if I would be able to withstand such a betrayal. I hope it won't be the case. And if it happens, there will be hurt and a very real pain. But I actually believe—and this is a considered response—that the answer is yes. I don't want my trust to be broken, but it helps me to periodically confront the bottom line. I do think the practice has been a substantial gift and its growing depth its own reward. And that, of course, begs the question: can the giver of such a gift ever really betray me?

The inner chatter subsides for a time. The mind grows quieter. I remember the near-death experience of 1997. I remember the terror. The years of yearning and despairing. The years of dryness. I remember shaking a fist at the heavens for their silence. Seven years later, the guidance came. Those were seven bloody long years. And that coming meant more than I imagined.

Years ago I wrote a poem about turning thirty. It closed with the lines: 'By thirty/ you know you want to walk/ away from ruined empires of fermented dream/ towards lands vast and unchoreographed/ where every step ahead is adventure/ and every step ahead, anchorage.'

This, I realize, is what Sadhguru has brought into my life. Adventure and anchorage. And he's made them simultaneous, the way I've wanted. The possibilities of an inner journey seem more exciting than I had imagined. At the same time, there is a deeper sense of rootedness, of being me than ever before. He's made the paradox come alive.

When I take away all the arguments, pro- and contra-, what I am left with is a quiet nub of trust. Some would counter that it is an unreasonable trust. But I think it is reasonably sturdy—not infallible, but nourished by reason, strengthened by scepticism. The acid test is that I believe my years with Sadhguru have decreased my dependence on his persona, not strengthened it. I can also see with some measure of clarity that there is more of me participating in my life than before. This seems to hold true—and it is just the depth and intensity that varies—for several of my fellow travellers at Isha. Something's working. And so, concerns and quibbles notwithstanding, the trust endures. I find myself stopping short in amazement again and again when I realize that he probably has no agenda other than the one he is open about: a commitment to guiding people towards their liberation. Can this be true? It seems to be. He is a strange man—a very strange man—but I think he's for real.

I don't have to agree with him, or approve of him, or even like him. But I do believe that when it comes, the Tennysonian moment, the time to 'cross the bar', when the breath draws to its ragged close, when the world as I know it crumbles, when my 3 a.m. fears of oblivion explode into reality, he'll be there. I suspect he doesn't have a choice. (The real gurus don't, I think.) He'll be unsentimental, as always, but swift, precise and decisive.

I cannot say this of anyone else I know. I'm not even sure what it means. But I believe that when the end comes, he'll do what he must. He'll do what he's best at. When the end comes, Sadhguru will—he must—he had better—see me through.